Contours of India's Foreign Policy

Changes and Challenges

Contours of India's Foreign Policy

Changes and Challenges

Mohammed Badrul Alam

Professor and Head, Dept. of Political Science,
Faculty of Social Sciences, Jamia Millia Islamia University,
Jamia Nagar, Okhla, New Delhi-110025. INDIA

Reference Press

New Delhi-110 002

Countours of India's Foreign Policy
Changes and Challenges

ISBN: 978-81-8405-082-0

₹ 975/-

First Published 2014

Published by:
Reference Press
4831/24, Ansari Road,
Darya Ganj,
New Delhi-110 002.
INDIA
Phones: 23260807, 41563444
Fax: 41563334
E-mail: info@essessreference.com
www.essessreference.com

Cover Design by *Patch Creative Unit*

Printed and bound in India at Salasar Imaging Systems.

Contents

SECTION-II : INDIA AND MAJOR POWERS

SECTION-III : INDIA AND THE MUSLIM WORLD

SECTION-IV : INDIA AND ITS NEIGHBOURS

Preface

The primary purpose of this book is to analyze, examine, evaluate and critique contours of India's foreign policy amidst change and challenges.

Generally, foreign policies are visualised through the prism of politico-security narratives. However, given the present interconnectedness of nation states through the process of globalisation, contemporary foreign policies envisage both political and economic aspirations of a particular nation-state. Moreover, it is through the force of a sound foreign policy that states try to neatly fit themselves into the anatomy of prevailing international system.

India enjoys formal diplomatic relations with most of the countries and its growing military and economic profile has meant that India considerable influence in global affairs. Even though India's foreign relations date back to pre-1947 years, yet its supreme and sovereign command over charting its relations with other countries commenced only after attaining independence from the British. Under the stewardship of Pandit Jawaharlal Nehru, India joined the Commonwealth of Nations and began to voice its solidarity with the independence movement going on in other third world countries. However, the cold war rivalry and the ideologically polarised world which emerged after the end of Second World became the eminent factors giving India's foreign policy a more coherent outlook. India's leadership decided to remain aloof from the Cold War politics and instead vouched for following a Non-Alignment Policy. However, in the immediate years following independence, India had to contend with security and territorial threats from Pakistan which witnessed India's foreign policy tilt towards Soviet Union so as to receive military support from Moscow. India's foreign policy has since then been shaped and conditioned keeping in view the security threat from Pakistan.

However, the end of the Cold War and the disintegration of the erstwhile Soviet Union came as a watershed moment for India's foreign policy. The economic reforms of early 1990's saw India heralding in the era of economic liberalisation and privatisation. The post-Cold War era witnessed India coming more close to the United States given the shift in India's strategic vision. The growing proximity between India and the U.S has meant that India has vastly gained in terms of the influence it exercises in affairs concerning the international community. India's relations with the west in general and the United States in particular have seen new milestones after the shocking events of 9/11. India's extensive contribution to the *War on Terror*, coupled with a surge in its economy, has helped India's diplomatic relations with several countries. Over the past three years, India has held numerous joint military exercises with U.S. and European nations that have resulted in a strengthened U.S.-India and E.U.-India *bilateral relationship*. The signing of Indo- US Civil Nuclear Deal in 2008 has been seen as a major foreign policy and strategic achievement for India. Growing proximity between India and the US has meant that the US even supports and endorses India's claims for permanent membership of the UNSC and vouches for a greater role for India in other important matters concerning international community.

However, much of India's success in future will depend on the effective implementation of its foreign policy and application of diplomatic resources and energy into that process. India will have to find ways and means to de-escalate the tension with its immediate neighbours and try to find out solutions to its disputes in an amicable manner. Moreover, India must strike a proper balance in its relations with all major powers including the US, Russia, Japan, Iran, and its growing neighboring major power, China.

Chapter One argues that India's foreign policy (IFP) and more importantly the micro-constituents of its decision making process, display new facets that need to be recognized. Ravi Prasad Narayanan explains how institutional actors – possess characteristics of skewed power mechanics since central institutions are far more powerful than comparable state equivalents and as foreign affairs is constitutionally the domain of the centre, states have no other option but to acquiesce.

Chapter Two explains how as an important stakeholder in the international parleys on the pressing environmental issues, Indian foreign policy also has a significant task at hand to safeguard the vital national interests of the country while joining other nations in finding mutually agreeable and lasting solutions to these problems. Rajendra Kumar Pandey attempts to critically analyse the changing contours of Indian foreign policy in its endeavour to negotiate appropriate and practicable responses to the global environmental challenges without compromising with the lives and livelihoods of the people of India.

Chapter Three provides a balanced, objective assessment of nuclear diplomacy of India and India's transition from a "nuclear apartheid" country to a "responsible" state and its strategy of nuclear energy alignments with multiple global players. Sitakanta Mishra discusses and explains in cogent details various critical viewpoints of prominent scholars who have tried to address India's nuclear diplomacy using content, empirical, technological and analytical approaches.

Chapter Four examine and evaluates how the global flow of labour and the consequent presence of numerous diaspora is a notable feature of contemporary politics and economics in general and that of India's foreign policy in particular. B.V.Muralidhar and M. Vishnu Prakash elaborate how India and its diaspora should be hands in glove for furthering their ties and also for the robust development so that India can become a credible power to reckon with.

Chapter Five addresses the trajectory shift in the relationship between India and the United States and how it should not be construed as the end of Pakistan factor. Mohammad Samir Hussain surmises that no matter how US engage with Pakistan, India's interest should be to strengthen closer ties with the United States and advance its strategic objectives.

Chapter Six situates the India's partnership with the EU as a partnership based on shared values and common commitment to democracy, pluralism, multi-centralism, human rights and religious freedom. Mohammed Badrul Alam dwells on India-EU enhanced cooperation in security issues, in particular counter-terrorism, cyber security and counter-piracy measures, as well as in other core areas such as trade, energy, innovation, health research, water and bio-resources, communication technology.

Chapter Seven examines how the relationship based on mutual trust and cooperation between India and Russia dates back to 1950s when India was experiencing the initial years of her independence from British colonial system and Soviet Union was observing sore relations with its rival super power United States in an ideologically divided world. Muzaffar Ahmad Ganaie discusses how India-Russia relations have withstood test of the time and have reached to a stage where both the countries look at each other as indispensible partners.

Chapter Eight focuses on India's relations with Africa at the local, regional and continental levels and attempt a prognosis on what the future holds. Sanjukta Banerji Bhattacharya elaborates how India, in its capacity as a partner in development, is playing the role of a key driver of growth in Africa and will continue to do so in years to come.

Chapter Nine highlights as to how in spite of competing geo-political interest, both India and China have cast aside their differences of the past and are cooperating in the field of economics. Amit Kumar Gupta describes how India and China are making very efficient use of their soft power resources so as to strengthen their ties and for putting an end to all their issues of contention.

Chapter Ten shows that India and Japan are acutely aware of the need for strategic and security cooperation between the two countries for ensuring order, stability and equilibrium among the region's great powers. Mohammed Badrul Alam explains how both the countries recognise that India-Japan cooperation and the process of engagement cannot be sustained on sheer expediency, episodic and transactional basis but has to be firmly rooted in shared values in both security and strategic terms.

Chapter Eleven analyses India's Look East Policy and its policy towards South East Asia was a major shift in the post-1991 phase. Biswajit Mohapatra summarizes as how India realized the opportunity of scaling up its economic growth as a whole and developed a region which had been neglected heretofore besides strengthening its ties with the countries of South East Asian region.

Chapter Twelve looks at the historic nature of the relationship between India and the countries of West Asia and how both sides have enjoyed warm ties since a very long time. Prasanta Kumar Pradhan summarizes as how West Asia can be a region where India can establish friendly ties with the countries, seek their cooperation on mutual issues of concern, which would give boost to its own economic and political clout in the region and beyond.

Chapter Thirteen discusses how India is committed to maintain strong economic and trade ties with Iran, an important geo-strategic power in Central and West Asia. Mahtab Alam Rizvi elaborates that in the light of current developments, the swiftly-changing international milieu and the associated strategic concerns, it is imperative for India and Iran to reorient their foreign policies toward each other.

Chapter Fourteen addresses how Post-ISAF (International Security Assistance Force) Afghanistan presents a scenario full of political and economic concerns for India's foreign policy makers which will largely be left unattended by U.S and its allies who seem to be in a hurry to disengage from the war torn country. Reyaz Ahmad Ganaie analyses how a stable and democratic Afghanistan will not only serve India's interests within Afghanistan alone but also limit to a large extent Pakistan's maneuvering of religious fundamentalism and terrorism as a state policy.

Chapter Fifteen tries to predict what shape the India-Pakistan peace process might take. Veena Kukreja analyses that given the rise of Islamist violence in Pakistan and the imminent looming threat to its internal stability in the wake of a US withdrawal from Afghanistan impending in 2014, this may provide an opportune time for cooperation between India and Pakistan.

Chapter Sixteen discusses the binary nature of India's foreign policy in the context of Pakistan and China. Dilip Mohite surmises that India's Ministry of External Affairs should work on consolidating its relations with China, which would alienate Pakistan, and also keep its strategic autonomy intact from any external pressure from U.S.A. or any other power.

Chapter Seventeen evaluates how the geo-strategic position of Bhutan and Nepal has transformed the relations with these countries into a vital importance to India since independence. Sarish Sebastian describes as how India and Bhutan have showed the world that peace and mutual benefits is possible through friendship and cooperation between two neighbors even with the high level of economic disparity and terrorism.

— Editor

Acknowledgements

This book has its origin from teaching a wide range of students in India, USA and Japan. My students at Nimapara College (Utkal University, Bhubaneswar, India) were the early inspirations for sharpening my writing skills. Later in New Delhi where I earned my M.Phil degree in American Studies at Jawaharlal Nehru University, my professors, Dr. B.K.Shrivastava, Dr. M.S.Venkatramani and Dr. R.P.Kaushik taught me aspects of foreign policy studies and its implications. My long stint working at the JNU library, American Center library and Indian Council for World Affairs (Sapru House) in New Delhi opened up my eyes to the scope and breadth of literature on almost all important facets of foreign policy discourse.

In the United States, where I attended Cornell University in Ithaca, New York, I earned my M.A and Ph.D degrees in International Studies. While at Cornell, many professors instilled in me the various intricacies and complexities of issues related to foreign policy and their impact in the shaping of India as a nation. The professors are: Dr. Richrad Polenberg, Dr. Mary Fainshod Katzenstein, Dr. Milton Jacob Esman, Dr.Walter Lafeber, Dr. Martin Shefter, Dr. Benjamin Ginsburg, Dr. Peter Katzenstein, Dr.Richard Rosecrance, Dr. Ami Ayalon, Dr. Stewart Blumin, Dr. Joel Silbey, Dr. Myron Rush, Dr. George McKahin, Dr.

Norman Uphoff, Dr. Steven Jackson. From the Cornell University Library, Mr.Ved Kayastha was of invaluable help in providing input and feedback whenever needed.

I am grateful to Dr. Bryan Reddick, Dean of Elmira College, New York, Dr. Anthony Layng, Professor of Anthropology, Dr. Robert Park, Professor of Political Science, Dr. Myra Glenn, Professor of History and Prof. Peter Ladley, Department of English, all from the same institution, for encouraging me at all times. Dr. Frank Czerwinski of the State University of New York at Cortland offered me useful advice whenever I sought it. My colleagues at Midway College, Kentucky, namely, Dr. Robert Miller, Professor of Religion, Dr. Judith Hatchet, Professor of English, provided me with useful research assistance.

In Japan, where I have been teaching at Miyazaki International College in Southern Kyushu since January 1998, the following people helped me in shaping my ideas and bringing in the right focus on India-centric courses. Among the colleagues who helped me are: Dr. Kate Greenfield, Dean; Dr. Getachew Felleke, Professor of Economics; Prof. Jun Maeda, Professor of Japanese Literature; Prof. Amanda Bradley, Professor of English Language; Dr.Jeong Pyong-Hong and Dr.Yasu Izumikawa, Professors in Political Science. My students at the Miyazaki International College in the course, "South Asian Societies and Cultures", provided interesting glimpses from the foreign policy literature as India pursued its national interest with utmost zeal. My friend working at other institutions in Japan also offered useful comments on this book project. Among those are: Dr. Joel Campbell (Professor of Political Science, Osaka University), Dr. Mika Mervioe (Professor of Political Science, University of Shimane), Dr. Jeffrey Folks (Professor of American Literature, Doshisa University at Kyoto), . Dr.Wilhelm Vosse (Professor of Political Science, International Christian University, Tokyo).

At Jamia Millia Islamia University, Delhi, where I am presently a Professor of Political Science, a number of my colleagues in the Department of Political Science including Prof.Rumki Basu, Prof.S.A.M.Pasha, Prof.Nisar Ul Haq, Prof.Furqan Ahmad, Prof.Muslim Khan, Prof.Mehtab Manzar, Dr.Farah Naaz, Dr.S.R.T.P.Raju, Dr.Naved Jamal, Adnan Farooqui, Dr.Krishnaswami Dara, and from the Economics department, Prof.Shahid Ashraf, Dr.Allim Baig, were great source of inspiration and motivation. A number of doctoral scholars including Sarish Sebastian, Kuldeep Singh, Reyaz Ahmad Ganie, Muzaffar Ahmad Ganie, Akhilesh Tiwari, Digvijay Singh Sekhawat, were of immense help in collecting the source materials.

I am extremely grateful to Sumit Sethi and his highly competent and capable associates at the Reference Press, Delhi, who not only showed keen interest but also agreed to publish the manuscript and put it on a fast track.

The greatest gratitude is owed to my mother, Mrs. Hedatun Nisa and brothers:

Dr. Mohammed Shamsul Alam and Mohammed Aminul Alam, and sisters: Dr. (Mrs.) Swaleha Khatun, Mrs. Rahima Khatun, Mrs. Sofia Khatun, my wife: Mrs. Gahartaj Rokeya and my children: Saira Alam, Zubair Alam, Sadaf Alam and Munawar Alam. Although quite demanding and at times frustrating, everyone allowed me the time and necessary emotional support I needed to complete my work. Much of my success is due to their love and affection at all times.

Prof. Mohammed Badrul Alam

Delhi, India

List of Contributors

Prof. Mohammed Badrul Alam
Head, Dept. of Political Science,
Jamia Millia Islamia University, Delhi

Dr. Raviprasad Narayanan
Assistant Research Fellow,
Institute of International Relations,
National Chengchi University, Taipei, Taiwan

Dr. Rajendra Kumar Pandey
Center for Federal Studies
Jamia Hamdard, Delhi

Dr. Sitakant Mishra
Research Fellow,
Center for Air Power Studies, Delhi

Prof. B.V.Muralidhar
Dept. of Political Science
S.V. University, Tirupati, AP

M.Vishnu Prakash
Dept. of Political Science
STSN Government Degree College
Kadiri, Anantapur, AP

Dr. Mohammad Samir Hussain
Research Associate
National Centre of International Security
and Defence Analysis, University of Pune

Muzaffar Ahmad Ganaie
Doctoral Research Scholar
Dept. of Political Science
Jamia Millia Islamia University, Delhi

Prof. Sanjukta Banerji Bhattacharya
Dept. of International Relations
Jadavpur University, Bengal

Dr. Amit Kumar Gupta
Dept. of Political Science
S.P.Mukherjee College
Delhi University, Delhi

Dr. Biswajit Mohapatra
Dept. of Political Science
North-Eastern Hill University
Shillong, Meghalaya

Dr.Prasanta Kumar Pradhan
Associate Fellow, Institute of Defense and
Strategic Analysis, Delhi

Dr. Mahtab Alam Rizvi
Associate Fellow, Institute of Defense
and Strategic Analysis, Delhi

Reyaz Ahmad Ganaie
Doctoral Research Scholar
Dept. of Political Science
Jamia Millia Islamia University, Delhi

Prof. Veena Kukreja
Dept. of Political Science
Delhi University, Delhi

Dr. Sarish Sebastian
Dept. of Political Science
I.P. College, Delhi University, Delhi

Prof. Dilip Mohite
Dept. of Political Science
M.S. University, Baroda, Gujarat

SECTION-I :
CONTEMPORARY ISSUES AND CHALLENGES

1

Indian Foreign Policy: Examining the Domestic/ External Linkage

Dr. Ravi Prasad Narayanan

INTRODUCTION

For over two decades since 1991, India's economic reforms have achieved a modicum of political acceptance for every governing party and coalition at the centre. Economic reforms do not exist in isolation and do leave an imprint on every facet of policy formulation and making. This essay argues that India's foreign policy (IFP) and more importantly the micro-constituents of its decision making process, display new facets that need to be recognized.

Dr. Raviprasad Narayanan is an Assistant Research Fellow at the Institute of International Relations and Assistant Professor, International Doctoral Program in Asia-Pacific Studies, National Chengchi University, Taipei, Taiwan. An earlier draft version of this paper was presented at a workshop titled *The Rise of India and its Strategic & Diplomacy Direction* atTaipei, Taiwan on 5 September 2012.

Perhaps the most significant and underrated facet is the role of 'domestic' actors that have the potential to influence (and alternately subvert) India's relations with its neighbours.

At an empirical level, unsettled security issues in South Asia display overt characteristics of conventional nature andIndia's boundary disputes with most of its neighbours being a persistent anomaly. Non-conventional security issues prevalent in the region, among other concernsincludewater disputes involving India, Pakistan, Bangladesh and Nepal. India's relations with Sri Lanka, otherwise strong, invariably get clouded by a powerful internal determinant – ethnicity. The ethnic dimension of the civil conflict in Sri Lanka has for the past couple of decades played an alarmist role in the internal politics of Tamil Nadu and the extremely violent manner in which the conflict was brought to a close in 2009 by the Sri Lankan army impacted Tamil Nadu with widespread sympathy – in official and non-official capacities - for minority Tamils of the island nation.

This chapter is premised on the following hypotheses:

- Coalition governments in India at the centre are dependent on powerful regional political parties for 'term continuity' and hence acquiesce their partners on policy issues.
- Regional parties are enlarging their political brief by engaging the centre on policy issues that involve relations with neighbors and sometimes embarrass the government by adopting postures that appear to contradict official policy.
- Bargaining on foreign policy issues between the centre and the states is emerging as a zone of contestation which in turn is a double edged sword that could lead to three possibilities - greater pluralism in IFP, or, the centre asserting its constitutional role in conducting foreign affairs, or, the beginnings of a contested policy

debate that accommodates regional interests into the framing of overall national interests.

This essay extrapolates Bangladesh-India relations and the role of West Bengal as an illustration of the central theme and hypotheses. The role of West Bengal in framing India's policy towards Bangladesh has always been important and in recent years has become more intensive owing to two primary factors, both domestic.

First, coalition compulsions have dictated that the Trinamool Congress (TC) currently ruling West Bengal was part of the ruling United Progressive Alliance from 2004 to 2012. The TC forcefully advocated West Bengal's position on various issues including relations with Bangladesh on the national stage. Second, The TC has not hesitated in differing with the centre on vital issues since its domestic support base is primarily regional – in West Bengal – and it does not want to appear as bartering away the state's interests.

I. Bangladesh-India relations and West Bengal

(a) Political relations, the boundary and enclaves

2011 was the year when Bangladesh – India relations reached their zenith. In a year of frenetic diplomatic activity that witnessed India's top political leaders including the Vice-President of India, Hamid Ansari; Chairman of the ruling UPA alliance, Ms. Sonia Gandhi; former External Affairs Minister S.M. Krishna; and former Finance Minister Pranab Mukherjee (currently President of India) all making visits to Bangladesh, the Indian Prime Minister, Manmohan Singh visited Dhaka from 6-7 September 2011.

For long, Bangladesh-India relations have been hobbled by two issues – lack of a boundary agreement with the rider of how to deal with "enclaves"[1] and the contentious issue of sharing river waters. A significant step in establishing rapprochement was made on 6 September 2011 when

Bangladesh and India signed a protocol to the Agreement concerning demarcation of the Land Boundary between India and Bangladesh – a development that finally decided to do away with "enclaves" on either side.[2] Of the enclaves that were part of the agreement the most contentious were the three sectors of Daikhata 56 (West Bengal), Muhuri River-Belonia (Tripura) and Dumabari (Assam)[3] that had often led to frayed tempers between India's Border Security Force (BSF) and the Bangladesh Rifles (BDR), now renamed the Border Guards Bangladesh (BGB) following a failed mutiny in 2009.[4]

These extraterritorial patches – 111 Indian enclaves in Bangladesh and 51 Bangladesh enclaves in India[5] - were ensconced not only on the wrong side of the political states they belonged to, but are an anomaly at a time when both the countries earnestly pursue a robust bilateral relationship. With the departure of the British and the violent partition of India that followed in 1947, the question of enclaves assumed a new veneer – that of its inhabitants wanting to belong to the country where the majority practiced either of the two religions practiced in the region. The choice was to either joina largely Hindu India or a Pakistan created in the name of Islam.[6]On the Indian side of the 'boundary' all the enclaves are in the district of Cooch Behar in the state of West Bengal.[7] Caught in the middle of the unsettled nature of the 'enclaves' were the people who inhabited these enclaves and for decades had little access to both sides, living in "stateless" limbo. For Reece Jones the residents of these enclaves "find themselves in an alternate space that is shaped by the processes of modernity but not incorporated into it."[8]The stateless nature of the inhabitants of these enclaves was accurately pointed out as a "Kafkaesque" situation by Willem Schendel with these pockets not having any access to health, education, communication and transport due to the bureaucratic and political apathy shown by both the countries.[9] Denied of political citizenship, with interrupted social interactions and situated within a legal vacuum the residents of these enclaves have lived a life of disruption and shameful bureaucratic apathy. The total area that needed resolving of the boundary was quite small with Indian enclaves in Bangladesh totaling around 70 square kms and Bangladesh enclaves in India not exceeding 28 square kms.[10] The long drawn issue over enclaves between India and Bangladesh is reflective of a rigid and frightening temperament displayed by the political and bureaucratic class in both the countries towards territorial integrity.

The only serious attempt to address the issues of the enclaves was done in 1974 when India's Prime Minister Indira Gandhi and newly independent Bangladesh's founding leader Sheikh Mujibur Rehman signed a Land Boundary Agreement in which the two countries had decided to exchange the enclaves with India agreeing to forgo compensation in lieu of the additional territory going to Bangladesh. In hindsight, it could be argued that this agreement was arrived at without any objection from the state of West Bengal since at that time it was governed by Siddhartha Shankar Ray, a prominent Congress leader and acolyte of Mrs. Indira Gandhi. However, developments after the signing of this treaty put paid to any hopes of resolution as the Indian parliament did not ratify the treaty while Bangladesh's did.

The importance of Manmohan Singh's 2011 visit to Bangladesh goes beyond the ten agreements, protocols and memorandums of understandings (MoUs) the two countries signed. The Indian Prime Minister in a historic first was accompanied by four chief ministers, whose provinces shared boundaries with Bangladesh. The four chief ministers – Tarun Gogoi of Assam, Lal Thanhawla of Mizoram, Mukul Sangma of Meghalaya and Manik Sarkar of Tripura represent the landlocked states of northeastern India, a region yet to benefit from India's vaunted economic growth. The presence of the provincial leaders would have been enriched further had the chief minister of West Bengal, Ms. Mamta Banerjee been part of the Indian delegation. Ms. Banerjee stayed out of the delegation at the last moment owing to issues that are dealt later in this essay.

The importance of West Bengal to conducting relations with Bangladesh cannot be understated for several reasons.First, the linguistic character of West Bengal and Bangladesh derives from a common cultural and linguistic identity.As a uniting feature the Bengali language was a political mobiliser when Bangladesh was called East Pakistan following the partition of India by the British in 1947. The stridency with which the rulers of West Pakistan tried to impose Urdu as a language on a resentful population in East Pakistan began the de-legitimization of West Pakistan's power in its eastern political geography.[11] By invoking language as a mobilizing tool political activists appropriated cultural symbols and also tapped into popular sentiments by articulating freedom, progress, equality and patriotism.[12]As symbolic factors, language and culture played a prominent role in "constructing collectiveself-consciousness in Bengal."[13]The academic and mid-level bureaucratic segments of society in East Pakistan were as committed to East Pakistan's independence from West Pakistan as the Awami League that represented the political expression of the people.[14]

(b) Strategic aspects - Economic issues, Infrastructure synergy, Water

The importance of Bangladesh to India's northeast begins with geographical proximity, and the landlocked states of northeast India would benefit if access to Chittagong port were to materialize. The port of Chittagong on the Bay of Bengal is a mere 75 kms from Tripura state, yet exports from that state have to route it from Kolkata port located

1700 kms away. If Bangladesh were to provide unhindered transit, the same distance whittles down to 400 kms! Currently, transportation costs from Eastern India, especially Kolkata (capital of West Bengal) to northeast India are prohibitive (distance and the unofficial rent seeking activities of various insurgent groups add to the eventual cost) and it is expected that if Bangladesh were to emerge as a trade and transit corridor it will reduce transportation costs to northeast India andbenefit Bangladesh which will derive transit fees. Also, to achieve win-win results, tapping the resources of northeast India appears an attractive prospect to Bangladesh – especially in the agro business sector. Bangladesh also wants to import power from India and the hydel potential of northeast India is an attractive option. It is expected that Bangladesh would receive 500 MW of power from India of which half would be at a preferential rate. A joint venture between the two countries on setting up a thermal power plant with a power generating capacity of 1320 MW is also expected to enhance grid connectivity. In brief, closer and more wide-ranging economic cooperation with Bangladesh bilaterally and potentially through an FTA will not only prove beneficial to both the countries but also end the economic isolation of northeast India.[15]

The two-way trade between the two countries in 2010-2011 was USD 5.099 billion with India's exports to Bangladesh accounting for USD 4.586 billion and imports US $ 0.512 million. Bangladesh is renowned for its textiles with its major customers being in northern and western Europe and India unilaterally decided to import duty-free 46 textile items from Bangladesh with immediate effect, during Manmohan Singh's 2011 visit to Dhaka.[16]India has also extended a credit line of USD 1 billion to Bangladesh that will be utilized for construction of roads and railway lines ensuring better connectivity between the two countries.

Enhancing peace and cooperation with Bangladesh

and encouraging the continuance of a democratically elected polity are India's primary aspirations. With a sharply polarized internal polity revolving around two coalitions – the ruling Awami league led by Sheikh Hasina and the Bangladesh Nationalist Party (BNP) led by Khaleda Zia – domestic politics in Bangladesh assumes hysterical overtones of the "foreign hand" every time a government tries to foster closer relations with India. The two parties have different visions of 'India' as well that finds expression in domestic politics. For India, a deeper relationship with Bangladesh will yield dividends on several fronts.

First, for long, militants of various insurgent groups based in northeast India have used the terrain of Bangladesh as a rear base. For close to two decades the United Liberation Front of Assam (ULFA) that called for an independent Assam operated out of Bangladesh. With the upswing in ties between the two countries, the ULFA was forced to come to the negotiation table with the government of India and their top leadership "handed" over by Bangladesh. Other insurgent groups have used Bangladesh as a transit point and location to source arms and ammunition form Southeast Asia that were then picked up from Chittagong and Cox Bazaar ports. If India were to get a firm grip over the insurgency in certain parts of its northeast, the solution lay through Bangladesh – better political ties, increased strategic cooperation and creating transportation infrastructure for connectivity.

Second, an issue that both countries need to address on a firm footing is to do with border management. India and Bangladesh share a 4096.7 kms long border that straddles various geographical features. A state-wise break-up of India's border with Bangladesh is as follows: West Bengal shares a 2216.7 kms border with Bangladesh; Assam has a 263kms border; Tripura has an 856 kms long border; Meghalaya shares a 443 kms border and Mizoram has 318 kms border with Bangladesh. In its entirety, the border runs along plains, rivers, hills, forests and inhabited spaces. With dense population on both sides and cultivations upto the border, the India-Bangladesh border is a haven for infiltration and smuggling. Infiltration into India has led to a piquant situation in Assam with "illegal migrants" being an explosive political issue. In order to prevent illegal migration the Indian authorities are erecting a fence that will cover 3296.87 kms of which work on 2535.80 kms has been completed.[17] It is expected that this fence will be a deterrent to illegal migrants and smugglers alike.

Third, Bangladesh and India share 54 common rivers. It was in 1972 that the two countries agreed to establish permanent Joint Rivers Commission (JRC) comprising experts from both sides. The fundamental principle of the JRC was to carry out a comprehensive survey of the river systems shared by both the countries in the fields of flood control and implement them."[18]The Ganga Waters Treaty signed on 12 December 1996 details water sharing of the river Ganga during lean season (1 January -31 May and theJRC between the two countries who hold regular meetings to address water woes – an aspect that is bound to become salient since there is going to be more pressure on this finite source in the coming years. The Ganga Water Treaty would be valid for a period of thirty years with the treaty assuring Bangladesh of a guaranteed flow of 35,000 cu ft/s during any critical period.[19]For Bangladesh an agreement over the sharing of waters from the Teestariver is important since it forms a flood plain and supports vital rice growing areas in northwest Bangladesh. The Teesta river floodplain is a highly irrigated area and the river barrage at Gozaldoba in India influences agricultural patterns downstream. Bangladesh seeks a fair deal of sharing fifty percent of the water flows, but the devil in the detail lies on the Indian side as 'Water' according to the Indian constitution is a subject of the state government and not the central government! While New Delhi is willing to go the extra mile to satisfy Dhaka, the view from Kolkata, capital of West Bengal, is different and local interests predominate.

During Manmohan Singh's visit to Dhaka in 2011 there was a lot of expectation over signing an agreement over the sharing of waters of the Teesta, Feni and six other common rivers, but this agreement did not materialize owing to the absence of Ms. Mamta Banerjee, chief minister of the province of West Bengal in India. Her absence was reflective of the contentious domestic politics over the sharing of river waters with Bangladesh, and Ms. Banerjee did not want to annoy her domestic constituencies by being party to an agreement that might be seen as "selling out" by powerful lobbies. While the mainstream media highlighted the absence of Ms. Mamta Banerjee as a slight to the prime minister of India as also to relations with Bangladesh, the details leading to her decision to stay away from the signing of an agreement are indeed complicated. To begin with, it appears that the data on river water flows over which the agreement was to be signed was decades old and not reflective of current reality. It appears that the reduced water flows in the rivers even during monsoons have not been taken into consideration. Complicating matters is the detail that water flows and river water management data in India is the exclusive domain of the Central Water Commission (CWC). There is no state-level equivalent of the CWC and hence there appears to be bureaucratic inertia in the sharing of data regarding the quantum of water flowing from the state of West Bengal into Bangladesh. Adding another layer to the issue is that many of the rivers flowing into West Bengal have their source of origin in some other states (like Sikkim, Assam and Arunachal Pradesh) and the states themselves have only very rudimentary coordination mechanisms – usually during a flood or other natural calamities.

The central government's dominance in deciding the course as regards foreign policy with neighbors giving short shrift to domestic concerns expressed by states like West Bengal is an aspect not to be ignored. For provincial level leaders, being part of an agreement that will affect local interests and lobbies will reflect in a negative outcome in the next round of an electoral mandate and this is a 'political risk' Ms. Banerjee could do without. With her party – the Trinamool Congress – having ousted the Communists and bringing about hopes of economic development in the state, Ms. Banerjee is left with no other option but to adopt a rigid stance when it comes to resource sharing with neighboring Bangladesh. In effect, local considerations, especially in West Bengal do have an important bearing in deciding foreign policy in the case of Bangladesh-India relations.

ANALYSIS

Undeniably, there are strong shades of emerging "linkages" in India's federal polity regarding the conduct of foreign relations with neighbors. How far these linkages dovetail with James Rosenau's "Linkage Politics" is a moot question.[20] For Rosenau "linkages" were the basic unit of analysis, but I wish to argue that in the Indian context the basic unit – linkages – is a highly contested domain where individual and institutional actors arbitrate, negotiate and adopt postures that may be at variance with overall national interests. In India's case, individual actors are more powerful in a coalition setting since most regional parties are tight units run by charismatic individuals who brook no challengers to their style of leadership. The latter – institutional actors – possess characteristics of skewed power mechanics since central institutions are far more powerful than comparable state equivalents and as foreign affairs is constitutionally the domain of the centre, states have no other option but to acquiesce. If West Bengal has reservations about certain aspects of the centre's relations with Bangladesh, it is only a matter of time before other states follow the cue and express their opinions more forcefully.

From available literature on the subject Kripa Sridharan is of the opinion that Indian states are on the ascendant regarding foreign policy advocacy owing to two trends - increasing regionalization of Indian politics with coalition governments becoming the mainstay, and economic liberalization encouraging states to become more pro-active vis a vis their neighboring countries.[21] There is thus space for new variables to enter into the foreign policy making arena in India, where ideational variables and practical necessities jostle with each other. In the words of Vipan Narang and Paul Stanil and, "...there is significant space for ideationalvariables to play an important role in shaping the trajectory of Indian foreign securitypolicy."[22] Adding to the debate are Subrata Mitra and Bernd Rill who state:

> "As things stood at the outset, foreign policy and strategic planning were almost exclusively in the hands of Nehru and his close advisers during his tenure as Prime Minister until 1964. More recently, this formerly relatively closed circle of policy experts has opened up to allow regionalpolitical forces (which have come to wield influence as coalition partners at the centre) to air their respective views on strategic planning."[23]

In its totality, the centre holds the upper hand while conducting foreign policy[24] but with political arrangements being coalitional, there is greater leeway for regional parties to express their opinions and dissent on external relations especially with neighbors. An aspect of importance relating to Bangladesh – India relations is that while the conduct of foreign affairs has been dealt by the Union List of the Seventh Schedule of the Indian constitution aspects related to water (supplies, irrigation, canals, drainage, embankments and storage) are the domain of the province. As a consequence a perceptible gap emerges between what the central government wishes to exercise in national interest and what the state government interprets as harming local interests. This apart there needs to be clear demarcation of powers that impinges upon foreign relations. To cite an instance in the words of Rafiq Dossani:

> "In West Bengal, the state police and Border Security Forces (a centrally-controlled paramilitary group) often work together to control the movement of migrants and goods from Bangladesh. The final authority over controlling the border is extremely unclear: the states have the authority to maintain law and order and to provide ration cards (a key form of identity) to each 'citizen,' but the central government has the (far stronger) authority to conduct relations with Bangladesh and protect national security.[25]"

Indeed, Bangladesh and India appear to have opened a new chapter in their relationship, but this development has several caveats attached to it. In Dhaka, the ruling Awami League is considered 'secular' and more in sync with fostering relations with India and securing benefits for Bangladesh. The political history of the Awami League founded by Sheikh Mujib and now headed by his daughter Sheikh Hasina is closely linked to India and especially the Congress party that heads the UPA coalition in New Delhi. Political stability in New Delhi has helped too with Manmohan Singh visualizing closer relations with Bangladesh as an extension of India's 'Look East' policy since Bangladesh is a geographical bridgehead to Myanmar and Southeast Asia. In Dhaka, the opposition BNP while grudgingly accepting the recent positive developments in

Bangladesh-India relations is reflectively suspicious of India. The BNPs hobnobbing with fundamentalist parties to retain power in its previous innings as ruling party in Bangladesh did not go down well in India since that period coincided with an increase in fundamentalism and religious intolerance in Bangladesh. A section of Bangladesh's polity is implacably hostile to India and that is a reality India has to accept and live with.

Sheikh Hasina's and Manmohan Singh's genuine endeavors for peace and cooperation are welcome and need to be institutionalized for long term benefits to the people and the region. If not handled with pragmatism and delicacy the opposite might happen since"a host of structural and domestic political variables" could end up"pulling the two states in opposite directions."[26]

REFERENCES

1 An "enclave" is a piece of land surrounded on all sides by foreign territory. See Evgeny Vinokurov, *A Theory of Enclaves* (Lanham, MD: Lexington Books, 2007) especially Ch.2 "What are Enclaves and Exclaves?" pp.9-54.

2 The enclaves and their peculiar set of problems emerged from the very hasty manner in which the Boundary Commission led by Sir Cyril Radcliffe – a British bureaucrat who had never been to India before 1947 – was given the task of dividing the country since partition had become inevitable before independence.

3 Haroon Habib, "Northeast, gateway to Bangladesh ties" *The Hindu* (New Delhi) 24 September 2011. Available at: http://www.thehindu.com/opinion/lead/article2479883.ece?css=print (Retrieved on 26 January 2012)

4 In February 2009, the Bangladesh Rifles (BDR) staged a violent mutiny against its leadership that was comprised of senior army officers. After four days of mayhem order was restored but not before 57 BDR army officers including the Director General, his deputies and sixteen sector commanders were killed. This incident forced Bangladesh to thoroughly revamp the BDR into the Border Guards Bangladesh (BGB).Civil – Military relations in South Asia make for interesting reading in the cases of Pakistan and

Bangladesh. See Veena Kukreja, *Civil-Military Relations in South Asia* (Delhi: Sage Publications, 1991).

5 Since different estimates of the numbers of enclaves exist in contemporary writings, this article bases the numbers of enclaves (111 Indian enclaves in Bangladesh and 51 Bangladesh enclaves in India) on the joint census conducted by the Joint Boundary Working Group of both the countries in 2011. See Raktima Bose, "Census in Indian and Bangladesh Enclaves ends" *Hindu* (Kolkata) 19 July 2011. Accessible at: http://www.thehindu.com/news/national/article2260223.ece (Accessed on 23 July 2012)

6 Although Bangladesh has a sizeable yet progressively declining Hindu minority comprising around 9.6 percent of the total population, at the time of partition in 1947, many were willing to identify with India and not with a Muslim dominated East Pakistan. See, Joya Chatterji, *Bengal divided – Hindu communalism and partition, 1932-1947* (Cambridge: Cambridge University Press, 1994), p.222.

7 In 1947 Cooch Behar was a princely state and was given the option of joining either India or East Pakistan. The then Maharaja of Cooch Behar chose to join India on 20 August 1949 – thereby creating the issue of enclaves.

8 Reece Jones, "Sovereignty and statelessness in the border enclaves of India and Bangladesh, "*Political Geography* (Amsterdam), Vol.28, No.6, 2009, p.374.

9 Willem vanSchendel, "Stateless in South Asia: The Making of the India-Bangladesh Enclaves" *The Journal of Asian Studies*(Cambridge), Vol. 61, No.1, February 2002, p.116.

10 "The end of the enclaves" *The Economist* (London), 7 September 2011. Accessible at: http://www.economist.com/blogs/banyan/2011/09/border-agreements (Accessed on 12 February 2012)

11 Afroza Anwary, "Frame Alignment and the Dynamics of the National Language Movement of East Pakistan:1947-1956" *Journal of Asian History* (Wiesbaden), Vol.45, 1/2, 2011, p.173.

12 AfrozaAnwary, *Ibid.*, p.185.

13 Shahadat H. Khan, "Radicalism in Bengali Muslim Thought: Kazi Abdul Wadud and the 'Religion of Creativity'" in Rafiuddin Ahmed (ed.) *Understanding the Bengal Muslims – Interpretative Essays* (New Delhi: Oxford University Press, 2002), p.175.

14 Hassan Zaheer, *The Separation of East Pakistan – The Rise and Realization of Bengali Muslim Nationalism* (Karachi: Oxford University Press, 1994), p.128.

15 Prebir De, Selim Raihan and Sanjay Kathuria, *Unlocking Bangladesh-India Trade: Emerging Potential and The Way Forward,* The World Bank, *Policy Research Working PaperNo.6155,* August 2012, p.29. Available at: http://elibrary.worldbank.org/docserver/download/6155.pdf?expires=1358414267&id=id&accname=guest&checksum=F836FFCAF1FC087F00EF9C2480A28F79 (Retrieved on 14 November 2012)

16 "India – Bangladesh Relations" Ministry of External Affairs, India, January 2012.

17 Chapter 3 on 'Border Management' in the Annual Report of the South Asia Terrorism Portal (SATP) 2007-2008.

18 Ishtiaq Hossain, "Bangladesh-India Relations: Issues and Problems" *Asian Survey* (Berkeley), Vol.21, No.11, November 1981, p.1119.

19 Philippe Sands, "Bangladesh-India: Treaty of Sharing the Ganges Waters at Farakka" *International Legal Materials,* Vol.36, No.3, May 1997, pp.519-528.

20 See James N. Rosenau, *Linkage Politics: Essays on the Convergence of National and International Systems* (New York: The Free Press, 1969).

21 Kripa Sridharan, "Federalism and Foreign relations: The Nascent Role of the Indian States'" *Asian Studies Review,* Vol.27, No.4, pp. 463-489.

22 Vipin Narang and Paul Staniland, "Institutions and Worldviews in IndianForeign Security Policy"*India Review,* 11:2, 2012, p.78.

23 Subrata K. Mitra and Bernd Rill (eds.) *India's New Dynamics in Foreign Policy* (Munich: Hans Seidel Stiftung, 2006), p.16.

24 A reading of Articles 51 and 253 of the Indian Constitution make it clear that the Union (Centre) holds wide powers in arriving at the conclusion of international treaties and obligations. See P.M. Bakshi, *The Constitution of India* (New Delhi: Universal Book Traders, 2000).

25 Rafiq Dossani and Srinidhi Vijaykumar, "Indian Federalism and the Conduct of Foreign Policy in Border States: State Participation and Central Accommodation since 1990," See *Stanford Journal of International Affairs*. Available at: http://www.stanford.edu/group/sjir/7.1.07_dossani.html (Retrieved on 12 August 2012)

26 Harsh V. Pant, "India and Bangladesh: Will the Twain Ever Meet?" *Asian Survey,* Vol.47, No.2, March/April 2007, p.232.

2

India and Global Environmental Challenges

Rajendra Kumar Pandey

Global environmental challenges have emerged as one of the most unconventional yet contentious issues confronting the different countries in the post-Second World War period. Indeed, the realm of international relations has experienced a marked departure from its traditional goal-posts of strategically-oriented state-led war and peace, to grapple with the problems emanating from the economic and social pursuits of life of people, particularly of the developed countries. Clearly, beginning with the burden of mechanised overproduction heralded by the industrial revolution, the subsequent energy-intensive lifestyle of people in certain countries has created a massive load on the endowments and resources of the earth that goes much beyond its carrying capacity. The resultant nature and extent of damages caused to ecology of the earth appeared alarming given the fact that the environmental degradations did not remain localised due to the largely seamless stretch of the atmospheric and aquatic elements of human ecosystem. So, for instance, the adverse impacts of excessive emission of greenhouse gases (GHGs) in a particular country or region of the earth is not confined to that area only, and the atmospheric concentration of such gases invariably leads to rise in the surface temperature of the earth that contributes its part in what is known as global warming. Environmental challenges have, therefore, been unanimously agreed to as international problems requiring a joint coping strategy of all the countries to secure the earth from the unintended ecological disasters that are in the offing if appropriate remedial measures are not taken well within time. Consequently, environmental issues have found prominence in the international agenda, and a series of negotiations and events have been organized to dwell deep into complexity of the problem and find practicable solutions for the same. However, after the initial deliberations when various stakeholders set on the task of deciding about the root causes of the environmental challenges and fixing responsibilities for the same, the fissures between the developed and the developing countries became apparent. Probably the most contentious issue in this regard turned out to be the notion of 'common but differentiated responsibilities.' This principle avers that 'although all nations had to accept responsibility for the world's changing climate, it was developed nations that were immediately responsible because they had benefited from the industrialization which was generally regarded as the source of the excess carbon dioxide emissions that had caused mean temperature increases.'[1] Accordingly, the foreign policies of different nations have been geared to jealously guard the national interests of the countries while participating in the international summits and negotiations on the global environmental challenges. As an important stakeholder in the international parleys on the pressing environmental issues, Indian foreign policy also has a significant task at hand to safeguard the vital national interests of the country while joining other nations in finding mutually agreeable and lasting solutions to these problems. The paper attempts to critically analyse the changing contours of Indian foreign policy in its endeavour to negotiate appropriate and practicable responses to the global environmental challenges without compromising with the lives and livelihoods of the people of India.

EARLY CONCERNS FOR ENVIRONMENTAL PROTECTION

Environmental issues remained almost non-existent in the mainstream discourses of international relations for a fairly long period of time in the post-war period for two obvious reasons. One, the nature and extent of environmental challenges were neither as alarming as they are today, and consequently, nor was there felt a need to mount international cooperation to cope up with such challenges. Two, the preoccupations of various countries with their own distinct national priorities were so pronounced at that time that no one seemed to be interested in engaging with a common cause such as environment. For instance, while the major powers were extremely busy in initiating moves and countermoves as part of their cold war strategy, the newly independent countries had the mammoth responsibility of heralding a rapid pace of social and economic development to meet the basic needs of their people. In such a scenario, much scope did not appear to be left for the common global concerns like environment to receive even an iota of attention of the important countries. At the best, occasional concerns for environmental protection were expressed when any untoward incident of environmental pollution or similar mishap would take place in any part of the globe. For example, the wreck of oil tanker

Torrey Canyon off the Cornish beach in 1967 that led to huge pollution in the marine ecosystem of the region sparked off an intense public debate on the need to preserve the marine ecosystem and prevent massive release of oil in oceans and seas in future. However, the overbearing obsession of governments with their political and strategic priorities presumably did not allow them to respond to the public aspiration on the issue. Similar absence of positive responses from other formal structures of states appeared to have motivated the creation of a number of non-governmental organizations such as Greenpeace to take up the cudgel for environmental protection. Under these circumstances, Indian foreign policy too, like others, remained engrossed with the priorities of national interest with almost total exclusion of environmental concerns figuring into her framework of international cooperation. Undoubtedly, in the times of intense cold war, the policy of non-alignment provided an appropriate alternative to India, to not only keep away from the dynamics of the cold war but also secure positive engagements with both superpowers as well as the other developing countries. Moreover, under Nehru's astute leadership India focused more upon Afro-Asian solidarity, not in the sense of evolving any competing power bloc against any of the superpowers but to foster mutual cooperation amongst them. This may be argued to be India's significant contribution to the cause of securing the interest of developing countries in the subsequent international environmental negotiations as the absence of southern solidarity in these negotiations would definitely have cost them dearly.

PURSUITS FOR SUSTAINABLE DEVELOPMENT

While the important actors of international relations seemed too occupied with the imperatives of their national interest to spare time and efforts for focusing attention on global environmental challenges, the responsibility to initiate some sort of international cooperative endeavour towards environmental issues came on the shoulders of those nations which did not have much stakes in the ongoing cold war. So, taking a proactive step on the subject in 1968, Swedish government proposed an international gathering of all stakeholders on the issue of human environment in order to draw the attention of both the governments as well as the general public on the significance and urgency of environmental problems. This proposal eventually led to the organisation of United Nations Conference on Human Environment (UNCHE) at Stockholm in 1972 where, for the first time, the developed and developing countries came face to face on the subject of conceptualising and debating the critical issues involved in protection of environment. In the face of the disturbing western design to portray environmental challenges as isolated issues rooted in the activities of the underdeveloped societies, the developing countries forcefully argued that environmental questions cannot be seen in isolation from their demands for rapid development, financial assistance, technology transfer and overall restructuring of international economic relations. Leading the charge from the front, India categorically stated that poverty has been the greatest polluter and castigated the developed societies for exploiting the resources of the developing countries to reach their present levels of affluence. Indian position in this Conference was overwhelmingly supported by the third world countries who sought to bring in black and white the ideological and political ramifications of the global environmental issues.

Another controversial matter of vital significance for the developing countries that emerged from this conference was the idea of eco-development.[2] Markedly posited in favour of developing countries, the concept of eco-development underlined the necessity of meeting the basic needs of people all over the world in an environmentally sound production system relying more on men than machinery. Two critical components of this discourse that apparently weighed heavily in favour of the developing countries were the imperatives of self-reliance, on the one hand, and the reliance on men than machinery, on the other. In other words, the operationalization of the idea of eco-development would require greater self-reliance on the part of the developing countries so that they could remodel their production system in an environmentally sound way. Similarly, increasing reliance on men than machinery would facilitate a productive utilisation of the massive manpower available in these countries. But these two critical components of eco-development would definitely compromise with the economic pursuits of the developed countries that thrived on their unequal trade with the developing countries in the first place, and that blindly evolved a production system which was unsustainably resource and machinery intensive. Unsurprisingly, therefore, after the conference, concerted efforts were afoot not only to discredit the idea of eco-development, the entire discourse on environment was sought to be given a new direction by focusing on the population growth in the developing countries as the core concern of environmental challenges. Moreover, the non-sustainable resource intensive production systems of the developed countries and their adverse implications for the global environment were surreptitiously underestimated to escape critical scrutiny in the public domain.

The political standoff between the developing and developed countries at Stockholm was apparently result of the growing assertiveness of the former on the issue of making the western world realise their accountability for damaging the environment and consequent responsibility of sharing of burden in undoing the same. But the developed nations were in no mood to relent, and instead, unleashed a mischievous propaganda to convince the international opinion that it was the growing population and concomitant poverty in the developing countries that had become bane of the human environment. The ideological manoeuvring of the developing countries at the conference was further weakened due to the voluntary absence of the Soviet Union and its allies in protest against the non-inclusion of East Germany as a conference participant. Nevertheless, the developing countries stood their guard at the conference and did not allow the developed world a walkover. Indeed, Indian diplomacy appeared at its best as it forcefully articulated the considered opinion of the developing countries that sustainable development could not be achieved unless the developed nations bear in fullest measure their responsibility of supporting the former in securing an environmentally sound production system through both financial assistance and technology transfer. Interestingly, Indian stand on the issue earned support not only from its traditional allies but also countries like China that was maintaining a good rapport with the American leadership of the time. It was, therefore, not surprising that in the final declaration of the conference a number of submissions of the developing countries were accepted despite reservations of the developed nations. For instance, Principle 9 of the Stockholm Declaration categorically stated that 'environmental deficiencies generated by the conditions of under-development and natural disasters pose grave problems and can best be remedied by accelerated development through the transfer of substantial quantities of financial and technological assistance as a supplement to the domestic effort of the developing countries and such timely assistance as may be required.'[3] Thus, this Declaration, in a way, set the tone for the future environmental negotiations in which the developing countries were likely to bargain hard with the developed ones in their pursuits for sustainable development.

Despite being the pioneering conference, the Stockholm Conference, at the best, was just able to bring out the complexity of issues in the global environmental protection and the rest of the matters were left for the other commissions and conferences to tackle. The strong disagreement between the developing and developed countries in their understanding of the causes of environmental degradation, and probable mechanisms and means of environmental protection minimised the chances of the conference being able to provide finer blueprint for sustainable development. Hence, the United General Assembly resolved to set up an independent World Commission on Environment and Development (WCED) under the stewardship of Gro Harlem Brundtland to look into the complex issues of environment and development, and suggest a practicable framework to bring about development without compromising with the imperatives of environmental sustainability. Additionally, part of the Commission's mandate was also to outline new methods of international cooperation that would enhance the understanding of the concept of sustainable development and allow it to develop further.[4] Later, in its report entitled 'Our Common Future', published in 1987, the Commission came out with the sustainable development approach to deal with the vexed relationship between development and environment. Elaborating the idea of sustainable development, the Commission succinctly pointed out: 'Sustainable development seeks to meet the needs and aspirations of the present without compromising the ability to meet those of the future. Far from requiring the cessation of economic growth, it recognizes that the problems of poverty and underdevelopment cannot be solved unless we have a new era of growth in which developing countries play a large role and reap large benefits.'[5]

Conceptually, thus, the idea of sustainable development seeks to strike a balance between the requirements of the developed countries and the aspirations of the developing nations. But the radical critics of sustainable development argue it to be ideologically loaded as it privileges economic growth over everything else. The poverty and underdevelopment is sought to be eradicated by the same mechanism which has been at the root of these problems. Ironically, the idea of sustainable development has emerged from those countries which themselves practice unsustainable use of natural resources unmindful of the environmental losses arising out of such practices. It is, therefore, argued that the politics of sustainable development lies in its being anti-south, anti-poor, and thereby, anti-ecological.[6] This precisely is the reason that the developing countries including India did not come out very enthusiastically on the idea of sustainable development as the primary approach to deal with the global environmental challenges.

Sustained belligerence of India in the international environmental negotiations was also quite evident in the ozone parleys even before the idea of sustainable development came into prominence. The country has been consistent in its position that the global environmental problems have been the creation of the developed world, and hence, the prime responsibility of taking remedial measures also lies on them. It emphasised that the developing countries need neither worry about the impending environmental crisis nor bother about the western gimmicks of coping with them. Given such an understanding of the global environmental challenges, India refused to participate in the Vienna Conference on the protection of ozone layer in 1985, and also did not sign Vienna Convention for the Protection of the Ozone Layer.

With just 0.5 percent of total world production of chlorofluorocarbons (CFCs), India had no role to play in the ozone depletion, and nor should it be asked to shoulder the responsibility of mitigating that. Similarly, while refusing to sign the Montreal Protocol, India reiterated its stand that, 'ozone depletion had been caused by the North's profligate use of CFCs over many decades, and therefore the responsibility for remedying the situation was also the North's; furthermore, the North had a moral responsibility to assist the developing countries by transferring the technology being developed by Northern chemical firms for CFC substitutes; finally given the grossly unequal production and consumption of CFCs by developed and developing countries, any protocol that sought to place similar restrictions on the use of CFCs on all countries was iniquitous and therefore unacceptable.[7] Eventually, India agreed to sign the Amended Montreal Protocol after most, if not all, of its concerns were addressed in the London Conference in 1990.

POLITICS OF CLIMATE CHANGE

In contemporary times, the issue of climate change has become the mainstay of global environmental negotiations. Various climate conferences and programmes, along with the environmental groups warned about the catastrophic consequences of climate change unless remedial measures are initiated to deal with the problem effectively. As a result, different governments agreed in 1988 to form the Intergovernmental Panel on Climate Change (IPCC) to deliberate on the variegated issues of the matter and suggest evolution of a suitable global strategy to meet the challenge. However, for obvious reasons, the industrialised countries developed cold feet on the matter on the plea that the precise causes and consequences of climate change are yet to be ascertained, and therefore, it would be premature to be drawn into the matter. On the other hand, the developing countries, particularly the small island states, became quite proactive and called for global negotiations to discuss the questions of responsibility for climate change, and also that of the division of the costs of a global response. Showing his utmost sincerity on the issue, Indian Prime Minister Rajiv Gandhi called for the creation of a Planet Protection Fund (PPF) in 1989 to assist developing countries in acquiring environment friendly technologies at reasonable costs. Amidst the wrangling between the developing and developed countries, the IPCC set into motion a series of conferences, preparatory meetings, and sessions of Intergovernmental Negotiations Committee (INC) to arrive at a consensus on Framework Convention on Climate Change. During these proceedings, strident positions were taken by both the developed and developing countries on various issues. Ultimately, feebly standing by the position of the developing countries, the IPCC evolved the unconventional idea of common but differentiated responsibilities whereby it called upon the countries for full cooperation in accordance with their 'common but differentiated responsibilities and respective capabilities, and their social and economic conditions.'[8] Though the Framework Convention did not meet all the requirements of the developing countries, it, nonetheless, established the argument that climate change is a common problem but needs differentiated efforts on the part of different countries to overcome the problem.

With a trendsetting advantage in the form of the UN Framework Convention on Climate Change (UNFCCC), India, along with other developing countries, was an enthusiastic participant at the United Nations Conference on Environment and Development (UNCED) held at Rio de Janeiro in 1992. The major concern of these countries at the Earth Summit, as the conference is popularly called, was to extract a holistic framework of environmental protection from the developed countries in which they were to be predominantly responsible for both emission cuts as well as paying for the cost of environmental protection. Moreover, the development related issues of the developing countries were to be addressed in such a way that they become a distinct beneficiary of these environmental commitments. Hence, when the UNFCCC was signed at the Conference, the developed countries were obliged to reduce their CFCs emissions to 1990 levels by the year 2020 without substantive concomitant obligations on the developing countries. Similarly, while finalizing the Convention on Biological Diversity, India stressed the need for international incentives for biodiversity conservation in developing countries by technology transfer from the developed to the developing countries on a preferential and non-commercial basis. Besides, it argued for the recognition and reward of informal innovation by local people in order to safeguard the farmer's rights. While many developing countries showed reservations on few of these demands, eventually in the final convention, most of the demands of the developing countries found place in it.

However, more divergent positions were taken by the two sides while negotiating the Rio Declaration on Environment and Development and finalizing the Agenda 21. The major contention of India here was to secure more and more leverage for the developing countries to foster economic development without overbearing concerns for environment. But in the case of the developed countries, their economic development was to be subjected to imperatives of environmental protection. The resistance of the developed countries on the issue ultimately led to a compromise formula whereby the action plan for sustainable development would be based on the principles of local community and market principles to integrate the goals of environmental protection and economic development.

Another advantageous proposition for the developing countries at the Rio Conference came in the form of the Forest Principle. It accepted the sovereign rights of individual states to exploit their forest resources within the general principles of forest protection and management. In general, Indian diplomacy appeared to be quite effective at the Earth Summit as it succeeded, to a large extent, in galvanizing the southern solidarity into a meaningful voice to secure their unfettered right to development in face of the concerted efforts of the developed countries to tie them with the same principles that applied to them despite the situations being markedly different in the two cases.

Notwithstanding the marginal achievements of the developing countries at the Rio Conference, the real intent of the developed countries was demonstrated while negotiating and implementing the operational apparatus of the UNFCCC i.e. the Kyoto Protocol. Technically, Kyoto Protocol to the UNFCCC commits the industrialised countries to make an average of a 5.2 percent of cut in their GHG emissions from a 1990 baseline that were to be achieved by the first commitment period of 2008-12. Such an initiative burdening them with emission norms became overbearing for many of them leading to an intense play of politics on the issue. Interestingly, initially under moral prodding of the developing countries, and immense pressure of their enlightened public opinion, most of the developed countries agreed to the various instruments signed at the Earth Summit. But when it came to implementing the commitments of those instruments, the real politics behind their façade became open. Though the Kyoto Protocol was signed in 1997, the requisite number of ratifications by the member states to make it effective took eight years and it could come into force in 2005 only. Even after that, two prominent developed countries – United States and Australia – did not ratify the Protocol on account of inconvenience caused to them by the principle of 'common but differentiated responsibility' to which they had acceded to in the beginning. What is, however, more challenging for the developing countries is the subtle but sure move on the part of those countries to get the developing countries like China, India and Brazil accept some commitments to limit emissions of GHGs in the second commitment period of the Kyoto Protocol, beyond 2012.[9]

Kyoto Protocol has, in fact, become the theatre of politics on the issue of climate change between developed and the developing countries. Under intense pressure from their conservative elements and corporate houses, the United States emerged as the most vocal votary of inclusion of the developing countries within the ambit of the Kyoto Protocol without itself becoming part of it. This has placed the developing countries in a piquant situation in which they have to reorient their climate change strategies in order to bring all the developed countries on board. This has also been perceived as a failure of India's environmental diplomacy in view of its inability to persuade all the developed countries to commit and honour their commitments on the emission of GHGs for the first commitment period, on the one hand, and save itself from the predating manoeuvres of the developed countries to make it a party to limit its GHG emissions, on the other. Now, the country is left with no option but to look for a viable strategy of negotiating emission norms with the developed countries without compromising with the imperatives of rapid economic development and the basic needs of its people.

Faced with the vexed issue of meeting the challenges thrown up by the global politics of climate change, Indian policy response has been ambivalent.[10] India's official position has been that 'no negotiations are possible without addressing the egregious equity issues due to the historical burden placed on poor countries by industrialised countries, who have not only been the main contributors to the existing stock of anthropocentric GHGs, but continue to emit at per capita rates that are manifold that of a poor country like India.'[11] Such a vehement stand by India has prompted the critics to describe the Indian position as imbued with negativism and bereft of any positive postulates to overcome the stalemate dogging the climate change negotiations. However, India has charged the western countries of backing out on the commitments made at the Rio Conference and the squabbling on the Kyoto Protocol exposed their dual face while it comes to preaching and practising on the norms of international environmental protection. Further, India reminds the industrialised countries of the understanding that the developing countries would not pay for the adaptation and mitigation efforts that would have to be made feasible for them through resource and technology transfers from the developed countries. Despite such a harsh political stand, a feeling appears to be gradually dawning on the echelons of Indian policy makers that sooner or later India will have to undertake some sorts of emission commitments in order to save the climate change negotiations from getting derailed. In this direction, while certain voluntary steps have already been taken by the government, those are not an evidence of India accepting the western logic on emissions by the developing countries. Rather, India has consistently been maintaining that long-term convergence of per capita emissions is the only equitable basis for a global unanimity on climate change that the developed countries refuse to accept. In this scenario, what could have been the best policy option for India remains a moot question. Official policy response over the years has been vague and episodic as there is no clear and consistent approach or framework that directs and guides these efforts.[12]

In final analysis, the global climate change politics has

taken India off the guard, and it is becoming increasingly difficult for the country to stand the high moral and ideological ground that it has been taking from the very beginning.

CONCLUDING OBSERVATIONS

India stands out prominently amongst the countries whose international pursuits for a very long period of time were so much engrossed in the global strategic, political, and economic considerations that environmental issues failed to get even a passing reference in the agenda of national set forth for their foreign policies. Despite having vast endowments of fragile natural ecosystems and quite unsustainable systems of production, the foreign policy makers could not foresee a time when the issues of environmental protection and sustainable development could emerge as the formidable agenda in the international politics. Hence, in the beginning, India appeared as a passive recipient of the loaded issues and concepts of environmental protection offered by the developed countries. Indeed, environmental concerns came to the centre stage of Indian foreign policy only when the issue was taken up by the United Nations on a priority basis by organizing various conferences and summits to garner support of the prominent nations for the cause of environmental protection and sustainable development. Nevertheless, once the belated realisation came to the echelons of Indian foreign office that environmental issues are increasingly attaining the proportions of prime international contention, concerted efforts were afoot to not only evolve a well thought out strategy on the issue but also gather support of other developing countries, given the commonality of interests amongst them. Since then India has been at the forefront in fiercely arguing the case of the developing world in the environmental negotiations and exposing the follies of the claims and submissions made by the developed countries. For instance, at the times of negotiations on sustainable development and climate change, India has been very vociferous in emphasising the primary responsibility of the developed countries for remedying the harms caused to nature. It forcefully voiced the conviction of the developing countries that the developed countries have had been the sole beneficiary of the processes and products of modern industrial revolution that lie at the root of the current global environmental degradations. Logically, therefore, they must bear the brunt of required remedial measures for environmental sustainability. Moreover, if the developing countries are asked to share the burden of environmental sustainability, they must be adequately enabled to discharge their responsibility by unconditional financial assistance, technology transfer, soft loans, reforming international political and financial institutions, and overall improvement in the social and economic conditions of life of the people in these societies. But the recalcitrance of the developed countries is not allowing the global environmental negotiations make much headway, and the commitments made by them are likely to go unmet. In such difficult situations, the developing countries have the double responsibility of not allowing the international environmental negotiations and obligations falter due to the defiance of the developed countries, on the one hand, and jealously guarding their interests in these negotiations, on the other. In a way, thus, this precarious situation has turned out to be a test case for the Indian foreign policy whereby its diplomatic acumen and persuasive skills shall be called upon to deliver the desired result.

REFERENCES

1 John Vogler, 'Environmental Issues', in John Baylis, Steve Smith and Patricia Owens, (eds.), *The Globalization of World Politics*, 4th edition, Oxford University Press, Oxford, 2008, p. 363.

2 K R Nayar, 'Politics of Sustainable Development', *Economic and Political Weekly*, May 28, 1994, p. 1327.

3 *Declaration of the United Nations Conference on the Human Environment*, http://www.unep.org/Documents.Multilingual/Default.asp?documentID=97&ArticleID=1503, Accessed on 20 June 2013

4 David D Kemp, *Global Environmental Issues*, Routledge, London, 2004, p. 19.

5 WCED, *Our Common Future*, Oxford University Press, Oxford, 1987, P. 40.

6 K R Nayar, *op. cit.*

7 Mukund Govind Rajan, *Global Environmental Politics*, Oxford University Press, Delhi, 1997, p. 63.

8 United Nations, *Framework Convention on Climate Change*, Preamble, http://unfccc.int/resource/docs/convkp/conveng.pdf, Accessed on 21 June 2013

9 R K Pachauri, 'Can India Lead?' *India International Centre Quarterly*, Vol. 34, No. 1, Summer, 2007, p. 101.

10 For critical analysis of Indian responses and policy choices on the issue of climate change, see, Michael A. Toman, Ujjayant Chakravorty and Shreekant Gupta, (eds.), *India and Global Climate Change: Perspectives on Economics and Policy from a Developing Country*, Oxford University Press, New Delhi, 2003; and, Navroz K Dubash, (ed.), *Handbook of Climate Change and India: Development, Politics and Governance*, Oxford University Press, New Delhi, 2011.

11 Devesh Kapur, Radhika Khosla and Pratap Bhanu Mehta, 'Climate Change: India's Options', *Economic and Political Weekly*, August 1-7, 2009, p. 36.

12 Navroz K Dubash, D Raghunandan, Girish Sant and Ashok Sreenivas, 'Indian Climate Change Policy', *Economic and Political Weekly*, June 1, 2013, p. 47.

3

India's Nuclear Diplomacy : From Apartheid to Multi-Alignment

Dr. Sitakanta Mishra[1]

India's Independence coincided with the dawn of nuclear era in world politics. The Cold War rivalry characterised by nuclear weapons race between the two Super Powers brought India's statesmanship the challenge of independent nationhood. Therefore, the diplomatic base of India's nuclear strategy was established in the Nehru years and believed to have served India well as the foundation of its approach to international nuclear and disarmament conference diplomacy.[2] Irrespective of repeated assertions of its security concerns and imperatives of nuclear disarmament for decades, India found itself as "nuclear apartheid".[3]Multilateral technology denial regimes were imposed on India after the 1974 nuclear test circumscribing its nuclear energy programme in subsequent decades.

However, after the second series of nuclear tests in 1998, India has embarked on a proactive nuclear diplomacy engaging the entire world that culminated in the Indo-US civil nuclear deal in 2008. The state of affair turned in such a way that "not even India could have expected that a trade embargo on nuclear and related commerce, evolved because of India, would be lifted purely for India".[4] Today, it has initiated civil nuclear cooperation with around twenty countries and two dozen industrial houses and aspiring for nuclear suppliers group (NSG) membership. The sections that follow stride through India's transition from a "nuclear apartheid" country to a "responsible" state and its strategy of nuclear energy alignments with multiple global players.

CHANGING CONTOURS OF DIPLOMACY

Many argue that aftermath the Pokhran II tests, the diplomatic base of India's foreign policy in general, and the strategic objective of its nuclear diplomacy in particular, has changed.[5] Also, the changed environment has given rise to many new ambiguities relating to India's approach to non-proliferation regime especially the CTBT and FMCT that the diplomatic establishment has to deal with. But there is a visible triumph of new Indian 'opportunism' over its past commitment to a 'principled' foreign policy and universal disarmament.[6] Raja Mohan points out that "India's nuclear story is indeed an exceptional one" for which the Bush administration has justified the nuclear accord with New Delhi.

Amrita Narlikar is of the view that" Indian negotiators across issue areas and over time, have the dubious distinction of epitomizing the near-constant use of the strict distributive strategy ... which is quite rational one."[7] While examining the claim of "radical changes" taking place in India's foreign policy style and substance, "certainly true that something in the Indian negotiating style has changed, says Narlikar.

For instance, India justified its refusal to sign the CTBT in 1996 not by appealing to the usual arguments about 'nuclear apartheid' but by referring to 'national security considerations'." India also sent important signal to the international community by taking on a no-first-use commitment. Rather than resorting to the usual defiance, India launched diplomatic initiatives at several levels to convince the West that it was going to be a responsible nuclear power. Contrary to others expectations India voted in support of the IAEA resolution on Iran's nuclear programme.

Subrat K. Mitra and Jivanta Schottli, on the other hand, views that "Indian foreign policy is less ambiguous in deed than it is in terms of doctrine".[8] In support, they cite the nature of post-Pokhran II nuclear diplomacy which was deftly handled in its conceptualization, implementation and subsequent damage-limiting diplomacy and produced an environment conducive to a new sense of realism in Indo-US strategic relations. It is to be seen how soon and how smoothly India is included in the NSG.

Broadly, there persist today a sense of unanimity among scholars regarding India's diplomacy that has "acquired a significant strategic space with its expanding engagements with various countries" and its nuclear diplomacy being the fulcrum of this paradigm shift. Certainly, "there is a success story to be found in India's nuclear diplomacy", Ashok Kapur said way back in 1976; but such success must be seen in the light of the external as well as internal constraints, policy ambiguities and compulsions that the diplomacy operates under. It is to wonder how the international reactions towards, and the diplomatic challenges out of, India's nuclear tests in 1998 were handled to pacify the global outrage. Why the countries that were critical about India's nuclear programme and had imposed technology embargos are now willing to put aside their principled position and trade nuclear with India? Does India's negotiating approach and/or the philosophical base of its global vision changed? In pursuit of examining the contours of India's nuclear diplomatic undertaking since 1998, and more specifically in the post-Indo-US civil nuclear deal, this chapter attempts to identify the criticalities of India's *nuclear multi-alignment* strategy.

THE 'MULTI-ALIGNMENT' DEBATE

A plethora of strategic studies in the post-Indo-US civil nuclear deal have advanced the idea that India today is positioning itself in the post-Cold War global diplomacy. C Raja Mohan names it as the "diplomacy of 'multi-alignment' that replaced its earlier emphasis on non-alignment."[9] According to Brahma Chellaney, India "having helped found the non-aligned movement today repositioning itself to be multi-aligned, *while preserving the core element of nonalignment* – strategic autonomy".[10] However, Kanwal Sibal views this "not an accurate description as India is not entering into multiple alliances". Rather, "this is an extension of nonalignment, in the context of the new world of globalization".[11]

Sibal's assertion corroborates a collective deliberation by a group of Indian analysts and policy makers (Sunil Khilnani, Rajiv Kumar, Pratap Bhanu Mehta, Prakash Menon, Nandan Nilekani, Srinath Raghavan, Shyam Saran, Siddharth Varadarajan) titled "NONALIGNMENT 2.0: A Foreign and Strategic Policy for India in the Twenty First Century" that attempted to identify the basic principles that should guide India's foreign and strategic policy over the next decade.[12] It reiterates that "strategic autonomy" has been the defining value and continuous goal of India's international policy and believes that this continues to remain at the core of India's global engagements even today. In pursuit of renovating that value and goal for the twenty-first century it stresses non-alignment as a strategy to be used for the strategic interests of India. But, the report's key recommendation, taking into account India's current strategic circumstances, that India should remain "nonaligned" well into the future and refrain from cementing strong strategic "alliances" with other actors is "deeply misguided and potentially even dangerous" and "India would be left perilously vulnerable", views Ashley J. Tellis.[13]

However, all acknowledge the fact that India is poised to be a major power but disagree to paraphrase a single terminology about the nature and contours of current diplomatic strategy that India has embarked on. The term 'multi-alignment', though sounds fancy and seems appropriate in relation to the phraseology of 'non-alignment', it has no precise definition or conceptual explanation yet. In an attempt to explore the contours of India's so-called 'multi-alignment' strategy, two narrations cited here.

(1) During the release of the Malayalam transliteration of his book *Pax Indica* on 9 December 2012, Shashi Tharoor expressed that:

> India is a non-permanent member in UN. At the same time, it is a SAARC member. India is a G-77 member as well as G-20 member. It is part of RIC, BRIC, IBSA, BASIC at the same time. After non-alignment, it is time for **multi-alignment** in international relations.[14]

To quote Thoroor, in another occasion:

> My vision of foreign policy is a means to enable the transformation of India by accelerating its growth, preserving its strategic autonomy, and protecting its people. We need to move beyond non-alignment to **multi-alignment**. My metaphor is that of the World Wide Web. In this increasingly networked world, we are going to have to work through *multiple networks*,

and the networks will sometimes overlap with each other, but sometimes they will be distinct; they all serve our interests in different ways.[15]

(2) In a policy review of the Hoover Institution (2006), C. Raja Mohan and Parag Khanna write:

While there is no guarantee that India will become more allied or aligned, there has been a continuous trajectory toward a diplomatic posture which is perhaps best described as "neo-Curzonian," after the British imperial viceroy and player of the "Great Game" Lord George Curzon. Ironically, India's neo-Curzonian worldview is the logical heir to one of the nation's strategic ur-texts, Kautilya's fourth-century B.C. Arthashastras, which locates India at the nucleus of concentric rings of potential friends and foes. A neo-Curzonian foreign policy is premised on the logic of Indian centrality, permitting *multidirectional engagement* – or "**multi-alignment**" – with all major powers and seeking access and leverage from East Africa to Pacific Asia.[16]

While Shashi Tharoor's assertions are more generic, based on the fact that the world has been increasingly networked and India needs to work through "multiple networks", Raja Mohan and Parag Khanna, with an analogical construct, define multi-alignment as "multidirectional engagement" like Lord Curzon's India centrality policy. However, both descriptions do not correlate with, in any sense, competition or alliance against any other state. Rather, it resembles to multiple partnerships and alliances for meeting India's vital national interests. Though the prefix "non" is replaced by "multi", the term "alignment" is in no way indicates a Cold War type situation (or the NAM) where India has to chose one against the other or stay aloof. Introspectively, after the end of Cold War, India's global engagements have been premised on a "forward foreign policy" emphasising simultaneously the revival of commercial cooperation, links with neighbourhood, developing energy supplies and assets, and pursuing of multistate defence/strategic partnerships. India's growing role in the global arena is now premised on the strategy of "multi-alignment which is the way forward and not non-alignment".[17] Whether India has fully recovered the Curzonian "360-degree vision" in its global outlook is still debatable as certain issue areas have remained unattended by Indian strategic calculations.

However, one can easily figure out the fact that, after the 1998 nuclear tests India has carved out a *360-degree nuclear vision* – engaging America and Europe for removing the technology embargo, negotiating the Central Asian and African republics, and convincing the East Asian countries and Australia about its nonproliferation credentials, for uranium supply while not shying away from potential strategic competition with nuclear neighbours. As a part of this vision India, in the first phase tries to access nuclear material and technology supply channels and in the long-term eyes to be a supplier itself through various treaty arrangements bilaterally and multilaterally.

TOWARDS NUCLEAR MULTI-ALIGNMENT

As part of India's post-Pokhran II nuclear diplomacy, the 14 round of talks between Jaswant Singh and Strobe Talbot culminated in US President Bill Clinton's visit to India and initiation of the Next Step in Strategic Partnership (NSSP). USA, the most vocal critic of India's nuclear option, was convinced to take note of India's compulsions. It is argued that the post-Pokhran II diplomacy has "changed the way the Indian elite began to think about external relations and diplomacy and the political will ... to find reconciliation that inevitably brought a new maturity and self-assurance to India's foreign policy."[18] India's self-assured diplomatic posture to deal with the exigencies of the tests explored many innovative approaches to engage multiple actors simultaneously. The Indian community in US who plays influential role in US administration was mobilized to garner support. Once the US made its peace with nuclear India, other US allies like Australia, Canada, Japan, and some North European countries fell in line supporting India's cause. Simultaneously, India's relations with Russia, France and China gradually reached a high level.

Subsequently, India's entire diplomatic attention was focused on to achieve a special waiver from technology embargo imposed by multilateral nuclear regime. With strong backing from US, India managed to ink the IAEA safeguards agreement followed by the NSG "clean waiver" from its existing rules, which forbid nuclear trade with a non-NPT member country. Ever since the conclusion of the 123 Agreement with the United States, Memorandums of Understanding (MoUs) for civil nuclear cooperation have mushroomed in India. At present, the civil nuclear network that India is carving spans six continents.

India's quest for nuclear energy in recent years can be viewed as the second phase of its nuclear networking which seems to be robust and smarter than the first phase – initiated as early as the 1950s, when Jawaharlal Nehru and Homi J. Bhabha set out to garner technology support for harnessing atomic energy for India's socio-economic uplift. Countries like USA, Canada, France, Britain, Germany and Soviet Union were part of the network. While the rationale and drive behind the first phase of network was to lay down a country-side nuclear technology infrastructure, the current phase of networking is driven by the reality of energy security of a rapidly growing India. Even if India's per capita energy consumption was to rise to 5,000 kWh from around 600 kWh of today, it would still suffer an energy deficit of 421 GW by 2050.[19] Even if its Gross Domestic Product (GDP) grows at 7-8 per cent per annum, the energy requirements of India are expected to grow at 5.6-6.4 per cent per annum over the next few years. This implies a four-fold increase in India's energy requirement over the next 25 years.[20] For a large country like India, bulk imports of fossil fuel are neither affordable nor strategically prudent. Given the country-wide nuclear infrastructure and scientific-technological skills that India is endowed with, nuclear power is a viable option to overcome future energy requirements and if things move right. Also, empirically, the Long Range Marginal Cost (LRMC) of nuclear energy or nuclear power supply at locations far away from other sources like coal or hydel would be cost-effective.[21]

However, the key to making nuclear energy as a viable option is availability of uranium which is in short supply in India. The country's reserves stand only at 78,000 tonnes of low-grade ore, which requires processing before it becomes usable for reactors.[22] Four mines in Singhbhum (Bihar) produce only 220 tonnes of uranium concentrate.[23] In addition, 120 tonnes come from byproducts like tailings from phosphate, zinc and copper mines. Besides the requirements for its weapons programme, India's operating civilian reactors require more than 600 tonnes of uranium concentrate annually. Two more mines, one in Meghalaya (Domiasat) and another in Karnataka, may increase the output to about 600 tonnes. All these may meet the requirements of the existing reactors but are not enough for the ambitious nuclear power generation that India is planning. Generating 47,000 MW of nuclear energy by 2025, as envisaged by the UPA government, will require huge amounts of uranium. For materialising such an ambitious programme, India will need as much as 100,000 tonnes of new ore but the chances of finding it within the country are slim. Therefore, India's strategy of multiple alignments with nuclear technology and uranium enriched countries is an imperative.

First of all, the civil nuclear deal with the US marks a watershed in India's nuclear diplomacy in general and in Indo-US relations in particular. It promises uninterrupted supply of nuclear fuel and technology. This has helped assimilating India into the nuclear mainstream to reap enormous economic, political and strategic dividends for the country. During his India visit in June 2013, Secretary of State John Kerry, in pursuit of setting a timeline for operationalising the civil nuclear agreement, announced that American nuclear equipment supplier Westinghouse Electric Co. would sign a "commercial agreement" to sell nuclear reactors to India's Nuclear Power Corporation by September 2013.[24]

When the USA gave the green signal and the IAEA safeguards agreement in August 2008, France was the first country to enter into a formal understanding (September 30, 2008) with New Delhi, as even the Indo-US deal was awaiting Congressional approval. The deal came into force with the exchange of instruments of ratification on January 14, 2010. This forms the basis of wide ranging bilateral cooperation from basic and applied research to full civil nuclear cooperation, including reactors, nuclear fuel supply, nuclear safety, radiation and environment protection and nuclear fuel cycle management. According to sources, France has agreed to provide 300 tonnes of uranium to India. A couple of days after the IAEA safeguard agreement was concluded, the French nuclear giant Areva signed a deal worth US$ 12.3 billion with NPCIL to provide India six new-generation reactors at Jaitapur in Maharashtra. In all, 35 French firms are eyeing the civil nuclear sector in India today.

Russia signed a broad-based agreement in the civil nuclear field with India on December 7, 2009, to ensure transfer of technology and uninterrupted uranium fuel supplies.[25] The agreement goes far beyond the Indo-US nuclear agreement, under which Russia has ensured fuel supply guarantee even if India conducts a nuclear test in the future. The pact promises enrichment and reprocessing rights and access to high end technology (light water reactors). India approached some uranium rich countries in Africa and Central Asia as well. According to sources, Russia's state nuclear energy company, *Atomenergoprom*, said that Russian nuclear fuel manufacturer TVEL has supplied the first batch of 30 tonnes of pellets on April 8, 2009, for India's PHWRs.[26] Under the agreement, Russia will set up four new reactors in Kudankulam and another nuclear park of 6-8 nuclear reactors in Haripur in West Bengal.[27]

The Indo-US civil nuclear cooperation turned full circle on February 4, 2010, when President Obama certified India's placement of its nuclear facilities under the IAEA safeguards. The economic-strategic benefits that the Indo-US nuclear deal would accrue have been painted vividly. According to the US-India Business Council (USIBC), the deal could add up to US $ 150 billion over the next 30 years.[28] In 2009, the US Commercial Nuclear Mission visited India with 60 senior executives of 30 nuclear power companies. L&T has signed an MoU with Westinghouse of the US for work involving engineering, procurement, construction and manufacturing activities for the AP 1000 modular nuclear reactors. The infrastructure company Punj Lloyd and the US based Thorium Power have signed an MoU to form a 50:50 joint venture to explore commercial nuclear power opportunities.[29] The proposed investment is US$ 1 billion.

Kazakhstan became the fourth country to sign a nuclear cooperation agreement with India in January 2009. The scope of the agreement involves export of uranium from Kazakhstan which is currently the world's second largest producer and caters for 15 per cent of the world's uranium needs.[30]While Kazatomprom, the state-owned nuclear holding company, aims at a comprehensive nuclear agreement, India wants to leverage its agreement with it not only to source uranium but also to use the company's 10 per cent stake in Westinghouse Electric Corporation and tap advanced nuclear technology.

The first African nation to sign a civil nuclear deal with India (on August 31, 2009) was Namibia,[31] which is the fifth-largest producer of good quality uranium in the world. Initially, under the Agreement on Cooperation in Peaceful Use of Nuclear Energy, the two sides will trade uranium and exchange expertise in designing of atomic plants, and train personnel.

India inked an Agreement for Cooperation in the Peaceful Uses of Nuclear Energy with Argentina during President Christina Fernandez de Kirchner's state visit to India on October 14, 2009.[32] The joint statement states that India and Argentina will use the synergies and vast experience of their nuclear scientists and technologists. Taking into account their respective capabilities and experience in the peaceful uses of nuclear energy, the two countries have agreed to encourage and support scientific technical and commercial cooperation for mutual benefit in this field. An Institutional Cooperation Agreement between the Argentina Council on Scientific and Technical Research (COICET) and Council of Scientific & Industrial Research (CSIR) India has been signed in this regard.

The world's largest producer and third-largest reservoir of uranium, Canada has signed a civil nuclear agreement with India on June 28, 2010, paving the way for Canadian firms to take part in India's multi-billion nuclear energy business over the next 10 years.[33] The Atomic Energy of Canada, Ltd. (AE CL) aims to enter into technology, marketing or even ownership partnerships with its Indian counterparts. L&T signed an MoU with AE CL during the visit of Stockwell Day, the Canadian International Trade Minister, covering development of the Candu ACR 1000 heavy-water moderated reactor for the Indian market.[34]

A declaration on civil nuclear cooperation between India and Britain was signed on February 11, 2010.[35] The UK's nuclear goods and equipment exports are worth 700 million pounds and its civil nuclear industry provides employment to 80,000 people. Its nuclear industry is also keen to provide 70 to 80 per cent of a new nuclear reactor in India. British companies specializing in nuclear safety and research have resumed contacts with India. However, potential British suppliers are in the private sector, therefore, the British government has raised objections to New Delhi's restrictions on nuclear commerce that is confined to the public sector.

Beside all these, nuclear cooperation agreements of various nature and aspects with another twenty countries are in the pipeline. They include countries such as, Belgium, Brazil, Mongolia, Uzbekistan, Kazakhstan, Uzbekistan, Ukraine, Nigeria, Sweden, Hungary, Germany, Spain, South Korea, South Africa, Niger, Japan, Australia, China, etc. Agreement with each of these countries may take longer time to conclude but they are equally important partners in India's ambitious nuclear energy programme.

However, nuclear deals are not the immediate solutions for increasing energy supply. One can mark the amount of time and effort needed between signing an MoU and translating it into a formal agreement for full nuclear cooperation. To be competitive and maximise the potential benefits of today's relatively simple nuclear market, India needs to make smart moves. The hunt for energy resources is a challenge, as can be seen in how China has repeatedly outbid India in Africa, Central Asia and Myanmar. For example, in Namibia, India will face tough competition from Chinese, Russian and Western companies that are also interested in the country's rich deposits. India's strategy to source nuclear technology and materials from diversified sources, no doubt, is impressive. But certain potential supplier countries have been surprisingly overlooked or neglected. Jordan possesses 2 per cent of global uranium reserves and has cordial relations with India. So far, no attention has been paid to Jordan which is planning to build its own nuclear power plants by 2015. Other countries in the region like Saudi Arabia, Syria and the UAE, are lucrative destinations for India. Until recently, India had overlooked the benefits of dealing with China in the nuclear energy sector.

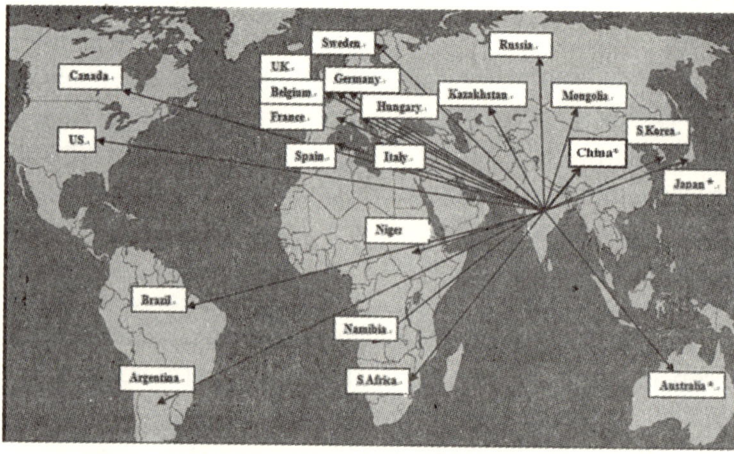

India's Nuclear Network: A 360° View

The latest round of diplomatic engagements with the reluctant suppliers like Australia, Japan and a critical China bring home the impression that India will ultimately break out of the 'nuclear apartheid' through a grand bargain with the world. Through sustained dialogue with these three countries and taking along the confidence of USA, India would be able to win for itself the NSG membership in the future. This would open up the Pandora's Box for India to energize its nuclear energy sector.

A NUCLEAR GRAND BARGAIN!

Amidst prolonged domestic opposition to new nuclear

projects, especially the Kudankulam stand-off, India has received positive gestures from three countries that have so far remained adamant to its requisites for civil nuclear energy. On May 20, 2013 in a Joint Statement during the visit of Chinese Premier Li Keqiang, China and India have agreed "for carrying out bilateral cooperation in civil nuclear energy".[36] On May 29, 2013, Prime Minister Manmohan Singh agreed over a Joint Statement with Japanese Prime Minister on the importance of such cooperation between the two countries.[37] On June 3, 2013, the Australian Prime Minister Julia Gillard expressed her main aim "to get away from the problem that prevented Australia into entering uranium sale with India" and now she is "working on the safeguards agreement".[38]

These all may have taken place coincidentally; but, if they really reach their logical conclusions, it would be a *grand bargain* to liberate India from the 'nuclear apartheid' once for all. However, the pace of the bargain and consequent achievements will depend on the degree of public acceptance, as well as expedition, of nuclear energy projects at home. Secondly, India needs to stock-take the flurry of nuclear pacts it has signed so far to evaluate how many of them really shown results. Thirdly, as national elections are due in Japan and Australia later this year and in India early next year, contours of the bargains may alter in consonance with the outcomes of the poll and the ideology of political party that assumes power. Therefore, it would be prudent to scrutinize all possible contours of the respective deals in advance while addressing genuine public concerns patiently.

(I) Contours of Sino-Indian Proposal

In the 20th May Joint Statement, Chinese Premier Li Keqiang and Prime Minister Manmohan Singh acknowledged that "expansion of civil nuclear energy program is essential component of their national energy plans to ensure energy security". Therefore, in line with their respective international commitments, the two countries "will carry out bilateral cooperation in civil nuclear energy". This certainly promises a new chapter in Sino-Indian relations and potential of stable addition to the booming bilateral economic relationship provided both countries keep away the nuclear trade from bilateral contentious issues.

In 1993, China had supplied low enriched uranium for Tarapur nuclear plant after USA in 1974, and France in 1993, stopped their supply. Ever since, India has overlooked the benefits of dealing with China in the nuclear energy sector. Though its uranium reserves comprise only one per cent of global reserves and even less than India's, China has an ambitious nuclear energy programme underway. China – a relatively late-comer to the civil nuclear industry – is gluing to the edge of a frontline nuclear energy nation. Following a two-pronged strategy, comprising both outbound activities and domestic capacity building, Beijing is fast becoming the 'favoured nuclear partner' for nuclear developments across the world. Partnering in nuclear front with China will certainly help India draw lessons from its strategy to become a "favoured guest" both as an investor in international projects and as a customer for its own domestic demands.[39]

First of all, absence of any nuclear cooperation between India and China would lead to unwarranted competition as both countries are targeting the same source for uranium procurement. Secondly, cooperation in civil nuclear field would foster bilateral exchanges which will restore some balance in India's foreign policy undertaking as it is criticized West-oriented. Thirdly, since China is planning a major expansion of its nuclear energy programme and is expected to become the second biggest consumer of the radioactive metal (around 20% of global uranium demand), New Delhi's partnering with Beijing would help both become stakeholders in each other's programmes. In the process, foreign companies involved in China may get attracted towards India's nuclear energy expansion programme.

However, imagining a Sino-Indian civil nuclear deal in line with the Indo-US nuclear deal at this point would be farfetched. At the initial stage both countries can focus their cooperation on safety and security, social acceptance, nuclear information management, uranium procurement issues and may be some technical exchanges. A few small cooperative steps initially would help setting the tone of nuclear cooperation and develop mutual understanding, especially on India's credentials for a Nuclear Suppliers Group (NSG) membership for which China is found to be a stumbling block.

(II) A Problematic Pact with Japan

Indicating a major shift in Japan's post-Hiroshima nuclear policy, the May 29th India-Japan Joint Statement has reaffirmed the importance of a civil nuclear cooperation between India and Japan. However, many in Japan view such a "pact is problematic especially in view of the fact that India is not a party to the nuclear nonproliferation treaty (NPT)".[40] In fact, clause 31 of the Joint Statement gives an impression that "India, Japan differ on Comprehensive Test Ban Treaty (CTBT)".[41] While the Japanese Prime Minister stressed the importance of bringing into force the CTBT at an early date, his Indian counterpart reiterated New Delhi's voluntary moratorium on nuclear test.

Moreover, the Japanese domestic critics view such a pact with India "would further undermine the effectiveness and relevance of the NPT system".[42] An editorial in the Japanese national daily newspaper *Asahi Shimbun* opined that "Tokyo should ask New Delhi to become a party to the NPT and sing the CTBT".[43] In protest against the start of negotiations, the 2010 Nagasaki Peace Declaration said, "a nation that has suffered atomic bombings itself is now severely weakening the NPT which is beyond intolerable".[44]

Although an actual India-Japan civil nuclear deal may take a few more years to finalise, it is to introspect now if Japan is really going to compromise on its principled nuclear stand with India; if yes, why? Second, what would be the terms of negotiation for India to win a deal with Japan while maintaining its strategic programme, reprocessing rights, and non-proliferation stand? Third, what benefits, technological or otherwise, will India accrue from Japan through the deal?

Taking into account Japanese economic situation in the post-Fukushima phase, Tokyo may come in term with India for its potential as a huge market for nuclear energy technology. As prospects for constructing new nuclear reactors in Japan is fading as a result of the 2011 disaster, the export of nuclear energy technology is of extreme interest to roughly 10,000 companies in Japan.[45] Experts view that "the economic trickle-down effects from exports are huge. ... Japan's technology is indispensible for the US and France ...." As US and France use Japanese-made parts for nuclear plants, the absence of a nuclear agreement between India and Japan slows down nuclear business deals for those two nations as well.[46]

To carry forward the deal, India may satisfy Japan by a separate bilateral pact or safeguards agreement ensuring its commitment on nuclear test moratorium and nonproliferation. As the stakes seem high for both India and Japan for such a pact, India should ensure Japan to agree to the terms of its nuclear liability provisions for any future purchases. However, outright acceptance of, or shifting attitude towards, NPT or CTBT at their present forms would be difficult for UPA government to convince the domestic public when national election is at the doorstep. India's sentiments and compulsions should be conveyed to Japan in clear and sound terms.

In reference to the benefits by dealing with Japan, India's aspiration for getting membership of international export control regimes like the NSG, Missile Technology Control Regime (MTCR), the Australia Group and the Wassenaar Arrangement, would be facilitated. The most important benefit India would gain through Japanese cooperation is in the area of nuclear safety by gaining Japan's experiences and lessons derived from the nuclear accident. However, in terms of other technological benefits, according to Dr A Gopalakrishnan, Japan does not have any comprehensive nuclear reactor technology of its own today. It will either be GE-Hitachi or Westinghouse-Toshiba plants, which are mostly license-based production in Japan, where technology control mostly rests with the US companies.[47] Therefore, to get reactors from GE or Westinghouse, India has to have separate understanding or play ball with Japan as these companies have term and condition agreements with Tokyo on third-country sales.

Secondly, for purchase of "Japanese reactors", India may not expect or receive much financing from them as Japanese finances are in shambles in the post-Fukushima years. Moreover, it would be prudent to wait until their "nuclear sector including their questionable quality control system is put back in order to repose confidence on them".

Nevertheless, the Japanese interest in resuming the debate for a civil nuclear deal with India is a big leap in Japan's nuclear policy. It is clear that Japan understands the symbolic and practical importance of a deal with India, especially after Australia lifted its ban on uranium exports to India in 2011. But the issue will remain highly controversial in Japan with formidable bureaucratic and political opposition. As a result, Abe has been consistently forced to reiterate his desire for India to sign the CTBT, if not the NPT. But there is a good chance that after the elections in the Japanese Upper House in July 2013, Abe may have the political strength to push through an agreement. "This would represent a major conceptual change in Japan's nuclear non-proliferation posture.... There could be wider implications than just making an exception for India".[48] Equally, this would be a major breakthrough in India's nuclear diplomacy after the Indo-US civil nuclear deal.

(III) Australia's First Non-NPT Customer

If things move as planned, India will be the first customer that is not a signatory to the NPT to get Australian uranium. Normally, Canberra bans export of uranium to countries that are not a party to the NPT. Making an exception to this policy has been a quite big political issue in Australia, despite India's strong non-proliferation credentials.

In fact, after initial hesitation, Australia had agreed in principle in 2007 to export uranium to India "subject to India agreeing to very stringent safeguards and conditions".[49] Defending the Australian government's decision to lift the ban on uranium sales to India, former Australian Premier John Howard spoke to Manmohan Singh (August 16, 2007) after which he announced negotiations between the two countries. But the Australian government's chief nuclear adviser Ziggy Switkowski expected a ban on further nuclear testing by India to be part of any deal. After the defeat of the Austrian Labor Party (ALP) in the 2007 federal election, the momentum and willingness to cooperate with India in the civil nuclear field had waned. However, during the visit of the new Australian Prime Minister Kevin Rudd to New Delhi in November 2009, India pressed hard for uranium sales.

After ALP coming into power in 2010, Prime Minister Julia Gillard resumed the debate and faced down many in her own party to force a change in Australia's uranium sale policy specifically for India. Senator Scott Ludlam views that India has a history of nuclear accidents, near misses and misadventure, and it is only a matter of time until a serious incident occurs.[50] He raises that India is buying uranium from foreign source to lock up own domestic reserves for weapon purpose; this would beget an arms race with Pakistan. Suffice it to say that Australia also supplies uranium to China which obviously frees up Chinese domestic reserves. Also, Ludlam views that the nuclear sector worldwide is in huge trouble at this moment and the Australian government at the behest of the mining industry are looking for any markets at all. India as an industrialising nation with a growing nuclear energy sector, the Uranium industrial lobby finds it as a green pasture.

Whatever may be the motives and drivers, while aiming for and working towards a uranium supply deal with Australia (which holds about a third of world's recoverable Uranium reserves) India must be ready with defined terms of bargain. To satisfy Australia's national resolve and non-proliferation sentiments, India needs to reassure Canberra may be in the form of a separate agreement in good faith for peaceful use of the uranium supplied. All these have to be finalised keeping in mind the federal elections in Australia scheduled in September this year and Parliamentary election in India in 2014.

Side Effects of the Bargain

India to achieve the aspired end of the discriminatory nuclear regimes that have circumscribed India's inherent right to tame the atom, specific deals with these three nations constitute a 'grand bargain' for India. The road and the process to achieve this would certainly not be smooth. Beside the procedural and conditional issues for such deals, India is likely to face complicacies and manage its implications on three critical spheres – domestic, regional and global.

With the opening of these negotiations, India would be the target of intensive anti-nuclear lobby operating in these countries which would exacerbate the domestic anti-nuclear movement in India. Early settlement of the Kudankulam issue and enhancement of public acceptance of new nuclear projects should be priorities for Manmohan Singh government. With a comprehensive 'nuclear information management' network, the nuclear establishment must address all public concerns before jumping into more new projects. Otherwise, India's image as a responsible nuclear power would be hampered when domestic opposition will hinder its global commitments through various deals it is signing for.

Also, India needs to mind Pakistan's probable reactions and moves, and its implications in a regional context, especially for getting through Japan and Australia's node for exceptional nuclear deals. It is to ponder, if China will not give Pakistan an edge over India in the nuclear area. It has already inked a civil nuclear deal secretly with Pakistan which is rapidly expanding its nuclear arsenals and missile inventory. With Chinese backing, Pakistan will leave no chance for pulling India's leg to hinder its entry into multilateral nuclear groups. The Sino-Pak strategic nexus would be more intensive in the years ahead with frustration out of India's diplomatic maneuvers. To manage Pakistan for a soft landing in its incessant struggle for maintaining strategic parity with India should be a major diplomatic task, as part of India's current nuclear diplomacy.

On the international front, India's strategic relations especially with Japan and Australia may have provoking ramifications on global power configuration. The US has been encouraging strategic partnership between US, Japan and India and also between US, Japan and Australia. This quadrilateral equation may attract critical attention of China. On the other hand, USA has also floated the idea of a triangular strategic equation between the US, India and China which would also attract critical attention of Japan. The proposed nuclear deals alongside India's strategic cooperation with all these actors would be a tight rope walk for New Delhi in the years ahead.

INSULATING THE NUCLEAR STRATEGY

In pursuit of ensuring nuclear energy as a viable source of national energy mix, India has visualized an ambitious nuclear energy expansion plan. It has initiated nuclear cooperation deals with around ten countries and a dozen industrial houses. As global leaders in nuclear energy commerce, countries like USA, France, Russia, Japan, Australia, China and a few Central Asian countries constitute India's core and determining partners. However, inherent adversarial and competing relations among them may land India sometime in awkward situations. For example, Manmohan Singh's visit to Japan in May and India's strategic partnership initiative with Tokyo has riled China. Beijing has accused Tokyo of attempting forge alliances with New Delhi to "encircle China". The ruling Chinese Communist Party-run *Global Times* on May 30 came out with an opinion titled "India gets close to Japan at its own peril".[51] This suggests that China views India-Japan relation is "animated by a shared strategic agenda of encircling and countering China".[52] This would be counter-productive for India's aspirations to get access to multilateral nuclear trading cartels.

Such developments might in fact give rise bloc politics which is completely against India's foreign policy ideals. "India does not fancy a situation in which it might have to choose one nation over the other" by overlooking its national interest.[53] Therefore, New Delhi will have to maintain equidistance from all while aligning with multiple nuclear partners but not get entangled to rivalries among them. India must express loud and clear to all concerned that New Delhi only mean nuclear business and nothing else. While setting its own house in order by taking along the domestic public in its quest for new nuclear projects, India has to devise a strategy to insulate its nuclear dealings from global/regional power politics. However, while bargaining for grand deals with important nuclear players, India has to take cognizance of US help in bringing India the much needed breakthrough.

REFERENCES

1 Ashok Kapur, "The Diplomatic Base of India's Nuclear Strategy, in *Pokhran and Beyond: India's Nuclear Behaviour*, New Delhi: Oxford, 2003, p. 73.

2 The term nuclear "nuclear apartheid" is used for describing the differentiated standards of national security; the perceived unjust international nuclear order where nuclear weapons and their role are paradoxically legitimized. Most nations are beneficiaries of a security this framework in which nuclear weapons powers provide extended deterrent protection, only Africa and southern Asia remained outside the paradigm. See, Jaswant Singh, "Against Nuclear Apartheid", *Foreign Affairs*, September/October 1998.

3 Ajay K Rai, *India's Nuclear Diplomacy After Pkhran II*, New Delhi: Pearson/Longman, 2009.

4 C Raja Mohan argues that radical changes or reorientations are taking place in India's foreign policy style and substance. For detail see C. Raja Mohan, *Crossing the Rubicon*, New Delhi: Penguin, 2000.

5 C Raja Mohan, "India's Nuclear Exceptionalism", in Morten Bremer Maerli and Sverre Lodgaard edited *Nuclear Proliferation and International Security*, London: Routledge, p. 154.

6 Distributive strategy, also known as the value-claiming strategy, comprises of 'a set of tactics that are functional only for claiming value from others and defending against such claiming'. Examples include very high opening demands, refusing to make any concessions, and holding the other issue hostage. Amrita Narlikar, "Peculiar Chauvinism or Strategic Calculation? Explaining the Negotiating Strategy of a Rising India", *International Affairs*, vol. 82, Issue I, 2006, pp. 59-76.

7 Subrat K Mitra and Jivanta Schottli, "The New Dynamics of Indian Foreign Policy and its Ambiguities", *Irish Studies in International Affairs*, vol. 18, 2007, pp. 19-34.

8 C Raja Mohan, "India, China and the United States: Asia's Emerging Strategic Triangle", Snapshot 8, The Lowy Institute's MacArthur Asia Security Project, February 2011, http://www.lowyinstitute.org/

files/pubfiles/Mohan,_India_Snapshot8_web.pdf, p. 1.

9 Brahma Chellaney, "The Quad: Australia-India-Japan-U.S. Strategic Cooperation", http://chellaney.net/2007/07/02/the-quad-australia-india-japan-u-s-strategic-cooperation/

10 Kanwal Sibal, "'Strategic' Relations Suit India", http://indiatoday.intoday.in/story/strategic-relations-suit-india-india-today/1/239437.html, December 26, 2012.

11 Sunil Khilnani et al., "NONALIGNMENT 2.0: A Foreign and Strategic Policy for India in the Twenty First Century", http://www.ris.org.in/images/RIS_images/pdf/NonAlignment.pdf, 2012.

12 Ashley J. Tellis, "Nonalignment Redux: The Perils of Old Wine in New Skins", http://carnegieendowment.org/files/nonalignment_redux.pdf, July 10, 2012.

13 "Multi-alignment in Global Relations for India Mooted", http://htsyndication.com/htsportal/article?arid=%22644338%22&pub=%22New+Indian+Express%22, December 9, 2012.

14 ON RECORD: 'TIME FOR MULTI-ALIGNMENT', Ashok Tuteja in conversation with Shashi Tharoor http://tharoor.in/press/on-record-time-for-multi-alignment/

15 C. Raja Mohan and Parag Khanna, "Getting India Right", *Policy Review 135*, Hoover Institution, Stanford University, February 1, 2006, www.hoover.org/publications/policy-review/article/7570, p. 2.

16 Jeffrey W. Legro, Professor of Politics from the University of Virginia quoted saying "Multi-alignment the Way Forward", http://www.thehindu.com/todays-paper/tp-national/tp-andhrapradesh/multialignment-the-way-forward-legro/article2972568.ece, March 8, 2012.

17 C Raja Mohan, *Crossing the Rubicon*, 2003

18 "Uranium Import can Stave Off Looming Energy Crisis: Kakodkar", *Hindu Business Line*, July 5, 2008.

19 "Energy Overview", http://www.indiacore.com/overview-energy.html

20 Joginder K. Alagh, "Economics of Nuclear Power in India", *Nu-Power International*, vol. 11, no. 1-3, 1997, p. 22.

21 "India Needs 1 Lakh Tonnes Uranium, says Kakodkar", *The Hindu*, April 11, 2006.

22 Hari Sud, "India's Quest for Uranium", October 9, 2009, UPI Asia.com

23 Niharika Mandhana and Biman Mukherji, "U.S.-India Nuclear Deal Still Far Off", *The Wall Street Journal,* June 26, 2013.

24 "India, Russia Sign Nuclear Deal", http://timesofindia.indiatimes.com/india/India-Russiasign-nuclear-deal/articleshow/5311267.cms

25 "Russia Confirms Delivery of Uranium Pellets to India", April 15, 2009, No. 43 / News in Brief, http://www.worldnuclear.org

26 "India and Russia Sign Civil Nuclear Agreement", http://www.hindu.com/2009/12/08/stories/2009120856260100.htm, December 8, 2009

27 "US Business Hails $150 Billion 'Opportunity' in N-Deal", October 2, 2008, http://www.prokerala.com/news/articles/a6409.html

28 P.B. Jayakumar, "Punj Lloyd-Thorium JV to Pump in $1 bn", *Business Standard,* January 18, 2009.

29 Utpal Bhaskar, "India to Ink Nuclear Deal with Kazakhstan by Month-end", http://www.livemint.com/2009/01/11235839/India-to-ink-nuclear-deal-with.html, January 11, 2009.

30 "India, Namibia Sign Uranium Supply Deal", August 31, 2009, http://www.thaindian.com/newsportal/business/india-namibia-sign-uranium-supply-deal_100240902.html#ixzz0dz2wJkK4

31 Anand, "India, Argentina Ink Civil Nuclear Pact & Agreements on Science and Technology", October 15, 2009, http://machinist.in/index.php?option=com_content&task=view&id=2393&Itemid=2

32 "India, Canada Sign Civilian Nuclear Deal", http://www.thestatesman.net/index.php?option=com_content&view=article&id=332728&catid=35

33 "L&T, Canadian Firm Ink Pact for Nuclear Reactor at Hazira", The Financial Express, January 23, 2009.

34 "Britain, India Sign Civil Nuclear Pact: Official", http://www.google.com/hostednews/afp/article/AL eqM5jHW OUA C32W7duhpXH2RWS hnmMXdw

35 "Joint Statement on the State Visit of Chinese Premier Li Kequiang to India", http://www.mea.gov.in/bilateral-documents.htm?dtl/21723, May 20, 2013.

36 "Joint Statement on Prime Minister's visit to Japan: Strengthening the Strategic and Global Partnership between India and Japan beyond the 60th Anniversary of Diplomatic Relations", http://www.pib.nic.in/newsite/erelease.aspx?relid=96288, May 29, 2013.

37 "Progress on uranium sale to India on expected lines: Australia", http://www.thehindubusinessline.com/news/international/

progress-on-uranium-sale-to-india-on-expected-lines-australia/article4777497.ece, June 3, 2013.

38 Antony Froggatt, "Chinese Nuclear Goes Global", http://www.chinadialogue.net/article/show/single/en/4957, June 06, 2012.

39 "Problematic Pact with India", http://www.japantimes.co.jp/opinion/2013/06/01/editorials/problematic-pact-with-india/, May 31, 2013.

40 "India, Japan Differ on CTBT in Joint Statement", http://articles.timesofindia.indiatimes.com/2013-05-29/india/39600490_1_indian-ocean-joint-statement-ctbt, May 29, 2013.

41 "Japan should Ask India to Join NPT First", Editorial, *Asahi Shimbun*, May 25, 2013.

42 Ibid.

43 PK Sundaram, "Nuclear Hazard in Tokyo, Delhi Embrace", http://www.atimes.com/atimes/South_Asia/SOU-02-070613.html, Jun 07, 2013.

44 Jun Tabushi, Yuriko and Masaaki Shoji, "Abe Pushes Ahead with India Nuclear Agreement, Despite Concerns", *The Asahi Shimbun*, May 30, 2013.

45 ibid.

46 "Japan to Sell Reactors to India!", email interaction with Dr A Gopalakrishnan on June 01, 2013.

47 David Brewster, "India, Japan and the Grand Bargain", http://www.indianexpress.com/news/india-japan-and-the-grand-bargain/1124537/2, Jun 04, 2013.

48 "Australia to Sell Uranium to India: Howard", http://www.expressindia.com/news/fullstory.php?newsid=90916, August 16, 2007.

49 "Uranium Sales to India Fuel Nuclear Arms Fears", http://www.sbs.com.au/news/article/1763258/Uranium-sales-to-india-fuel-nuclear-arms-fears, May 06, 2013.

50 Liu Zongyi, "India Gets Close to Japan at its Own Peril, http://www.globaltimes.cn/content/785656.shtml#.UcE_n-fA7Ic, May 30, 2013.

51 K Sundaram, "The Emerging Japan-India Relationship: Nuclear Anachronism, Militarism and Growth Fetish", *The Asia-Pacific Journal*, vol. 11, issue 22, no. 1, June 2, 2013.

52 Manpreet Sethi, "India's Iran Dance", http://thediplomat.com/flashpoints-blog/2012/02/13/indias-iran-dance/, February 13, 2012.

4

Prospects for India's Foreign Policy: Engaging the Indian Diaspora

B.V.Muralidhar
M.Vishnu Prakash

A nation's development depends upon the sincere hard work put by its people consistently. However here the word people should be taken in much broader sense and that includes the diaspora, whose love for their motherland makes them to serve even in their absentia. The global flow of labour and the consequent presence of numerous diaspora is a notable feature of contemporary politics and economics.

The term Diaspora literally means 'scattering' or 'dispersion'. Derived from the Greek word *dia* (over through) and *speiro* (to sow, to scatter), the word "Diaspora" was originally used to refer to the dispersion of the Jews to the lands outside Palestine after the Babylonian captivity. Since the late twentieth century, the notion of diaspora has been used to describe any ethnic population who resides in the countries other than their own historical homeland. The term diaspora has been approached in various ways. Cohen (1997) proposes a typology in which he classifies Diasporas as: victim diaspora, labour and imperial diaspora, trade diaspora, cultural diaspora, and global de-territorialized diaspora[1].

According to several, if not most theorists, there is a dense web of affiliation between Diaspora and their country of Origin. Diaspora communities in the host country usually reconstruct the class, ethnicity, religion, political affiliation, and language that they belonged to in their homeland. Hence, Diaspora as a social form is based on a diasporas' continued ties, imaginary or actual, with a homeland despite separation from that homeland.

Migrants not only take with them their skills and expertise to their new locales, but also their culture, living styles and collective memories. Over the ages, this has been a common thread, irrespective of nationality or ethnicity. Over the past two millennia, three broad patterns of migration have occurred: ancient and medieval migration to colonial powers; migration to the industrial nations immediately after World War II; and recent migration to developed countries for better career opportunities and living conditions, where the internet, affordable airfare, and cheap communications help to maintain close ties with one's homeland.[2]

Due to radical developments in technology and communications over the last decade, new approaches have emerged in the study of diasporic communities. Diaspora from this point of view is defined as a phenomenon of globalization. It is used to refer socio-economic and political networks of ethnic groups of people which internationally connect Diasporas to their homeland as well as to other members of the same ethnic groups living elsewhere. These networks also provide the possibility of participation in production and reproduction of a kind of transnational culture. Although links, both formal and informal, between diaspora and their presumptive homelands have existed in the past, the recent developments constitute a far more widespread and qualitatively different phenomenon which can be called as Domestic Abroad.[3]

Lauding achievements of about 25 million overseas Indians *spread* across 130 countries, he said the community can serve as an "important bridge" between the "home" and the world. Overseas Indian *Affairs Minister Vayalar Ravi* addressing the 5th Biennial Diaspora conference said "Overseas Indians have made significant contributions to the economies of their countries of adoption and have added in considerable measure to knowledge and innovation".[4]

The Indian diaspora is estimated to generate an annual income equal to about 25 per cent of India's GDP. As per a World Bank report, India with $ 69 billion topped the list of countries receiving remittances in 2012, followed by China ($ 60 billion).[5]

Overseas Indians comprise People of Indian Origin and Non Resident Indians, who today are amongst the best educated and successful communities in the world. In every part of the world, the Overseas Indian community is recognized and respected for its hard work, discipline, non-interference and for successfully integrating with the local community.

It is common knowledge that the earlier migrants who formed the basis of an Indian diaspora mainly involved 'cheap' manual laborers leaving India in large numbers to meet the enormous quantitative demand for indentured workers that arose in the plantations, mainly in south-east Asia and the Pacific, but also in the Caribbean and the African countries immediately after the British had abolished slavery in 1834 leading to what is sometimes also called the 'brawn drain'. The 'brain drain', a quality exodus of India's cream of highly skilled professionals comprising doctors, engineers, scientists, teachers, architects, entrepreneurs, and more recently the IT workers, and nurses on the other hand, appeared a century-and-a-quarter later.

Mohandas K. Gandhi, the "Father of the Nation," had been prominent in the diaspora and had begun his experiments with civil disobedience movements while in South Africa. The Indian nationalists had linked their case for independence with the discrimination faced by Indians in other British colonies. From the 1920s onward, the Indian nationalist movement had acknowledged and lauded the contribution of overseas Indians to the struggle for freedom.

Initially, beginning in the early 1960s, the brain drain from India was associated with the public recognition that the Nobel Prize had brought to the gifted PIO scientists like Har Gobind Khorana (Medicine 1968) who had naturalized into American citizenship at that time, or Subramanyan Chandrasekhar (Physics 1983), who having naturalized in 1953, had made the United States his home. Gradually, following the landmark 1965 amendments to the US Immigration and Nationality Act, the migration of professionals became a mass phenomenon through the 1970s and onwards, with the Indian professionals enjoying the distinction of being one of the best-educated, highly employable, and high-income earning ethnic groups of the US census data, yet in their own country disdained as 'deserters' of the 'motherland India', either openly or subtly.

From the post-mid-1960s, it has continued in the twenty-first century, flowing westward and contributing *inter alia* to the concentration of Indian diaspora's 10 percent share in the USA. It was only towards the end of 1990s that the success and achievements of the Indian diaspora in the US drew real attention of the developed countries in the West and the East alike, subsequently or simultaneously followed by a change of attitude in India too towards its diaspora.

Apart from the US, within the European Union (EU) in the West the largest economic entity in the world today two-thirds of the entire Indian diasporic community still resides in the UK. Here too, the Indian community is one of the highest-earning and best-educated groups, achieving eminence in a variety of fields comprising business, information technology, the health sector, the media, and entertainment industries. In Canada, with just 3 percent share in a population of 30 million, Indo-Canadians have recorded high achievements in the fields of medicine, academia, management, and engineering. [6]

In the East, there are 30,000 Indian citizens in Australia; and New Zealand has also witnessed a rise in the entry of Indian professional immigrants, those engaged in domestic retail trade, medical, hospitality, engineering, and IT sectors, and countries like Japan, Korea, and Singapore are trying to attract Indian talent in large numbers, testifying the importance of the Indian diaspora in international development.

The size, spread and the growing influence of Overseas Indians today are truly impressive. The Indian Diaspora spans the globe and stretches across all oceans and continents. Estimated at over 25 million, India has the world's second largest overseas community—next only to China, characterized as far more diverse when compared to the Chinese counterparts. Overseas Indians constitute a significant and successful economic, social and cultural force in the world. The Overseas Indian community is the result of different waves of migration over hundreds of years driven by a variety of reasons— mercantilism, colonialism and globalization. In the last three decades of the 20th century the character of migration began to change and a 'New Diaspora' led by high skilled professionals moving to the western world and semi-skilled contract workers moving to the Gulf, West and South East Asia emerged.

In a rapidly globalizing world the diasporic community is both the result as well as the driver of globalization. The Indian Diaspora is characterized by distinct communities across the globe whose uniqueness has been determined by their separation from the home country by space and time. Thus we have the 'Old Diaspora' represented by People of Indian Origin who are the decedents of those who migrated in the 19th century as part of the indentured labor. This community has overcome considerable adversity and today represents an eminently successful Diaspora in the host countries. Several of the representatives of this community today occupy a leadership position in several walk of life and exercise considerable influence on the 'political- economy' as well as the development of their host countries.

Equally we have a large 'new Diaspora' that is essentially a 20th century phenomenon wherein workers—blue, grey and white—as well as professionals went in search of opportunities to the western world. Today the Indo-American, Indo-Canadian, Indo-British, Indo- Australian communities etc. represent remarkable and pioneering success in the knowledge-based sectors as scientists, technologists, academics and entrepreneurs.[7] They are beginning to exercise in recent years visible political influence and shape policies that might impact on India. The role of the Indo- American community in the conclusion of the Indo-US civil nuclear deal is an important example of Diaspora advocacy.

Overseas Indians have made significant contributions to the economy of the country of residence and have added in considerable measure to knowledge and innovation.[8] An Overseas community can and does serve as an important 'bridge' to access knowledge, expertise, resources and markets for the development of the country of origin. The success of this bridge is often predicated upon two conditions: the ability of the Diaspora to develop and project a coherent, intrinsically motivated and progressive identity and the capacity of the home country to establish conditions and institutions for sustainable, symbiotic and mutually rewarding engagement. Home countries are now beginning to recognize the need to pursue and promote the dynamic of the Diaspora and development. India's engagement with its Diaspora is symbiotic: the strands of both sides of the relationship are equally important to create a resilient and robust bond.[9] The common thread that binds them together is the idea of India and its intrinsic values.

To engage with the Diaspora in a sustainable and mutually rewarding manner across the economic, social and cultural space is at the heart of the mutual relationship. As a new India seeks to become a global player of significance, the time has come for a strong and sustained engagement between India and Overseas Indians. The time has also come for Overseas Indians to benefit from the exciting opportunities that India provides.

Diasporas play an increasingly significant part in the development of nation-building in poor countries and in ones which have undergone major transformation, such as Eastern European and former Soviet states. This is due to a number of factors, including access to economic resources, greater ease in communication and travel, and the large number of expatriate professionals and entrepreneurs who have skills and experience to offer. The foremost means of diasporic nation-building comes through individual remittances, followed by hometown associations and charitable initiatives that directly affect economic development, poverty reduction, and capacity building. Governments of migrant-sending and receiving countries, international agencies, and academics are now paying considerable attention to the relationship between diasporas and development.[10] Innovative national and international programs for "tapping the diaspora" have been put in place so that home countries can access expatriate expertise, knowledge, and experience.

From the perception of a highly-educated or skilled knowledge worker supposedly 'draining' India of its knowledge wealth and human resources, professional Indian immigrants have come to be seen as 'angels' with a perfected image of transnational "global citizen" of the twenty-first century within the short span of the closing decade of the twentieth century. [11]

This paradigm shift in the perception about professional migrants leaving India, has taken place in phases though from the 'brain drain' of the 1960s and 1970s to the 'brain bank' of the 1980s and 1990s, and subsequently to 'brain gain' in the twenty-first century. This complete turnaround of perception in moving from one model of the Indian diaspora to the other gets reflected in the current official and public euphoria in India over the rising immigration quotas in the developed host countries, mainly the US and the UK, the EU, Canada, Australia and New Zealand, Japan, Malaysia, Singapore, and so on.

It is today the world's largest film industry, surpassing Hollywood with an annual output of over 1000 movies. Thanks to satellite TV and internet, Bollywood movies and Indian soap operas have reached a growing global audience that has become increasingly familiar with Indian society and culture. Another one of India's most successful and long-lasting exports, yoga, is now practiced around the world as a form of exercise, and Indian cuisine, with its distinctive use of spices, has become popular worldwide. More directly, cricket has proved to be a strong soft power resource for India, with cricket diplomacy having notably positive effects in reducing Indo-Pakistani tensions.

There are today millions of Indians spread as far as Fiji, Malaysia, Mauritius, South Africa and Trinidad. While many of these Indians originally migrated as laborers for the British Empire in the 19th century, a new wage of richer and educated expatriates have found their way to the US, Canada and Australia in the last decades. These immigrants have come to play major roles in the political spheres of these different countries. The educated Indian-American community has played an important role in improving Indo-US relations by lobbying American politicians and by giving a positive image of India to the American public is one example. Indian-American legal luminary *Sri Srinivasan* was sworn in as a *judge* in the US Court of Appeals for the *DC Circuit*, the second most powerful court in the *United States* after the Supreme Court.[12]

While economic power is usually considered a hard and material asset, a country's economic development model could also be interpreted as a soft power resource to the extent that its accomplishments prove attractive to others. The recent global successes of Indian information technology firms such as Infosys Technologies and Wipro, the achievements of other multinational companies such as the Tata Group and the Reliance Group; and the now global reputation of the Indian Institute of Management (IIMs) and Indian Institute of Technology (IITs) have contributed to the development of a new image of India as an economic powerhouse. The stereotypical image of underdeveloped, impoverished India has now been removed by the impression of a modern and dynamic economy attracting now foreign investments and workers from different parts of the world. The world is waking up to India's crucial role as the largest democracy and as a dynamic economy.

To serve the dual purpose of sustaining an expensive higher education system, and meeting *short-term* labor shortages, both the UK and the US, with other countries following suit, have adopted a policy of allowing foreign students in their universities respectively, to stay on and work, rather than return to their countries of origin on completion of their degrees (*The Hindustan Times,* March 2005). In addition, the destination countries gain political mileage in the form of a bonus: The foreign students become their long-term ambassadors in the international political arena. India has thus become a 'must destination for internationally renowned educational institutions shopping for "knowledge capital" - i.e., to woo the Indian student'.[13]

Examining the role of Diaspora in the reduction of poverty in their home countries, Newland and Patrick (2004) study how China, India, the Philippines, Mexico, Eritrea and Taiwan court their Diaspora. They illustrate 6 contrasting patterns. In the case of China, India and Taiwan, Newland and Patrick note that the interest in Diaspora is more business oriented, and that these countries seek Diaspora contributions to national development more than their assistance in poverty reduction. They state that:

Taiwan has pursued a "brain trust" model, focused on attracting human capital from the Diaspora. China has long worked to attract direct investment and open trade opportunities through overseas Chinese communities. India's recently launched Diaspora policy is multipronged, pursuing direct investment, portfolio investment, technology transfer, market opening and out-sourcing opportunities.[14]

The Indian government has set strategies to pursue investment, trade and technology transfer through the Indian Diaspora. The huge sale of bonds guaranteed by the State Bank of India and available only for Indians living abroad is one of the examples of courting Diasporic investment, or in this case, compensation funds. In fact, the "Resurgent India Bonds" was an action to finance compensation for the economic impact of nuclear tests in 1998. Sengupta (1998) in his article in New York Times, titled 'India Taps into Its Diaspora' writes: The Indian Government has been trying for several years to raise foreign investment from its expatriates — Non-Resident Indians, they are called, or less flatteringly in India, Never-Returning Indians.[15]

The Indian government tried to attract immigrants with advertisements (such as "You don't need to be a financial wizard, you need to be an Indian") in their local media, and launched a marketing campaign in US and Europe which attempted to encourage nonresident Indians to purchase bonds. They sold £2.3 billion just over two weeks; a great success. "The experience was repeated in 2000 with another bond issue, the India Millennium Deposits, which raised over £3 billion".

In analyzing the economic impact of migration, Kapur[16] focuses on the mechanisms that transmit and amplify the diaspora's economic effects on their home country. These include the diaspora's overseas network; their role as credibility-enhancing agents for economic actors back home; and their impact through financial flows, especially foreign direct investment and remittances.

Realizing the importance of the Indian Diaspora the Government of India constituted a High Level Committee under the chairmanship of Dr.L.M. Singhvi in the year 2000 and it recommended dual citizenship for persons of Indian origin, simplification of investment in India from abroad, formation of a government body to liaison between India and its Diaspora etc., in its report. From then, there were various steps and schemes introduced to strengthen the bond between India and its Diaspora. Mention may be made of few like:

1. Voting rights to non-resident Indians.
2. PIO University.
3. Pravasi Bharatiya Divas (PBD)
4. Pravasi Bharatiya Samman Awards (PBSA)
5. Tracing the roots.
6. Know India Programme.

7. Scholarship for the children of Indian Diaspora.
8. Problems relating to Overseas Indian marriages.

The Ministry of Internal Affairs has proposed to launch a new service / scheme for Pension and Life Insurance (PLI) coverage for the Overseas Indian workers having Emigration Clearance Required (ECR) passports, who have emigrated overseas on employment/contract visa.[17]

The scheme aims to accumulate savings for facilitating their resettlement on their return and also to provide pension and life insurance coverage in their old age.

The Indian Council of Cultural Affairs is promoting cultural relations between diaspora with India. The 150th birth anniversary of Rabindranath Tagore was celebrated with gaiety and joy by all the Diasporas. Cultural festivals and Bollywood shows deeply enhances the bond and ties between India and the diaspora.

The diaspora has major expectations from India to assist it in realizing its aspirations of bonding with it, and remembering its cultural roots with pride. Most of them regard this as intrinsic to their development, both material and spiritual. NRIs and PIOs are unanimous in their belief that handing down India's rich culture to their descendants is a sine qua non for the forging of ties between future generations of the diaspora and India.

The Indian Diaspora has contributed the host countries and received laurels. Australia has commended the growing Indian diaspora in the country for its contribution in enhancing bilateral links. In a joint statement issued following the fifth Australia-India Foreign Ministers Framework Dialogue, Smith said the "Indian diaspora in Australia is making a tangible contribution to enhancing bilateral links".[18]

The increase in the size of the Indian diaspora has achieved a favorable tilt in policy lobbying especially in the developed countries. For example *Indian diaspora* is the largest ethnic group in the UK and Hinduism with 1.5 per cent of the population is the third most popular religion in the country.[19]

There is a great need to seek the assistance in humanitarian, technology, finance, managerial skills etc., from the Indian diaspora to meet the challenges in the 21st century. Yet even where humanitarian responses arise, corrosive diaspora politics may be present. There have been claims that various Tamil organizations collected money for Sri Lankan tsunami victims that was in fact used for weapons and materials for the Liberation Tigers of Tamil Eelam (LTTE) and also supporting insurgent activities in India and elsewhere. India should take cautious step in introducing any drastic change in policy that affects the Indian diaspora .This is an irreversible trend that policymakers should be conscious of when reconsidering any adjustments to immigration and integration policies.

The contribution of the Indian diaspora to the motherland is immense and still lot is to be done. Personalities like Lord Swaraj Paul, the Prime Ministers of Mauritius Navin Ramgulam and Sir Anerood Jugnath, the former President of Republic of Singapore S. Ranganathan, the former Governor-General of New Zealand Sir Anand Satyanand, Bobby Jindal, the present Governor of Louisiana, USA, Srinivasan, *judge* in the US Court of Appeals for the *DC Circuit* are some of the sons of India who made the country proud.

India and its diaspora should be hands in glove for furthering their ties and also for the robust development. India has huge potential to become a credible power. This is high time for its residents and non-residents, to forge strong relationship and work together for its all round development.

REFERENCES

1 http://www.cerium.ca/IMG/pdf/Building_Bridges_The_Role_of_the_ Indian_Diaspora_in_Canada_Literature_Review_-2.pdf

2 http://www.indiaamericatoday.com/article/indian-diaspora-past-present-and-future#.dpuf

3 "The Domestic Abroad: Diasporas in International Relations", Latha Varadarajan, October 2010, Oxford University Press.

4 http://economictimes.indiatimes.com/news/nri/nri-investments/india-considers-introduction-of-diaspora-bonds-to-attract-investment-from-nris/articleshow/20719748.cms

5 http://www.thehindubusinessline.com/economy/india-tops-global-remittances-list-received-69-billion-in-2012/article4636594.ece

6 http://horizon.documentation.ird.fr/exl-doc/pleins_textes/divers10-04/010047992.pdf

7 http://moia.gov.in/writereaddata/pdf/Annual_Report_2010-2011.pdf

8 http://www.tribuneindia.com/2013/20130107/edit.htm

9 http://d2dglobalsummit.cfo.gov.ph/2011/download/Materials/Diaspora_Toolkit_Book.pdf

10 http://www.migrationinformation.org/Feature/display.cfm?ID=313

11 http://www.jnu.ac.in/library/IMDS_Working_Papers/IMDS_Dec_2009_WP_12_33-420001.pdf

12 http://economictimes.indiatimes.com/news/nri/nris-in-news/indian-american-sri-srinivasan-sworn-in-as-top-us-court-judge/articleshow/20644763.cms

13 http://www.imi.ox.ac.uk/pdfs/migration-and-development-perspectives-from-the-south

14 http://www.migrationpolicy.org/pubs/Beyond_Remittances_0704.pdf

15 http://www.nytimes.com/1998/08/19/nyregion/india-taps-into-its-diaspora-expatriates-buy-bonds-for-love-country-7.75.html?pagewanted=all&src=pm

16 "Diaspora, Democracy and Development: The Domestic Impact of International Migration from India", Devesh Kapur, 2010, Princeton University Press.

17 http://moia.gov.in/writereaddata/pdf/Annual_Report_2010-2011.pdf

18 http://www.thaindian.com/newsportal/world-news/australia-commends-indian-diasporas-contribution_10063280.html

19 http://articles.economictimes.indiatimes.com/2012-12-11/news/35749850_1_cent-indian-diaspora-population

SECTION-II :
INDIA AND MAJOR POWERS

5

Paradigm Shift in Indo-US Relations and the Pakistan Factor

Mohammad Samir Hussain

INTRODUCTION

The United State's policy toward India and Pakistan in the past almost five decades has been that of zero-sum game that neither serves the US interest nor South Asian interest. Pakistan was the major beneficiary of the US approach in the past. The United States in the past failed to introduce an independent strategy toward India and Pakistan that would better serve the interest of both sides. However, in recent times there witnessed a dramatic change in US policy stand towards the South Asian rivals.[1] The US today successfully maintains close relations with both countries. The change in the geo-political and geo-strategic environment demands the US to engage closely with them. The United States understands the significant role India and Pakistan have to play in helping the former to achieve its strategic objectives. The present US policy provides the options of having closer relations with both South Asian countries based on their respective interests. This is very well manifested after the turn of the twenty first century where the US close ties with Pakistan did not come at the cost of its transforming relations with India. The United States relationship with India and Pakistan is no more zero-sum game. Such a change in the US policy is aimed exploring maximum advantage by closely engaging with India and Pakistan.

The chapter argues that the trajectory shift in the relationship between India and the United States should not be construed as the end of Pakistan factor. United States would like to enjoy close relations with both South Asian rivals and not repeat the mistake committed in the past-engaging one at the cost of other. In that the paper has made an attempt to answer for the following questions: Why there emerged a paradigm shift in the US approach towards India and Pakistan? What has been the Pakistan reaction towards the US shift in approach? How would India benefit out of this shift in the US approach? What would be the future the US stands towards the South Asian rivals? Finally the paper concludes by saying that no matter how US engage with Pakistan, our interest should be to strengthen closer ties with the United States and advance our strategic objectives.

HISTORICAL BACKGROUND

During the cold war period, the US enjoyed close relations with its strategic ally Pakistan at the cost of India. Indo-US relations during the cold war period were off-colored due to certain reasons. Mutual irritation, misunderstanding, distrust of each other intentions were part and parcel of the cold war period of Indo-US relations. Soon after its independent, India adopted a policy of non-alignment and started improving closer ties with the erstwhile Soviet Union. India adopted a policy of non-alignment to protect its national independence. On the other hand the United States adopted a policy of containment of communism and to achieve this very objective it started having close relations with Pakistan. With this the problem really started cropping up. The different approach adopted by India and the United States brought the two in opposite sides.

When India refused to became a partner for the US in the fight against communism, Pakistan became a very close partner to the US in the fight against communism. After which Pakistan joined the US founded military organisation such as Central Treaty Organization (CENTO) and South East Asia Treaty Organisation (SEATO). And the US started supplying military equipment and weapons to Pakistan as part of its effort to bring the relations closer.[2] India and US adopt a different stand on various international issues such as Korean crisis in 1950s, French activities in Southeast Asia where India was against while the US supported French activities. However, the high points in Indo-US relations came in 1962, when India came under the severe attack from China in the Northeast Frontier Agency and the Ladakh section of Kashmir. The Kennedy administration responded positively to Nehru's appeal for a military support. However, this move was not sufficient to strengthen the relationship between India and the United States.

The relationship suffered a serious setback in 1965 when America failed to prevent Pakistan from using the weapons which they had supplied. And the United States even suspended the aid which it promised to provide before the war.[3] But the lowest point in Indo-US relations came in 1971, when the United States without any reliable evidence charged India of attacking Pakistan. The United States even dispatched its naval task force of the seventh fleet spearheaded by the nuclear powered aircraft carrier Enterprise to the Bay of Bengal in support of Pakistan.

Further damage was done by the underground nuclear tests of India on 18th May, 1974.[4]

The situation changed after the Soviet military intervention in Afghanistan in 1979. India sought to open up its relations with the US and Washington responded positively to it. Both countries tried their best to improve the relations. It was justified by the US Secretary of State Alexander Haig to the US embassy in Delhi instructing them to "respond favorably to any arms purchase requests the Indians might bring up."[5] But the effort did not pay off when in May 1989 the Bush Administration imposed a sanction against Glavobosmos of Russia and India Space Research Organisation and even banned the sale of combined acceleration vibration climatic test system to India on the ground that it may be used for missile and nuclear capability.[6]

POST COLD WAR US RELATIONS WITH INDIA AND PAKISTAN

The end of the cold war rivalry between the United States and the erstwhile Soviet Union witnessed good signs for the start of new relations between the two largest democracies, India and the United States. Three reasons may be cited for this sudden change in the nature of the relations between India and the United States. First, the end of the cold war; secondly, the emergence of economic liberalization in India and the receding relevance of Pakistan to the United States.

The decision of the Indian Government to liberalise its economy was instrumental in attracting the attention of American towards India. It was the foreign policy priorities of the United States in the early part of 1993 to have a closer engagement with ten of the fastest growing markets in the world. India was counted among the top ten countries of the world along with China. After the cold war India's need for a capital and America's search for a better and lasting market to sell their products brought the two countries closer to economic and trade relations. American interest in Indian economy is also influenced by the presence of large quantity and quality of human resources.[7]

However, the issue of nuclear non-proliferation, disarmament and the Kashmir issue did not allow the relations to move freely in a positive manner. Former US president Bill Clinton main focus was on preventing the proliferation of nuclear weapons. For which, the United States wanted to bring India under the Nuclear non-proliferation treaty (NPT) and Comprehensive test ban treaty (CTBT). On the contrary India was not in favor of NPT and CTBT owing to its discriminatory treatment as both the treaty makes a clear discrimination between the states of the world into nuclear have's and have not's. When the nuclear issue was going on, India without any concern about the international reactions, carried out a series of five underground nuclear tests on 11 and 13 May 1998. In a harsh response to the tests, the US President Bill Clinton imposed sanctions against India under section 102 of the Arms export control Act.[8]

On the other hand, when Pakistan failed to met the satisfaction of the United States over the nuclear issue, Pressler Amendment was imposed upon Islamabad. Pakistan was annoyed by this move because it was not expecting the US to take such step that worked against its interest. With this, all forms of military assistance to Pakistan came to a halt, thereby resulting in a huge setback in US-Pakistan relations. Pakistan even criticised the United States saying that it was a result of its exhausted utility to America. However, the one time waiver of the Pressler amendment under the Brown amendment in 1996 cleared the way for further supply of military weapons and equipment to Pakistan. India again was not happy because it came at the time when the relationship between the two world's largest democracies was slowly gaining momentum towards a purposeful one. It only sent a wrong message to India that United States was not seriously concerned about India's security problems arising from Pakistan. For the sake of Pakistan, the United States was not cared about India's security.[9] Thus, the Bill Clinton Administration was not able to break past from its traditional US policy toward South Asia.

India was not satisfied when it was declared that the US policy toward Kashmir will be guided by three principles - one is that the US considers all of Kashmir to be disputed territory, on both sides of the LoC. The other two principles dealt with bilateral negotiation between India and Pakistan and the willingness of the US to assist in the process if that is desired by both sides. India felt unhappy with the first principle that has gone against the spirit of Simla agreement.[10] This was further worsened by the statement of the Assistant Secretary of State, Ms. Robin Raphael, that in the US policies and perceptions, Jammu and Kashmir remained a disputed area.[11] However, very soon the US Administration realised the mistake committed on its part. In a bid to not allow such issue to become a roadblock, the US State department arranged a meeting between Mr. Peter Tarnoff and the Indian Ambassador Mr. Siddhartha Shankar Ray in which the former assured India that the US still consider the Simla Agreement as a basis for resolving the Indo-Pak differences over Kashmir. Finally the US had to return back to its previous position.[12]

In an effort to reduce the damage done and to strengthen the relationship, former US president Bill Clinton paid a landmark visit to India in March 2000 after a gap of more than two decades by any US president. On this occasion, both the countries signed a number of agreements indicating the mutual desire to move the relationship toward a "forward looking" and politically constructive partnership.

The joint statements issued by the US President Bill Clinton and Indian Prime Minister Atal Bihari Vajpayee reveal the growing interest of both sides to build a lasting relationship.[13]

US RELATIONS WITH INDIA AND PAKISTAN BY THE TURN OF 21ST CENTURY

There was a paradigm shift in US approach toward the two South Asian rivals by the turn of the twenty-first century. Former US President George W. Bush was instrumental in bringing about a paradigm shift in Washington approach towards India and Pakistan. Unlike Bill Clinton, former U.S. President George W. Bush was not concerned about third party reactions to the expanding India-United States booming relationship. By the turn of the twenty-first century and in particular after the horrific events of 9/11, United States was determined not to repeat the same mistake and instead wanted to have deeper engagement with both sides. Such a shift in the US approach was fuelled by the need to manage and achieve regional stability by ensuring that nuclear clash between the two South Asian does not happen. Since then, US has manifested greater interest in the region.

What played a part in helping to bring about a shift in the US stand toward India and Pakistan? Two factors were crucial to this shift - one is that by the turn of twenty-first century, India was viewed by Washington as a growing economic and military power that had significant role to play and secondly, Pakistan despite of being its long-time close ally was perceived to be no where near India and was facing a problem of political and economic instability. There was also a possibility of it becoming a failed state. This was only aided by India's unconditional support to the US national missile defence initiative in May 2001 and in the fight against terrorism. India even provided escort to the US ships carrying valuable goods passing through the Malacca straits.

All of these factors have led the US to finally decide that Pakistan factor will not be permitted to circumscribe the long-anticipated India-US relations. And any India-Pakistan bilateral issue shall not be allowed to prevent the relationship from transforming.

Mr. Colin Powell, former US Secretary of State, stated in his testimony before the Senate Foreign Relations Committee in early 2001 that, "India, soon to become the most populous country in the world has the potential to help keep the peace in the vast Indian Ocean area and its periphery. We need to work harder and more consistently to assist India in this endeavor, while not neglecting our friend in Pakistan."[14] How US managed to have balance relations with both India and Pakistan can be smelled from the following sub-sections.

The change of the US perception of India is reflected in the National Security Strategy document of US published in 2006 saying that, "we have set aside decades of mistrust and put relationship with India, the world's most populous democracy, on a new and fruitful path- India is a great democracy and our shared values are foundation of good relations". This was further strengthened by the Quadrennial Defence Review (QDR), published in February 2006 which noted that India is emerging as a great power and a key strategic partner. The review paper further added that there is a need to stress on transforming the Indo-US relationship into a global partnership in the areas of mutual concern and interests.[15]

For Pakistan too the events of September 11 brought some relief when it was declared by United States as a 'frontline state in achieving the objective of defeating Al-Qaeda and Taliban. The US need for logistic facilities and intelligence information about the Al-Qaeda and Pakistan need for constant US support coalesced into transforming the relationship between Pakistan and United States.

Pakistan due to its close proximity to Afghanistan offered United States with two naval bases, three air force bases and its airspace. Moreover, it deployed more than 70,000 troops along the Afghan border and even launched more than 38 major successful operations to flush out foreign terrorists. The US officials acknowledge Pakistan support in the fight against terrorism.[16] Pakistan's support to United States entails both opportunity and challenges. The opportunity is that of regaining the lost relationship. With this, the US would be supplying arms and equipment assistance to Pakistan that has been stopped after the nuclear tests. While the challenge before Pakistan is that they have to cooperate with the US forces in the fight against al-Qaeda and Taliban based in Afghanistan with whom it had a close traditional ties. For the sake of regaining the lost relationship with US, Pakistan reluctantly will have to sacrifice ties with Taliban. However, the main rationale behind why Islamabad took such a huge step was to ensure that the US is with them in dealing with India on Kashmir and other related issues. And also to ensure that it have a hold in Afghanistan by establishing a friendly regime in Afghanistan.[17]

Pakistan and United States signed 'defence cooperation agreement' in 2002 under which, Pakistan had allowed the US to make use of its military equipment for training and other military exercises. The agreement was a turning point in a way that the US authorized Pakistan for the supply of the US air traffic control radars to enhance surveillance capability worth $110 million. Followed by the designation of Pakistan as a "major non-NATO ally" in March 2004. Then in April 2003, former US President George W. Bush allocated Pakistan with $200 million as security related assistance and even announced a five-year $3 billion aid package for Pakistan which commenced in 2005. According to former US Secretary of State, Mr. Colin Powell, "the US assistance package to Pakistan constitutes one of the 'largest US assistance programmes' in the world."[18] As a result of which, since 2001 Pakistan enjoyed being the largest recipient of the US security assistance including arms transfer. In the year 2006, Pakistan emerged as the biggest arms recipient from United States.

Given the kind of arms supply and assistance that Pakistan received from the US, K. D. Chadha, India's former Chief of Air force said "Pakistan's affiliation with the United States aroused "ambitions and delusions of grandeur" in Pakistan's power elite. Military officers exposed to American training and doctrines "began to see themselves as invincible superior beings. They held the Indian military forces... in derisive contempt. Arrogant, flamboyant and impregnated with American doctrinal proclivities, they were more than convinced that militarily India was a push-over."[19] This is followed by what former India's Defence Minister Mr. Pranab Mukherjee said on 12 December 2004, in reaction to the 9/11 commission report that calls for supply of arms and equipment to Pakistan that the supply of sophisticated weapons such as F-16 aircraft, lethal missile arrangements and naval surveillance reconnaissance aircraft to Pakistan by the US would jeopardize the peace process between the two countries. Defence Minister argument is based on the fact that these weapons are meant for big wars and not to fight terrorism.[20] From this view, we can only conclude that American assistance to Pakistan has only provided energy and power to deal with India. It also gives a clear indication that the US has keen interest in Pakistan for promoting its interests.

On the other side, the United States has created a history by concluding the long overdue civilian nuclear cooperation agreement with India and not offering the same to its long time close ally Pakistan. The US administration under the leadership of President Bush was very much committed to strengthening close ties with India that became strategically important in the emerging world order. He better understood that robust strategic partnership cannot be achieved when India is a target of the US nuclear policy. Had President Bush and his administration not convinced US Congress to exempt India from certain Atomic Energy Act provisions, the successful conclusion of the civil nuclear cooperation could not have taken place. These waivers includes-

a. that the partner country should not have exploded a nuclear explosive device in the past. This waiver is necessary because India had exploded a series of nuclear device in May 1998;

b. that the partner country must have all its nuclear facilities and activities under fullscope safeguards. This waiver becomes necessary because India has rejected to place its strategic nuclear weapons programme to the international safeguards and;

c. that the partner country is not currently engaged in the development and production of nuclear explosive devices. This waiver is required because there is no freeze or capping of India's strategic weapons programme. India will continue to carry out its nuclear weapons programme. Prime Minister Manmohan Singh special envoy Shyam Saran has made it very clear that if the US Congress considers the 123 Agreement currently drafted as being in contravention with their understanding of the Hyde Act, the agreement would be voted down.[21]

The Paradigm shift in the US nuclear policy toward India was made possible due to the strategic shift in the recognition of India as a major global player that has a significant role to play in ensuring regional and global peace and security, thereby shaping a prosperous and constructive world. India has in the past and present shown its willingness to take responsibilities for preventing the horizontal proliferation of nuclear weapons. It was during his address at the Golden jubilee function of the Department of Atomic Energy on 23 October 2004, Indian Prime Minister Manmohan Singh stated that, "India is a responsible nuclear power. We are fully conscious of the immense responsibilities that come with the possession of advanced technologies, both civil and strategic. While we are determined to utilize our indigenous resources and capabilities to fulfill our national interests, we are doing so in a manner that is not contrary to the larger goals of nuclear nonproliferation." The Prime Ministers statement clearly reflected the fact that India is very clear about its responsibilities once India got the opportunity to share nuclear related materials with other countries.[22]

FUTURE US STAND ON THE KASHMIR DISPUTE

With the successive US Administration committed to sustained engagement with India and Pakistan, the focus has shifted from direct and active intervention to promoting a composite dialogue between India and Pakistan. The US intervention would come only after the consent of the two countries. The US should help both countries in finding the common ground for solving the problem.[23]

The former US Administration led by George W. Bush dislike of mediation in resolving the Kashmir dispute has given way to facilitation between the two countries. The US will not give up working closely with both countries on the issue because of the fact that both are nuclear power countries that came very close to large scale war on two occasions after the detonation of nuclear tests by both countries. The US very well understands the fact that given the stand taken by the South Asian rivals, the resolution of dispute is not likely to take place very soon, so there is a need for the US role in preventing another major crisis from occurring. This was very clearly spelt out by former US Ambassador to India Robert Blackwill that 'the United States would facilitate two-party talks between India and Pakistan, but that it would not provide substance, a road map, or a blueprint'. A task force sponsored by two important American foreign policy institutions subsequently recommended (in September 2003) that the administration appoint a high-level official to aid and abet the India-Pakistan dialogue, especially on Kashmir, and assume a more "forward leaning" posture in attempting to deal with India-Pakistan crises before they start.[24]

However, the resolution of the Kashmir dispute has nothing to do with the US. It is up to the South Asian rivals on what steps they take on the issue. The role of the US should be only to ensure that both sides engage in a serious and purposeful dialogue that would prevent any unwanted incidents from happening. Given the aggressive nature of Pakistan, United States should pressurise Pakistan to stop cross border terrorism which would create an environment for the start of the purposeful dialogue. So far, it has been very clear that Pakistan proxy war and cross border terrorism has only delayed the prospects of resolution. Both sides should be encouraged to maintain understanding, increase trade and confidence building measures (CBMs).[25]

US RELATIONS WITH INDIA AND PAKISTAN: ROAD AHEAD

Today when the relations between India and the US are growing in a way that has never existed before, the US is willing to accommodate India's security concerns arising out of Pakistan aggressive attitude while not losing its security ties with Pakistan. The US administration is very much willing to see amicable relations between the two South Asian rivals that would offer the opportunity of closely strengthening the relationship with both countries without worrying about the pressure from one side on the other. The task ahead of India in the coming years should be to concentrate on getting closer to the United States while not concerned about the tone of the relationship with Pakistan because for the US, relationship with Pakistan is the key to achieving its security and strategic objectives which is also important for India. However, at the same time India should also ensure that Pakistan does not use its relationship with the United States against India. It continues to be relevant for India what India's former Prime Minister Ms. Indira Gandhi said many years back before her visit to Washington in 1982 that, "We don't want the US to give up its friendship with Pakistan. But we don't see why that should affect its attitude toward us." This is followed by what India's former India's Ambassador to Washington, Mr. P.K. Kaul said, "Pakistan will always remain a problem, but instead of making it the key determinant one should make it one of fifty terms." If India and United States is really serious about getting the relationship stronger then both sides must have to stick to this formula. Then continue to work hard to removing the divergence over Pakistan. The US would be required to stop appeasement of Pakistan that has no doubt endangered India's security concerns. India in any way should not come under any US pressure to make concessions to Islamabad.[26] However, the US inclination towards India or Pakistan in the coming years is likely to be determined by the following factors:

a. India's growing economic and military relationship with the US;
b. The level of Pakistan's relevance to the US; and
c. India's stand in the key international affairs;
d. India's pro-active role in international affairs.[27]

CONCLUSION

Washington will continue to follow a policy of increased and pragmatic engagement with South Asian rivals to achieve its regional and global objectives. No matter how deep the relationship India enjoy with the United States in the coming decades, India cannot expect United States to completely ignore Pakistan, its long time partner and will continue to be an important partner for other purposes where the US has a huge stake including fight against terrorism, external influence, etc. The United States will continue to follow a policy of appeasement towards Pakistan because it still believes that Islamabad has a lot to offer in the changing world scenario. Any future US stand on Pakistan illegal activities has a huge stake on India-US strategic relationship. But what is most important is how India and United States take care of the issue in terms of not allowing such issues to circumscribe further prospects of the long term strategic ties. At this critical juncture, our interest should be to strengthen closer ties with the United States and advance our strategic objectives.

India on the one side, views Pakistan as a real problem to its security concerns while the US still continue to perceive Pakistan as a close ally in the fight against terrorism. It is not an easy task for the United States to totally ignore Pakistan that holds the key to some of its long-term interests. But given the kind of relations that India enjoys with the United States in the past one decade, one can only say that the past zero-sum policy of the US is not likely to repeat once again. The dehyphenation policy offers very little room for the Pakistan to influence United States against India. And on the other side offers India very good opportunity to keep growing its relationship with the United States. This is very much reflected in what the US Secretary of State Condoleezza Rice said during her interview with Mr. Shivraj Prasad that, "we have tried very hard, as a matter of fact, to make the point that this is not a hyphenated relationship." She further added that the US ties with each South Asian partner ought to be viewed on their own terms. But the success of the dehyphenation policy of the US toward India and Pakistan is yet to come. Since, it fails to ensure that Pakistan's aggressive attitude toward India has ended.[28]

REFERENCES

1 Ashley J. Tellis, "The Merits of Dehyphenation: Explaining U.S. Success in Engaging India and Pakistan", *Washington Quarterly* (Washington, DC), vol. 31(4), Autumn 2008, p. 22.

2 Ashok Sharma, "Indo-U.S. Strategic Convergence: An Overview of Defence and Military Cooperation", *Claws Paper* no. 2, New Delhi, 2008, pp. 3-4.

3 Norman D. Palmer, *The United States and India: The Dimensions of Influence* (New York: Philadelphia: Praeger Publishers, 1994), pp. 21, 24-30.

4 Ibid, pp. 47, 53-55.

5 Cherian Samuel, "Indo-US Defence Cooperation and the Emerging Strategic Relationship", *Strategic Analysis* (New Delhi), vol. 31(2), March 2007, pp. 214-15.

6 David S. Chou, "U.S. Policy toward India and Pakistan in the Post Cold War Era", *Tamkang Journal of International Affairs*, p. 35.

7 Narottam Gaan, "India and the United States Spinning a Strategic Engagement: Convergences and Divergences", *BIISS* journal (Bangladesh). vol. 27(4), October 2006, pp. 359, 369.

8 David S. McDonough, "Relations between the US and India: Towards a De Facto Strategic Partnership", November 2003, p. 2.

9 Arthur G. Rubinoff, "Legislative Perceptions of Indo-American Relations", in Ashok Kapur, et. al., (eds.), *India and the United States in a Changing World* (New Delhi: Sage Publication, 2002), pp. 435-36 and Monish Tourangbham, "The Pakistan Factor in India-US Relations: Is it Finally Muted?", *World Focus* (New Delhi), vol. XXIX(7), July 2008, pp. 274-75.

.0 Reeta Chowdhari Tremblay, "Indo-US Relations and the Kashmir Issue", in Ashok Kapur, et. al., (eds.), *India and United States in a Changing World* (New Delhi: Sage Publication, 2002), pp. 522-23.

11 Subhash Shukla, *Foreign Policy of India* (New Delhi: Anamika Publishers, 2007), p. 49.

12 Reeta Chowdhari Tremblay, n. 10, p. 524.

13 Bhabani Mishra, "India-US Relations: A Paradigm Shift", *Strategic Analysis* (New Delhi), vol. 29(1), January-March 2005, p. 85.

14 C. Raja Mohan, "A Paradigm Shift toward South Asia", *Washington Quarterly* (Washington, DC), vol. 26(1), Winter 2002-03, pp. 141-44 and also see Ashley J. Tellis, n. 1, pp. 23-25.

15 VK Kapoor and Vinod Anand, "Indo-US Relations on an Ascending Trajectory", *U.S.I Journal* (New Delhi), vol. cxxxvi(565), July-September 2006, pp. 355-56.

16 Touqir Hussain, "US-Pakistan Engagement: The War on Terrorism and Beyond", *Regional Studies* (Islamabad), vol. XXIV(1), Winter 2005-06, p. 9.

17 C. Raja Mohan, n. 14, pp. 144-45.

18 Shalini Chawla, "Pakistan's Conventional Arms Acquisitions: Priorities and Prospects", *Air Power Journal* (New Delhi), vol. 3(1), Spring 2006, p. 120-23.

19 Stephen P. Cohen, *India Emerging Power* (New Delhi: Oxford University Press, 2002), pp. 273-74.

20 Manohar Singh Batra, "India-Pakistan Relations in the Twenty-First Century", in V.D. Chopra (ed.), *India's Foreign Policy in the 21st Century* (New Delhi: Kalpaz Publications, 2006), p. 169.

21 Lecture by Prime Minister Special Envoy Shyam Saran on, "India and the Nuclear Domain", Strategic *Digest* (New Delhi), vol. 38(3), March 2008, p. 261.

22 Refer to, "Prime Minister Address at the Golden Jubilee Function of the Department of Atomic Energy on 23 October. 2004", available at http://pmindia.nic.in/speech/content.asp?id=36

23 Saleem Kidwai, "US and South Asia: Post 9/11 Scenario", in Saleem Kidwai (ed.), *US Policy toward South Asia: Focus on Sixty Years* (New Delhi: Academic Excellence, 2008), p. 37.

24 Stephen Philip Cohen, *The Idea of Pakistan* (New Delhi: Oxford University Press, 2005), p. 322.

25 Saleem Kidwai, n. 23, pp. 44-45.

26 Satu Limaye, "The Changing Place of Pakistan in US-India Relations", *Contemporary South Asia,* vol. 1(1), 1992, pp. 118-24.

27 Subhash Kapila, "United States Obsession with the Kashmir Issue: An Analysis", *South Asia Analysis Group* (Noida), Paper no. 403, 30 January 2002.

28 Ashley J. Tellis, n. 1, pp. 36-37.

6

An Overview of India-European Union Relations

Mohammed Badrul Alam

EU-India relations date back to the early 1960s. India is amongst the first countries to set up diplomatic relations with European Economic Community. Subsequently, bilateral agreements were signed in 1973 and 1981. The 1994 co-operation agreement (signed on 20 Dec 1993) is a wide-ranging 3rd generation agreement that encompasses issues beyond trade and economic co-operation. India's partnership with the EU is a partnership based on shared values and common commitment to democracy, pluralism, multi-centralism, human rights and religious freedom.

The institutional basis for EU-India political dialogue is a *Joint Political Statement* signed simultaneously with the 3rd generation Co-operation Agreement. The Commission Communication for a "EU-India Enhanced Partnership" of June 1996was a leap forward and it contributed to put the Commission in the forefront of EU-India relations. The

Commission Communicationof 16 June 2004 was another milestone, as it set out concrete proposals to up-grade the relationship to a Strategic Partnership. The Council in its Conclusions of 11 October 2004 endorsed the Commission's approach. The agreement at The Hague Summit in November 2004 to launch Strategic Partnership and to implement an Action Plan set the scene for another big stride in bilateral relations. The Action Plan agreed at the 6th Summit in Delhi on 7 September 2004 spells out concrete areas where the EU and India can be proactive and influential actors in political, economic and social developments across the globe.

ECONOMIC AND DEVELOPMENT CO-OPERATION

The 1994 Co-operation Agreement provides for an EC India Joint Commission as the central mechanism to oversee and guide the entire range of co-operation activities between India and the EC. Three separate sub-commissions, on Trade; Economic Co-operation; Development Co-operation, cover a more comprehensive agenda. These sub-commissions report directly to the Joint Commission.

The EU-India Joint Commission meeting confirmed the determination of India and the EU to operationalise the commitments made in the "Joint Action Plan" adopted at the EU-India Summit. Broad agreement was achieved on issues such as the negotiation of an EU-India maritime transport agreement; discussions on an horizontal civil aviation agreement; the designation of members of the newly-established "EU-India CEO Round Table"; the EU-India dialogue on employment and social affairs; industrial policy issues; the protection of intellectual property rights; bilateral cooperation on environment and climate change; science and technology; education, civil society exchanges and cultural cooperation as well as the programming of EC development assistance to India. The Joint Commission agreed to establish a bilateral ad hoc steering group to monitor regularly the implementation of the Joint Action Plan on a regular basis.

Helsinki summit of October 2006 envisaged EU-India trade to reach its optimum potential with the conclusion of a bilateral Free Trade Agreement to boost trade and commerce. Political dialogue between EU and India ranged from energy and environment to transport and employment along with significant progress in fields such as civil aviation, maritime transport and renewable energy. By joining efforts, the EU and India, the world's two largest democracies strived to have a great impact in addressing global challenges such as peace and security, governance and climate change.

Commissioner for External Relations and European Neighbourhood Policy, Benita Ferrero-Waldner and Trade Commissioner Peter Mandelson, have portrayed India as a country with enormous potential as a global player as well as a vital partner in the South Asia region. Recognising India's successful economic transition, the focus was on development cooperation programmes thus providing support for its efforts to attain the Millennium Development Goals in a credible and constructive way. For this two-fold approach, EU earmarked €470 million for new cooperation projects in India from 2007 to 2013.

Since the 1990's India-EU bilateral relations have progressed from trade in goods mostly in traditional sectors, and development and economic cooperation into a Strategic Partnership. Today, in addition to core trade, investment and cooperation issues, the relationship includes serious policy dialogues on a constantly increasing number of burning issues such as energy and environment, climate change, and culture, regular exchanges at civil society level and between parliamentarians between EU and India.

The EU continues to be India's main trading partner accounting for one-fifth of her total trade as well as the biggest source of actual foreign direct investment into India. Bilateral trade in goods touched 46 billion euros in 2006. India by 2010 was the eighth largest trading partner of the European Union, behind China and Russia. The EU is also one of India's leading partners in development and economic cooperation. The two countries cooperate regularly at the multilateral level whether at the UN or the WTO. The EU supports the efforts towards regional cooperation in South Asia under the aegis of SAARC. India has also recently joined the Asia Europe Meeting (ASEM) which provides a new forum for the two sides to work together on issues of mutual interest and concern. Cooperation in the field of Science and Technology is growing rapidly. Currently new joint cooperation initiatives are being launched in the field of environment, energy, materials, nanotechnology, agriculture and biotechnology.

Germany, United Kingdom and Belgium are main EU trading partners of India. Between 2000 and 2006, EU trade in goods with India grew by around 80%, with exports increasing from 14 bn euro to 25 bn and imports from 13 bn to 23 bn. As a result, the EU deficit in trade with India rose from 1 bn in 2000 to 2 bn in 2006. In 2006, India accounted for 2.1% of EU exports and 1.7% of EU imports.

Among the EU Member States, Germany (6.3 bn euro or 26% of the total) was the largest exporter to India in 2006, followed by Belgium (4.6 bn or 19%) and the United Kingdom (4.0 bn or 16%). The United Kingdom (4.5 bn or 20%) was the largest importer, followed by Germany (3.9 bn or 17%), Belgium and Italy (3.0 bn or 13% each). The largest surplus in trade with India in 2006 was concluded with Germany (+2.5 bn) and the largest deficit in Spain (-1.2 bn). Around 80% of EU exports to India in 2006 were machinery and vehicles and other manufactured articles, while other manufactured articles accounted for more than 60% of imports. Furthermore the main EU exports to India were unworked diamonds and aircraft, while the main imports were worked diamonds and clothes. The figures below provide a detailed distribution of trade items and the product grouping (import and export) between India and the European Union, as was the case in the year 2012:

European Union, Imports from... India

SITC Codes	SITC Sections	Value (Millions of euro)	Share of Total (%)	Share of total EU Imports
	TOTAL	37,295	100.0%	2.1%
SITC 6	Manufactured goods classified chiefly by material	8,435	22.6%	5.0%
SITC 8	Miscellaneous manufactured articles	7,823	21.0%	3.6%
SITC 7	Machinery and transport equipment	6,377	17.1%	1.4%
SITC 5	Chemicals and related prod, n.e.s.	5,262	14.1%	3.3%
SITC 3	Mineral fuels, lubricants and related materials	5,056	13.6%	0.9%
SITC 0	Food and live animals	2,347	6.3%	2.8%
SITC 2	Crude materials, inedible, except fuels	1,032	2.8%	1.4%
SITC 9	Commodities and transactions n.c.e.	455	1.2%	0.6%
SITC 4	Animal and vegetable oils, fats and waxes	212	0.6%	2.3%
SITC 1	Beverages and tobacco	159	0.4%	2.1%

European Union, Imports from... India

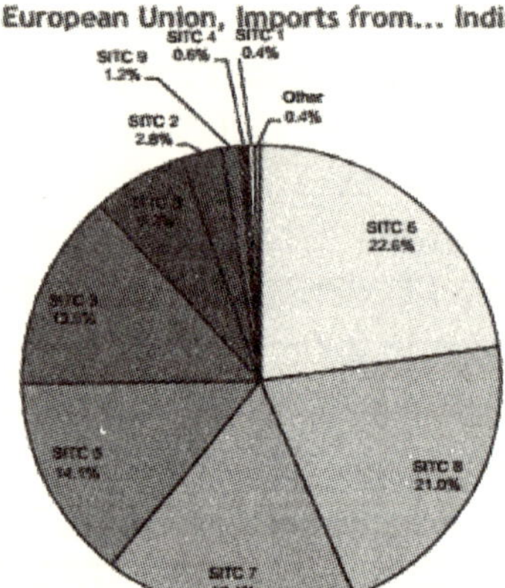

European Union, Exports to... India

SITC Codes	SITC Sections	Value (millions of euro)	Share of Total (%)	Share of total EU Exports
	TOTAL	38,468	100.0%	2.3%
SITC 7	Machinery and transport equipment	14,621	38.0%	2.1%
SITC 6	Manufactured goods classified chiefly by material	12,387	32.2%	6.0%
SITC 5	Chemicals and related prod, n.e.s.	4,454	11.6%	1.6%
SITC 8	Miscellaneous manufactured articles	2,670	6.9%	1.9%
SITC 2	Crude materials, inedible, except fuels	2,531	6.6%	5.9%
SITC 3	Mineral fuels, lubricants and related materials	340	0.9%	0.3%
SITC 9	Commodities and transactions n.c.e.	303	0.8%	0.6%
SITC 0	Food and live animals	207	0.5%	0.3%
SITC 1	Beverages and tobacco	105	0.3%	0.4%
SITC 4	Animal and vegetable oils, fats and waxes	50	0.1%	1.1%

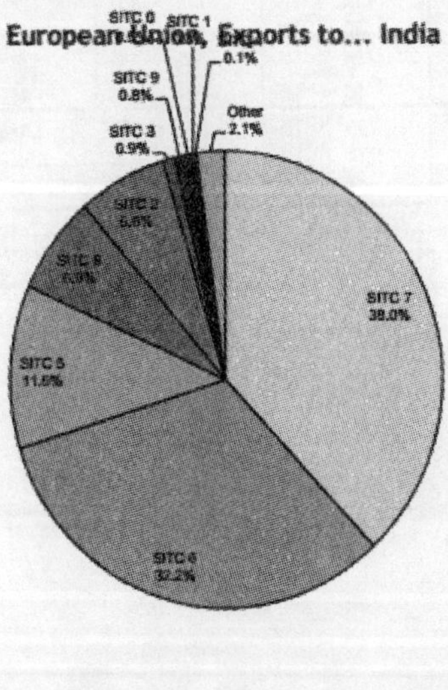

Fig. 1. European Union Trade with India (By SITC Section 2012)
*** The sums of the individual SITC product categories are less than the totals due to confidentiality reasons.**
Source: DG Trade Statistics, 2013
Original Source: EUROSTAT (Comext, Statistical regime 4)

European Union, Imports from... India

SITC Rev.3 (UN, WTO/ITS) & AMA/NAMA** (WTO) Product Groups	2008		2010		2012		Share of Partner in EU Imports (2012)
	Millions euro	%	Millions euro	%	Millions euro	%	
0000 - Total	29,540	100.0%	33,308	100.0%	37,295	100.0%	2.1%
1000 - Primary products	5,452	18.5%	7,710	23.1%	8,979	24.1%	1.2%
1100 - Agricultural products (Food (incl. Fish) & Raw Materials)	2,507	8.5%	2,559	7.7%	3,381	9.1%	2.5%
1200 - Fuels and mining products	2,946	10.0%	5,151	15.5%	5,597	15.0%	0.9%
2000 - Manufactures	23,872	80.8%	25,373	76.2%	27,718	74.3%	2.9%
2100 - Iron and steel	2,339	7.9%	1,171	3.5%	1,557	4.2%	5.8%
2200 - Chemicals	3,318	11.2%	4,029	12.1%	5,262	14.1%	3.3%
2300 - Other semi-manufactures	3,827	13.0%	3,910	11.7%	4,585	12.3%	5.5%
2400 - Machinery and transport equipment	5,017	17.0%	6,172	18.5%	6,377	17.1%	1.4%
2410 - Office and telecommunication equipment	854	2.9%	1,449	4.3%	1,052	2.8%	0.6%
2420 - Transport equipment	1,718	5.8%	2,481	7.4%	2,391	6.4%	2.2%
2430 - Other machinery	2,445	8.3%	2,243	6.7%	2,934	7.9%	1.8%
2500 - Textiles	2,140	7.2%	2,213	6.6%	2,119	5.7%	10.0%
2600 - Clothing	4,333	14.7%	4,675	14.0%	4,467	12.0%	6.4%
2700 - Other manufactures	2,898	9.8%	3,203	9.6%	3,351	9.0%	2.3%
3000 - Other products	163	0.6%	184	0.6%	461	1.2%	0.6%
Agricultural Products (AMA)	2,074	7.0%	2,035	6.1%	2,783	7.5%	2.7%
Non-Agricultural Products (NAMA)	27,276	92.3%	31,097	93.4%	33,944	91.0%	2.0%
Other Products	190	0.6%	175	0.5%	568	1.5%	3.2%

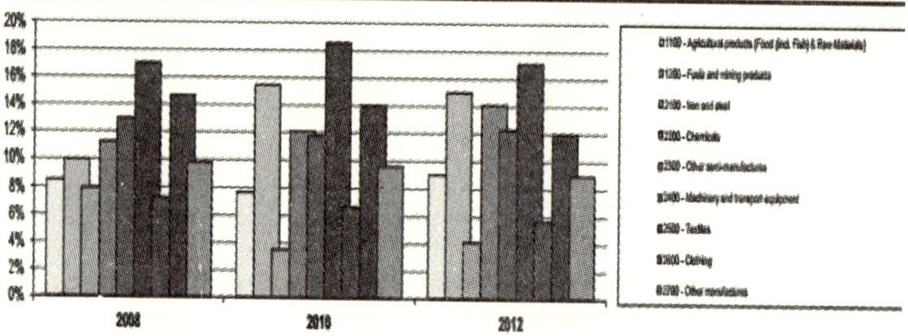

European Union, Exports to... India

SITC Rev.3 (UN, WTO/ITS) & AMA/NAMA** (WTO) Product Groups	2008		2010		2012		Share of Partner in EU Exports (2012)
	Millions euro	%	Millions euro	%	Millions euro	%	
0000 - Total	31,349	100.0%	34,866	100.0%	38,468	100.0%	2.3%
1000 - Primary products	3,091	9.9%	3,259	9.3%	4,404	11.4%	1.5%
1100 - Agricultural products (Food (incl. Fish) & Raw Materials)	570	1.8%	718	2.1%	1,028	2.7%	0.8%
1200 - Fuels and mining products	2,520	8.0%	2,542	7.3%	3,376	8.8%	2.0%
2000 - Manufactures	27,361	87.3%	30,300	86.9%	32,950	85.7%	2.5%
2100 - Iron and steel	1,690	5.4%	1,582	4.5%	1,447	3.8%	3.4%
2200 - Chemicals	3,007	9.6%	3,865	11.1%	4,454	11.6%	1.6%
2300 - Other semi-manufactures	6,558	20.9%	8,070	23.1%	9,550	24.8%	8.0%
2400 - Machinery and transport equipment	13,938	44.5%	14,191	40.7%	14,621	38.0%	2.1%
2410 - Office and telecommunication equipment	1,776	5.7%	1,714	4.9%	1,208	3.1%	1.5%
2420 - Transport equipment	3,185	10.2%	2,938	8.4%	3,626	9.4%	1.3%
2430 - Other machinery	8,849	28.2%	9,170	26.3%	9,581	24.9%	2.8%
2500 - Textiles	170	0.5%	188	0.5%	204	0.5%	1.2%
2600 - Clothing	34	0.1%	44	0.1%	59	0.2%	0.3%
2700 - Other manufactures	1,964	6.3%	2,333	6.7%	2,594	6.7%	1.7%
3000 - Other products	504	1.6%	519	1.5%	313	0.8%	0.6%
Agricultural Products (AMA)	264	0.8%	352	1.0%	472	1.2%	0.4%
Non-Agricultural Products (NAMA)	30,525	97.4%	33,564	96.3%	37,022	96.2%	2.4%
Other Products	560	1.8%	950	2.7%	974	2.5%	5.7%

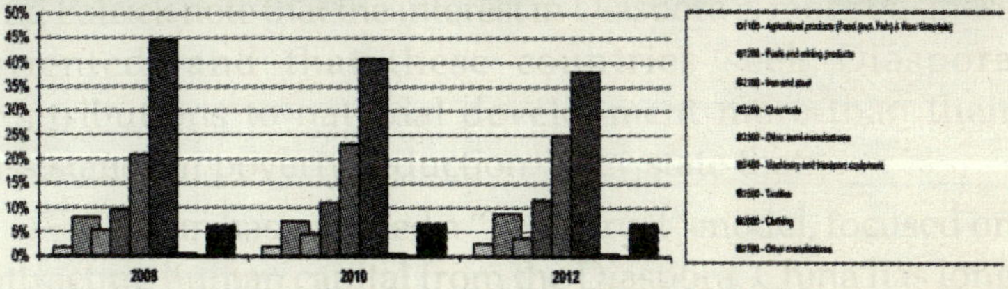

Fig. 2. European Union's Imports and Exports with India (By Product Grouping*)

***The sums of the individual SITC product categories are less than the totals due to confidentiality reasons.**

**** Based on: http://www.wto.org/english/tratop_e/markacc_e/namachairtxt_dec08_e.pdf**

***Source*: DG Trade Statistics, 2013**

***Original Source*: EUROSTAT (Comext, Statistical regime 4)**

Considering the growth in Indo-EU trade relations, the parameters for an ambitious Free Trade Agreement (FTA) was set up in the report of the EU-India High Level Trade Group in October 2006. In accordance with the report, negotiations for a comprehensive FTA were started in June 2007. However, talks for the long-pending India-EU Free Trade Agreement (FTA) are still ongoing and is yet to be finalized, considering the fact that both sides have failed to bridge substantial gaps on crucial issues, which include insurance and data security status for the IT sector. Nonetheless, India enjoys trade preferences with the EU under the Generalized Scheme of Preferences (GSP) and additionally, the EU is providing trade related technical assistance to India, with a view to assist India in its efforts to better integrate into the world economy. Considering this fact, the total trade between India and EU stood at 94.43 billion USD during April-February 2012-2013, which is a whooping rise from the trade volume of 25.6 billion USD in the year 2000. (Livemint 2013, European Commission 2013). The trade balance between the two regions is highlighted in the following figure:

European Union, Trade with India millions of euro, %

Period	Imports	Variation (%, y-o-y)	Share of total EU imports (%)	Exports	Variation (%, y-o-y)	Share of total EU Exports (%)	Balance	Trade
2008	29,540	11.1	1.9	31,349	7.5	2.4	1,809	60,889
2009	25,413	-14.0	2.1	27,477	-12.4	2.5	2,064	52,890
2010	33,308	31.1	2.2	34,866	26.9	2.6	1,559	68,174
2011	39,683	19.1	2.3	40,558	16.3	2.6	876	80,241
2012	37,295	-6.0	2.1	38,468	-5.2	2.3	1,173	75,764
2012Q1	9,661	.	2.1	10,012	.	2.5	350	19,673
2012Q2	8,732	.	2.0	9,282	.	2.2	551	18,014
2012Q3	9,185	.	2.0	9,327	.	2.2	142	18,512
2012Q4	9,718	.	2.2	9,848	.	2.3	130	19,565
2013Q1	.	.	.	.	.	.	.	.
2013Q2	.	.	.	.	.	.	.	.
2013Q3	.	.	.	.	.	.	.	.
2013Q4	.	.	.	.	.	.	.	.
Average annual growth (2008-2012)		6.0			5.2			5.6

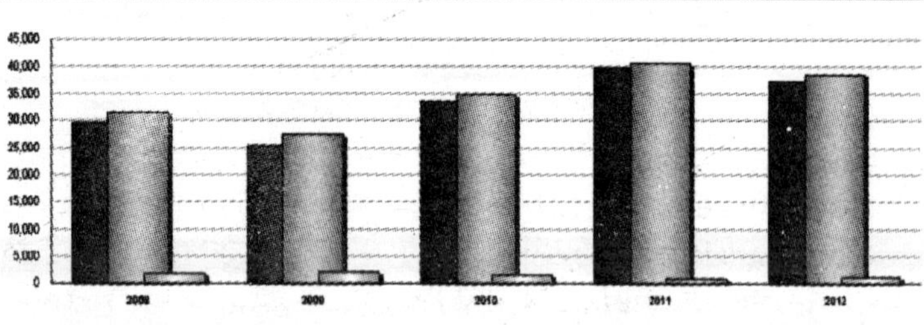

INDIA, Trade with the European Union — millions of euro, %

Period	Imports	Variation (%, y-o-y)	EU Share of total Imports (%)	Exports	Variation (%, y-o-y)	EU Share of total Exports (%)	Balance	Trade
2008	29,767	12.9	13.8	27,632	16.0	21.1	-2,135	57,399
2009	26,434	-11.2	14.5	25,045	-9.4	21.3	-1,389	51,479
2010	32,070	21.3	12.2	31,343	25.1	18.8	-728	63,413
2011	40,170	25.3	12.2	39,625	26.4	18.2	-545	79,794
2012	.	-	.	.	-	.	.	.
2012Q1	11,227	-	11.8	9,832	.	16.4	-1,395	21,059
2012Q2	10,119	-	11.4	8,967	-	15.8	-1,152	19,086
2012Q3	10,496	-	11.1	9,321	-	17.0	-1,175	19,816
2012Q4	.	.	.	.	.	.	.	.
2013Q1	.	-	-	.	-	-	.	.
2013Q2	.	-	-	.	-	-	.	.
2013Q3	.	-	-	.	-	-	.	.
2013Q4	.	.	.	.	.	.	.	.
Average annual growth (2008-2012)		.			.			-

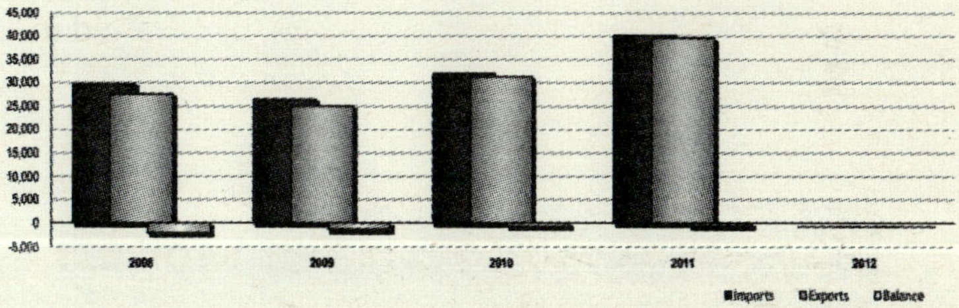

Fig. 3. European Union and India's Trade Balance Against Each Other
***Source:* DG Trade Statistics, 2013**
***Original Source:* EUROSTAT (Comext, Statistical regime 4) and IMF (DoTS)**

In addition to the above figure, the figure below sums up the overall trade (trade in goods, trade in services and Foreign Direct Investments) between India and the European Union, for the years, 2010, 2011 and 2012:

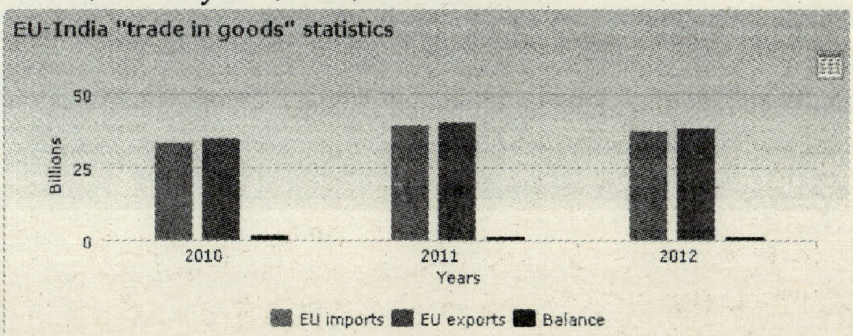

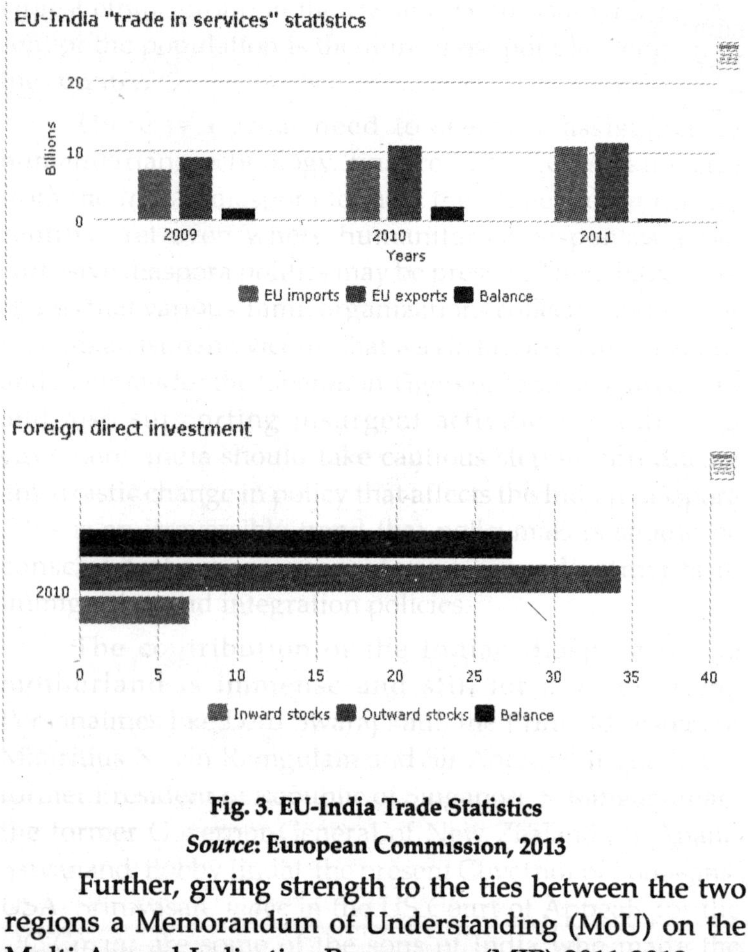

Fig. 3. EU-India Trade Statistics
***Source*: European Commission, 2013**

Further, giving strength to the ties between the two regions a Memorandum of Understanding (MoU) on the Multi-Annual Indicative Programme (MIP) 2011-2013 was signed between the EU and India in February 2011. A review confirmed the need to further support and facilitate social sectors like health and education, in particular secondary education and vocational training. For 2011-2013, the EU intends to fund fellowships for Indian students and professors (Erasmus Mundus), as well as projects in the fields of energy, environment, sustainable development and trade related technical assistance.

The European Union and India held their 12th annual summit in New Delhi on 10th February 2012. From EU side, European Council President Herman Van Rompuy, European Commission President José Manuel Barroso, EU Trade commissioner, Karel De Gucht and from India, Prime Minister Dr.Manmohan Singh, Foreign Minister S.M. Krishna, Trade Minister A. Sharma and National Security Adviser, S.S. Menon took part in the summit discussions. The participants emphasised the importance of the EU-India Strategic Partnership and its growing potential. Agreements were reached for enhanced cooperation in security issues, in particular counter-terrorism, cyber security and counter-piracy measures, as well as in other core areas such as trade, energy, innovation, health research, water and bio-resources, communication technology.

REGIONAL DIALOGUES AND EXCHANGES IN SHARED AREAS OF INTEREST

Various issues and topics that concerns today's world politics, are among those range of issues over which the two regions share some sectoral interests. As such the two sides have established various working groups and have organized policy dialogues and exchanges to address these issues. The following are an overview of these co-operations: (Europa 2013, Mukhopadhyay 2010)

Clean Development and Climate Change : Citing grave concerns on the degrading environmental level and rising global temperature, the EU-India Summit of 2008 adopted a Joint Work Programme (JWP) on energy, clean development and climate change. Until now two policy dialogues have been organized on the issues of environment and energy, and each of the countries have committed towards cooperating in the field of clean development and climate change.

Environment : EU and India have established a Joint

Working Group on Environment (JWGE), which is co-chaired by the Director General for Environment (DG ENV) of the European Commission and India's Ministry of Environment and Forests. It meets on a yearly basis, develops high level visits, and from time to time organizes India-EU Environment Forums (EF) with businessmen, academicians and members of the civil society as its participants.

Energy Cooperation : EU and India have made a Joint Declaration on Energy, which was adopted at the India-EU Summit in Delhi on 10th February 2012. The agenda of the Summit included issues of energy security and six essential areas were identified as priorities for bilateral cooperation, which included, clean coal, energy efficiency of products, energy efficiency in buildings, grids (including integration of renewables), cost-effective ways to promote renewable energies and safety (off-shore and nuclear). It has also been decided by the two sides that the EU-India Energy Panel would meet at least once every year at senior most level.

Counter Terrorism Cooperation : The EU-India Summit of November 2009 attempted to revitalize the EU-India Counter Terrorism Cooperation. Both sides have committed towards strengthening the UN Counter Terrorism Implementation Task Force (CTITF), and also have pledged to enhance negotiations between Europol and particular Indian Agencies, like the Central Bureau of Investigation (CBI).

Nuclear : World wide India is now being viewed as an important market for nuclear investment. Thus, India has now been given the privilege to participate in the International Thermonuclear Experimental Reactor (ITER) project since 2005. The year 2009 saw the conclusion of the Euratom-India Agreement on fusion energy research. Currently, negotiations of an India-Euratom Agreement on cooperation in civil nuclear energy research are underway.

Migration and Mobility : In the age of globalization mobility of their citizens, that is, people-to-people contact is a key component of the dynamic EU-India partnership. In the framework of the EU Global Approach to Migration and Mobility (GAMM), EU-India relations are currently driven by a High Level Dialogue on Migration and Mobility (HLDMM).

This is an important bilateral comprehensive forum for information exchange on all migration-related and mobility-related issues. The most recent HLDMM took place in New Delhi on 2 July, 2012. The dialogue led to the identification of four priority areas for future bilateral cooperation. These include:

1. Safe and legal migration.
2. Combating irregular migration.
3. Migration and development, and
4. Sharing of information and practices regarding international protection of those in need.

Science and Innovation : Under the S&T Cooperation Agreement signed in 2001, Science and Innovation cooperation between the two regions has ever expanded. This cooperation is further strengthening with the Indo-European partnership agreed at a Ministerial Meeting in 2012 that brings together the research and innovation resources of India and other EU Member States.

Statistical Cooperation : On 10th February, 2012, a Memorandum of Understanding (MoU) on statistical cooperation between Eurostat and the Indian Central Statistics office was signed at the EU-India Summit. Both sides are thus, currently engaged on a programme of cooperation in the field of Statistics.

Higher Education : A Dialogue on Higher Education was launched between the two regions in May 2011. The dialogue covered issues such as skills development, quality assurance, and the recognition of qualifications. And now concrete cooperation takes place through the Erasmus Mundus Programme (EMP) and under projects on vocational training and skills development.

The European Business and Technology Centre (EBTC) : The EBTC in New Delhi serves the interests of the European industry (with a focus on Small and Medium Enterprises [SMEs]) and research communities. Newer branches of the Centre are now opened in Mumbai, Bangalore, and Kolkata, which provides one-stop information on rules, regulations, standards, best practices, key market barriers, and general trade and investment-related matters.

In short, EU offers to contribute to India's overall development in a tangible way by

a. Strengthening the economic reforms, the small and medium business sector and stable and sustained market economy.

b. Assisting India in its relentless pursuit for a genuine social, structural and political transformation based on vibrant democracy, cultural diversity, secularism, pluralism and rule of law.

c. Cooperating with India in combating terrorism globally.

d. Actively supporting the integration of India into International Political Economy and in the process of globalization.

e. Reducing poverty and initiating self help measures in rural areas and strengthening democratic order at the grassroots level.

f. Continuing the process of dialogue between India and EU aimed at sustainable development.

g. Promoting the development of medial as an agent of positive change in society.

REFERENCES

- DG Trade Statistics, 2013, 'India: EU Bilateral Trade and Trade with the World', (Online Web), Accessed, June 15, 2013, URL: http://trade.ec.europa.eu/doclib/docs/2006/september/tradoc_113390.pdf
- Europa, 2013, 'Background Note: India EU Relations', (Online Web), Accessed, June 10, 2013, URL: http://europa.eu/rapid/press-release_MEMO-13-52_en.htm
- European Commission, 2013, 'Trade: Countries and Regions', (Online Web), Accessed, June 14, 2013, URL: http://ec.europa.eu/trade/policy/countries-and-regions/countries/india/
- Gerhard Wahlers, ed., 2007, India and the European Union, New Delhi, Konrad Adenauer Stiftung
- Livemint, 2013, 'India-EU FTA Talks Fail to Bridge Gaps', (Online Web), Accessed, June 16, 2013, URL: http://www.livemint.com/Politics/jO5DSVLjGMUay9mopfMPGL/IndiaEU-FTA-talks-fail-to-bridge-gaps-ministerial-meet-unl.html
- Mukhopadhyay Alok Rashmi, 2010, 'EU-India Counter-Terrorism Cooperation: Post Lisbon Prospects', IDSA Comment, (Online Web), Accessed, June 12, 2013, URL: http://www.idsa.in/idsacomments/EU-IndiaCounter-TerrorismCooperationPost-LisbonProspects_armukhopadhyay_260210
- Sachdeva Gulshan, 2012, 'The Eurozone Crisis and India-EU Ties', IDSA Comment, (Online Web), Accessed, June 12, 2013, URL: http://www.idsa.in/idsacomments/TheEurozoneCrisisandIndiaEUTies_gsacjdeva_070212

7

India and Russia Relations: Towards Pragmatism

Muzaffar Ahmad Ganaie

India-Russia relationship is credited for being one of the 'tried and tested' relationships, notwithstanding the demise of the Soviet Union and end of cold war which exposed both the countries to new realities of post-cold war international political system. The relationship based on mutual trust and cooperation between the two states dates back to 1950s when India was experiencing the initial years of her independence from British colonial system and Soviet Union was observing sore relations with its rival super power United States in an ideologically divided world. Initially the relations between two sides were very cold and unfriendly. The unleashing of cold war between US and USSR which in the words of T.N Kaul kept Russian leaders "so engrossed in their dealing American and western Europe that they had little time to devote to or discuss Asia in general and India in particular, and the absence of incentive in Asia made the

Soviet Union Ignore India. They did not possess sufficient resources to divert their attention to many parts of the world. India was a soviet neighbour in geographical terms only and did not share any common cultural, economic or historical bonds".[1] Besides these factors it was India's policy of non-alignment and her decision to remain in British Commonwealth of Nations even after independence, making Soviet premier Joseph Stalin to call Indian Prime Minister Jawaharlal Nehru an 'underdog of British imperialism'[2], greatly hindered the development of cordial and friendly relations between the two states. Not only the Soviet leadership even the Soviet press and academicians were also highly critical of Indian leadership and their policies labelling India a 'semi-independent state', Gandhi a 'bourgeoisie reformist' and Nehru a 'lackey of British imperialism'.[3]

However, after the death of Stalin in 1953, the attitude of Soviet leadership towards India drastically changed and leaders of the countries found enough reasons to redefine their relationship. Soviet Union on its part realised the importance of India as a leader of NAM to secure the support of non aligned group of nations through Indian leadership, to reduce the American and Chinese influence in the region by developing close relations with Asia's second largest country and as a country with which it shared common views on a number of global issues like anti-colonialism, multilateralism, anti-racism, anti-apartheid etc. India on its part, realised the importance of Soviet Union to safeguard its vital national security interests threatened by western military aid to Pakistan and Pakistan's formal joining of western alliance system.[4] The relationship gartered momentum in late 1950s when the Sino-Soviet relationship developed cracks on the one hand and on the other hand Sino-Indian relations deteriorated due to a border dispute, making Soviet Union to take much more interest in India's security needs. In 1962, the two sides signed a major defence agreement for the supply of military hardware to India.[5]

The support two countries provided to each other on certain regional and global issues further cemented their bilateral relationship. For instance in 1956, to the pleasure of Soviet Union, India greatly condemned the Anglo-French invasion in Egypt but remained silent on Soviet intervention in Hungary, it even supported the Soviet Union to vote down a UN resolution calling for the withdrawal of troops from Hungary.[6] Commenting on this attitude of India A.D Gorwala writes that India was not "able to bring itself to record a vote [at UN] condemning the Soviet Union for its barbarous suppression of national freedom in Hungary. The farthest India could go was to allow itself mild verbal reprobation and that too after public opinion throughout the country, moved for once to real emotion, strongly criticised its lukewarm attitude".[7] Likewise Soviet Union supported Indian action in Goa when it vetoed a resolution moved by western powers denouncing India as an aggressor and extended wholehearted and unconditional support to Indian stand on Kashmir issue.

Indo-Soviet relationship reached to its zenith in 1970s when two sides signed 20 years Treaty of Peace, Friendship and Cooperation in 1971 which proved a milestone in bilateral relationship. Early 1970s was a period marked by major strategical developments. On the one hand Sino-American breakthrough facilitated by Pakistan was achieved and on the other hand crises in Eastern Pakistan erupted which pushed millions of refugees from the region in to Indian Territory thus making Indian intervention in the region necessary. At the height of these developments came a warning form Henery Kissinger to India: "If war broke out between India and Pakistan and China became involved on Pakistan's side, we [America] would be unable to help you against China".[8] It was in the backdrop of these events that India signed a Treaty of Peace, Friendship and

Cooperation with Soviet Union which played a very important role in protecting India's sovereignty and territorial integrity and acted as a counterweight against Pakistan-China-America axis. Article 9 of the treaty calling up on the parties to "enter into mutual consultations when either of the parties is subjected to an attack so as to remove the threat and to take appropriate measures to maintain security of the region" [9] greatly deterred the American and China's involvement in the 1971 war.

Indo-Soviet relationship received a setback in 1991 following the sudden disintegration of Soviet Union and its replacement by Russia as a successor state. Russia under President Boris Yeltsin and Foreign Minister Andrey Kozyrev pursued a de-ideologised foreign policy with a western tilt to bailout the ailing Russian economy and in this process neglected Asian countries, particularly India. Even much to the pleasure of western powers Russia voted in favour of a resolution moved by Pakistan in 1991 for denuclearisation of South Asia, reversed its stand on Kashmir and urged India to join Nuclear Non-Proliferation Treaty,[10] thus relegating the relations to background. However failure on the part of Western countries to reach out to Russia made Yeltsin to revive the relations with traditional partners. In an attempt to reinvent the spirit old friendship between the two countries, Boris Yeltsin visited India in 1993. During his visit he seriously addressed the problem of uninterrupted supply of military hardware and spare parts to Indian defence forces. The visit culminated in signing of the Treaty of Friendship and Cooperation but unlike the treaty of 1971,it did not contain any security clause. After the visit of Yeltsin mutual exchange of visits between the leaders of two countries continued which greatly helped to take bilateral relationship to respectable heights.

A watershed event in the Indo-Russian relationship came in 2000 when Russian president Vladimir Putin Visited

India. It was during his visit that two sides signed a Declaration on Strategic Partnership. This strategic partnership was elevated to the status of a "special and privileged Strategic partnership" in 2010.[11] Besides the declaration on Strategic Partnership 10 more agreements were signed covering defence, science and technology and agriculture sectors. Moreover, during the visit it was also agreed to establish the institution of annual summit level meeting and since 2000 the leaders of two countries are meeting alternately in each others capital every year which has greatly helped to take relationship to newer heights.

DEFENCE TIES

Defence cooperation constitutes a vital component of Indo-Russian strategic cooperation. The foundation of this cooperation was laid down in early 1960s when India purchased a Soviet transport aircraft in 1961 followed by supersonic MIG-21fighters deal signed in 1962. By the end of the decade India was flooded with military equipments and weapon systems of soviet origin.[12] Today over 70 per cent of India defence forces are equipped with military hardware of Soviet/Russian origin. India is significant purchaser of Russian military hardware and its importance for the Russian military industrial complex can be viewed by the fact that India buys more military equipments and hardware from Russian defence Industry than Russia's own defence forces[13] and recently India has replaced China as biggest client of Russian defence industry.[14]

The cooperation between two sides in defence sector is not merely a buyer-seller cooperation but one based on joint research and development, joint production and marketing of weapon systems which is likely to continue for a longer time. The joint projects undertaken by two countries include joint production of Brahmos missile system, licensed production of T-90 battle tanks, Fifth

Generation Fighter Aircraft, Multirole Transport Aircraft etc. Brahmos is cruise supersonic missile which can be launched from land, sea, and air platforms. This is probably the fastest cruised missile in the world and has already been deployed in the Indian army. The decision on the joint production of Brahmos missile system was taken in early 1998 and because of years of joint efforts four variants of the missile have been developed. The total cost of the missile is estimated to be $ 10 billion and a number of countries have shown a great interest to acquire this defence technology.[15] Under a major collaboration programme, two countries inked an intergovernmental agreement in 2007 for joint development of Fifth Generation Multi-Functional Fighter Aircraft. The work on the project will be completed by 2015 and aircraft will be deployed in air force in 2017. The aim of the project is to develop aircraft analogous to American F-22 Raptor and F- 35 Joint Strike fighter.[16]

Russia has also made a significant contribution to India's space programme. Thamba Equatorial Rocket Launching Station at Thiruvanthapuram was set up with Soviet assistance. Moreover the experimental satellites, Arayabatta and Bhaskara—I and II were also launched with Soviet cooperation.[17] Currently two countries are cooperating in number of high technology based space projects which include Human space Flight project, youthsat project and Chandrayaan-2, unmanned lunar mission. These projects are the outcome of an intergovernmental agreement on "cooperation in the area of exploration and use of outer space for peaceful purposes", signed in 2004. Two sides are also cooperating in development, launch and use of Russian GLONASS Satellite Navigation System. The system with both civilian and military application will reduce Indian dependence on American Global Positioning system.

Despite the great strides made in the defence cooperation over the years, the relationship is facing a number of challenges. Cost overruns, delayed deliveries, untested weapon systems and substandard spare parts supplied by Russian defence Industry have greatly bedevilled indo- Russian military ties. The failure on the part of Russian contractors to facilitate in time deliveries has become a sore point in bilateral relationship, in this connection the example of Admiral Gorchakov is noteworthy. The Russian aircraft carrier, Admiral Gorshkov was scheduled to reach Indian waters in August 2008 under a deal signed in 2004. Then under a revised schedule the aircraft carrier was supposed to be delivered by December 2012, but technical problems have further delayed its shipment by several months, meanwhile the cost of the aircraft carrier has risen several times. Under a contract signed in 2004 India was supposed to pay $ 974 million to Russia to refit the aircraft carrier, but as things turned out Russia could not stick to the terms of 2004 contract which threatened Indian withdrawal from the deal. However in 2010 during the visit of Russian Premier Vladimir Putin to India the controversy was put to an end and final price of the project was set as $2.33 billion. Another example is that of nuclear powered Akula-II class submarine. The submarine was supposed to be handed over to India in 2008 on ten years lease but was delivered in 2012.[18]

Russia is also blamed for providing sub-standard systems and spare parts and sometimes the military equipments have been delivered to India without their key components. Phase III fighter planes were delivered to Indi without critical components. Likewise T-90 battle tanks were supplied to India without missile firing systems.[19] Taking seriously all these problems Indian Parliamentary Standing Committee has strongly recommended Indian government to reduce its heavy dependence on Russian defence industry. The committee has also urged the government that future defence deals must be concluded only through open competitive tenders.[20]

Another notable challenge faced by Russian defence industry is increasing competition posed by western countries. The failure on the part of Russian MIG-35 to win $ 10-12 billion fighter aircraft deal is perhaps indicative of the fact that Russian monopoly in India defence market is facing a serious challenge from western competitors. The bid for the purchase of 126 Medium Multirole Combat Aircraft was finally won by French defence company Dassault Rafale.[21] Moreover India's drive for modernization of its military equipments and weapon systems motivated by China which is modernizing its defence forces with latest and sophisticated technology is also a cause of concern for Russian military industrial complex. Since Russia which itself is looking towards western countries to receive cutting edge and sophisticated technology[22] can not satisfy Indian needs, in such a scenario India will also like to diversify its sources of arms and technology acquisitions to keep pace with China's modernization drive. But keeping in view the nature of ongoing defence projects between two countries and their traditional and deep rooted defence ties Russia will continue to be India's Major defence partner in foreseeable future.

TRADE AND ECONOMIC RELATIONS

Trade and economic relations remain a weak link of otherwise fruitful Indo-Russian bilateral relationship. Though the volume of trade is growing steadily touching $10 in 2012 but it is far below than the potential keeping in view the size of the two economies and their vast resource base. Looking back, Soviet Union was one of the most important trading partners of India and in 1980s it emerged as India's largest trading partner replacing United States.[23] However after the fateful soviet transition trade and economic relations received a set back and in 1992 the volume of bilateral trade shrinked to half-a-billion US dollars from

$5.5 billion in 1990.[24]

Though the trade between two countries is making steady progress and both the countries are striving to take it US $20 billion by 2015 but in the past two decades composition of trade between the two countries has gone through some remarkable changes. The export of traditional items like tea, coffee, tobacco, cotton yarn, cotton fabrics etc. from India to Russia has declined sharply. The decline registered in the export of tea and coffee is partly because of tough competition posed by countries like Srilanka, Kenya, Brazil etc. However the export of Pharmaceutical products has been able to maintain a healthy growth rate. The export of medicines, pharmaceuticals and fine chemicals items witnessed a threefold increase in a period of seven years (from 2000 t0 2007)[25]. Besides this the export of non traditional items like readymade garments and transport equipments has also increased to considerable levels.[26]

A notable aspect of Indo- Russian economic and trade relations is poor performance of India in Russian market in comparison to Russian performance in Indian market resulting in trade balance heavily tilted in Russia's favour and what is even more disturbing is that this imbalance has been growing over the years. The imbalance grew from $1.6 billion in 2007-08 to $ 2.8 billion in 201-2012.[27] The reasons responsible for the poor performance of India in Russian market include lack of information among Indian traders regarding Russian trading institutions, underdeveloped insurance market, ineffective payment system and strict visa policy. [28] Another worrisome aspect is narrow base of trade basket which needs to be diversified to give boost to economic and trade relations.

Lack of adequate trade roots is also acting as a stumbling block in bilateral trade relations. The current trade root is long and time consuming. In this context the quick operationalisation North-South trade corridor will be a welcome step. It will facilitate easy movement of goods across the countries, will reduce the transportation cost by 30 percent and transit time by 50 percent.

Despite the problems which over the years have surfaced in the bilateral trade relations, both the countries are making positive efforts to take it to respectable levels. A number of Indian companies are making huge investments in Russia to give a boost to bilateral trade. India's ONGC Videsh Limited owns 20 percent stake in Sakhalin-I off shore gas project and has invested $ 2.7 billion in the project. In order to involve Russian companies in India's oil and gas exploration projects, an intergovernmental agreement was signed during the visit of Russian president Dmitry Medvedev to India in 2010. The agreement could go a long way in increasing the share of Russian FDI in India, which stands at dollar one billion, primarily in telecommunication sector.[29] Moreover, some leading India pharmaceutical companies are collaborating with their Russian counterparts to enhance trade ties. During 2012 visit of Vladimir Putin an agreement was signed between Elder Pharmaceuticals of India and Pharma Eco of Russia to set up a manufacturing plant in Russia.[30] In order to increase the volume of two way investments $ 2 billion pact has been signed between State Bank of India and Russian Foundation of Direct Investment. The pact will provide financial assistance to joint venture projects.[31]

To promote business to business ties, institutional mechanisms like Indo-Russian Forum on Trade and Investment (established in 2007), India-Russia CEO'S Council (established in 2008), India-Russian Business Council (established in 2007), India-Russia Trade, Investment and Technology Promotion Council (established in 2007) and the India-Russia Chamber of Commerce have also been put in place.

COOPERATION IN ENERGY SECTOR

India is one of the fast developing economies of the world with ever increasing energy requirements and is expected to become world's third largest consumer of energy by 2030 after US and China but nature has blessed it with limited sources of energy to meet its growing demands of energy. On the other Russia is world's largest producer of natural gas and second largest producer of oil, [32] making it one of the India's most suitable partner in energy sector. Underlining the importance of Russia for India's energy security, former Indian Petroleum Minister Mani Shankar Ayer said in 2004 that : "In the half-century of Indian independence, Russia has guaranteed our territorial integrity, and in the second half it may be able to guarantee our energy security."[33] However cooperation in this sector is yet to gain much needed and deserved momentum. So far, India has not been able to show a strong presence in Russia's hydrocarbon sector. It has so for been able to acquire 20 percent share in Sakhalin-I off shore gas project where it has invested $ 2.7 billion, which happens to be largest investment abroad and has purchased Imperial Energy Company for $ 2.5 billion. However the reluctance shown by Russian authorities to do business with western companies in the energy field has greatly increased the chances of India's broader involvement in Russia's oil and gas exploration projects and India is expected to get access to Sakhalin-3 gas exploration project.[34] Russia's importance for India also lies in the fact that it can ensure India's access to vast oil and natural gas reserves of Central Asian Republics where Russia still remains a dominant player. Cooperation between the two sides in key gas pipeline projects like TAPI (Turkmenistan-Afghanistan-Pakistan-India) could go a long way in satisfying India's bourgeoning energy needs.

In the nuclear energy field, cooperation between two sides is much more comprehensive and diversified which has gathered momentum after Nuclear Suppliers Group exempted India from cartel's guidelines in 2008. Currently Russia is building two 1000 MW nuclear reactors at Kundankulam which are expected to be commissioned by this year. The agreement for the construction of four additional 1000MW nuclear reactors at same site has also been concluded. Russia will supply fuel for these reactors throughout their life span. During the visit of Russian President Vladimir Putin to India in 2012 two sides agreed on an ambitious roadmap to strengthen cooperation in civil nuclear energy field. Under the roadmap Russia will construct 16 t o 18 nuclear reactors in India of 1000 MW each. This would cost India around $45 billion in next two to three decades.[35] An interesting aspect of ongoing cooperation is that it is not only based on supply of nuclear reactors and fuel to India but on joint research and development, joint exploitation of uranium deposits, joint construction of nuclear reactors and their marketing to third world countries.[36]

CONCLUSION

India-Russia relations have withstood test of the time and have reached to a stage where both the countries look at each other as indispensible partners. Theirs is the relationship based on mutual trust and shared world views from which both the countries have gained enormously. Though India's relations with other countries, particularly United States have improved remarkably in last couple of years, but Russia continues to be India's privileged partner. In the words of India's Defence Minister A.K. Antony: "Russia remains India's number one strategic Partner and in many respects, there are no alternatives to the cooperation with Russia in foreseeable future".[37] Though there are certain irritants in the relationship particularly in commercial and defence sectors, which need an immediate attention from both the countries. Both the countries must focus more on bilateral trade ensuring a proactive role for private sector. Increased people to people contacts and cultural links could also go a long way in elevating bilateral relationship to new heights.

REFERENCES

1 Quoted in N. Jayapalan, (2011), *Foreign Policy of India: 1947-1987,* Atlantic Publishers, New Delhi, pp. 153-154.

2 B.M Jain, (Fall, 2003), "India and Russia: Reassessing the Time-Tested Ties", *Pacific Affairs,* Vol. 76, No.3, p.376.

3 N. Jayapalan, op.cit. No.1, p. 153.

4 Muchkund Dubey, (September 22, 2012), "Indo-(Soviet) Russian Relations", *Mainstream,* Vol. L, No. 40.

5 Dr. Surya Narain Yadav and Dr. Indu Baghel, (2009), *India's Foreign Policy: Opportunities and Obstacles in the post-Cold War Era,* Global Vision, New Delhi, p.258.

6 Harsh V. Pant, (2013), "India Russia Ties and India's Strategic Culture: Dominance of a Realist world view", *India Review,* Vol. 12, No. 1, p.3.

7 Jayanta Kumar Ray, (2011) *India's Foreign Relations: 1947-2007,* Rutledge, New Delhi, pp. 538-539.

8 Quoted in Harsh V. Pant, op.cit. No.6, p. 4.

9 Arun Mohanty, (September 10, 2011), "The Indo-Soviet Friendship Treaty and its Legacy", *Mainstream,* Vol. XLIX, No.38.

10 Dr. D.K. Sharma, (2011), *Indian Foreign Policy,* DPS Publication, New Delhi, p.275.

11 Nivedita Das Kandu,(March 12, 2010), "Vladimir Putin's Presidency and India-Russia Relationship". Available at: http://valdaiclub.com/asia/43221.htm, accessed on 6/6/2013.

12 Jayanta Kumar Ray, op.cit. No.7, pp. 570-71.

13 Deepa M. Ollapally, "The Evolution Of India's Relations With Russia: Tried, Tested and Searching for Balance" in Sumit Ganguly (ed.), (2010), *India's Foreign Policy: Retrospect and Prospect,* Oxford University press , New Delhi. P.233.

14 Patryk Kugiel, (4 January 2013),"India- Russia relations: An Enduring Partnership", *PISM Bulletin,* No. 2 (455).

15 Tatiana Shaumyan, "Russian-Indian Bilateral Cooperation" in P.

Stobdan (ed.), , (2010), *India-Russia Strategic Partnership : Common Perspectives* ,Institute for Defence Studies and Analyses, New Delhi, p 159-160.

16 Ibid. p. 158.

17 Muchkund Dubey, op.cit. No. 4 .

18 Harsh V. Pant, op.cit. No. 6. p. 8.

19 Sanjeev Pillay, (4 July 2009), India-Russian Defence Relations: On The Wane?" Available at: http://www.ipcs.org/article_details.php?articleNo=2902, accessed on 22/7/2013.

20 Stephen Blank,(Spring/Summer 2008), "Moscow's Strategic Triangle In A Time Of Transition", *The Journal OF East Asian Affairs*, Vol.22, No. 1, p. 138.

21 Richard Weitz, (July 2012), "The Maturing Of Russia-India Defence Relations", *Journal Of Defence Studies*, Vol.6, No. 3, p 87.

22 Rod Thornton, (July 2012), "India Russia Military Cooperation : Which Way Forward", *Journal of Defence Studies*. Vol. 6, No. 3, pp.100-102.

23 Muchkund Dubey, op.cit. No. 4

24 Arun Mohanty, (December 5, 2009), "India Needs A stronger Partnership with Russia in Emerging Multipolar world" *Mainstream*, Vol. XLVII, No. 51

25 R. G. Gidadhubli, (Jan. 17-23, 2009), "Indo-Russia Economic ties: Advantage Russia", *Economic and political weekly*, Vol. 44, No. 3, p.22.

26 Jayanta Kumar Ray, Op.cit No.7, p. 56.

27 R. G. Gidadhubli, (January 26, 2013), "Putin's visit to India — Advantage Russia", *Mainstream*, Vol. LI, No. 6.

28 R. G. Gidadhubli, op.cit. No. 25.

29 Ranendra Sen, "The Evolution of India's Bilateral Relations With Russia". Available at: http//www.aspenindia.org/pdf/the_evolution.pdf, accessed on 25/7/2012.

30 R. G. Gidadhubli, op.cit.No. 27.

31 Ibid.

32 Deepa M. Ollapally, op.cit. No. 13, pp. 236-237.

33 Quoted in Anuradha M. Chenoy, "India and Russia", in Atish Sinha and Madhup Mohta(eds.), (2007), *Indian Foreign policy :challenges and opportunities*, Academic Foundation, New Delhi, p. 737.

34 Jayanta Kumar Ray, op.cit. No. 7, p. 568.

35 Rajiv Sharma, (December 26, 2012), "India, Russia to Embark on $ 45 bln Nuclear Energy Roadmap", Available at : http;// www.indrus.in/articles/212/12/26/india_russia_to_ embark_on_ 45_bln_nuclear_energy_roadmap_2/9/html.

36 Arun Mohanty, (April 9, 2011), "Indo-Russia Strategic Partnership: a Reality Check", *Mainstream*, Vol. XLIX, No. 16.

37 Quoted in Rod Thornton, op.cit. No. 22 , p.110.

8

India - Africa Relations: From the Past Forward

Sanjukta Banerji Bhattacharya

"The 21st century is often described as the Asian century. India wishes to see the 21st century as the Century of Asia and Africa, with the people of the two continents working together to promote inclusive globalization." — **Manmohan Singh**[1]

Africa today is in the limelight as a resource-rich continent, resources that other countries, including India, need, but till almost the middle of the last century, Africa was known as the 'dark continent', and in the second half of that century after most of the sub-Saharan states had become independent, it was headlined for all the wrong reasons. Coups and counter-coups were common; bad governance, one party rule and even one-person dictatorships prevailed in many states; poverty, starvation deaths, famine, both natural and man-made were synonymous with several African states even as dictators and foreign multinational companies (MNCs) exploited Africa's huge natural resources and amassed immense wealth; assassinations of leaders, long wars of independence followed by civil wars, foreign intervention, apartheid – were the news that filtered out from Africa. Given the low per capita incomes (PCI) and gross domestic products (GDP) as well as the lack of strategic significance of most African states in the context of the Cold War, there was little international interest in what was happening in that continent except for the interest of the Unites States (US) and the Soviet Union in some southern and east African states where Cold War equations led them to intervene and prop up clients. The US, France and the United Kingdom (UK) were also interested in Africa's natural resources and exploited them with impunity, and here, France particularly, played an important role, supplying client states with military hardware and indulging in other clandestine means to keep desirable authoritarian rulers with whom they had special trade relations, in power. India, China and other countries of the developing world had little to do with African states, because they themselves were dealing with the economic, political and social problems of growing into mature statehood. There was talk of South-South partnership, but such ideas remained ideas in the context of the incapacity of countries of the 'South' to independently partner each other, not only because of the unequal nature of international trade, but also because they lacked financial and other resources to invest in any other country. Moreover, African states were declared as 'basket cases' and even Western donors began to cut down on their aid to several countries because of the frustrating manner in which such aid disappeared without any improvement in the economic status of the country concerned or any infrastructure development. From the 1980s, the World Bank and the International Monetary Fund (IMF) began to press for structural adjustment programmes (SAP) to be implemented as the price that countries had to pay for further loans or aid, and structural adjustment was not restricted only to the economy, but also meant changes in governance.

The SAPs may have prompted change despite initial hardships; changes in the international environment may also have had a role to play, and this implies not just the end of the Cold War but also globalization, economic liberalization and the emergence of a completely new set of players in world politics and the economic arena; and finally, the emergence of new players also meant the entrance of 'new kids on the block' so far as Africa was concerned, with new ways of doing business, wanting to partner African states rather than exploit them, thereby drawing them into the merging markets of an increasingly globalized world.

Today, Africa presents a very changed scenario. Even though many countries are not yet completely politically stable, there is a general trend towards multi-party democratic governance with regular elections. Though levels of corruption may still be high and transparency levels low, the situation is far better for most states than even ten years back. Continental institutions under the relatively new African Union (AU), which places governance and human rights standards at a high premium, are developing and this implies that stability and accountability are goals that are reachable. In the new environment prevailing in most states, it is easier for the new players to do business since they can be assured that their investments will not disappear with nothing to show for it. New players, on their part, in order to develop further, need new markets for their products and resources for their growing industries. Most countries of the world already have heavy economic linkages with developed or other countries, and resources are more often than not pledged to companies for decades in advance. African countries, on the other hand, because of earlier circumstances, were far less committed to other countries and in fact, much of their resources had yet to be discovered, leaving them relatively free to draw contracts with emerging states. China and India were the two emerging powers that were in need of new partners in their bid for growth, and they were among the first of the new players in Africa. The fact that relations with these countries has paid off is amply evident in the fact that the African middle class is rapidly expanding and the continent hosts some of the fastest growing economies of the world. The present paper will focus on India's relations with Africa at the local, regional and continental levels and attempt a prognosis on what the future holds.

I

To understand the present, a brief background of India's past relations with Africa is necessary. Contact with Africa goes back thousands of years though the exact nature of this relation is clouded due to non-availability of historical data. The first mention of trade in East African slaves between India and Africa can be found in the Graeco-Egyptian maritime manual, *Periples of the Erithraen Seas,* written around the first century A.D., but actual evidence of such slaves can be found from the time of the Sultanate, when Muslim rulers brought Abyssinian slaves to their Indian courts, who later became indigenized as *siddis* and *habshis* and got absorbed in the population to a large degree with only around 76,000 *siddis* still maintaining a separate selfhood under the category of Scheduled Tribes in contemporary India.[2] On the other hand, there was movement of people from the Indian sub-continent to Africa as well, perhaps going back to the sixth or seventh centuries B.C.[3] While it is known that coastal trade existed from very early times, not much is known about Indians who settled in Africa though it is believed that certain Sudanese tribes may be of Indian origin. After the colonization of both India and Africa by Europeans, there are recorded accounts of Indians being imported into African countries as labour to work in plantations or railways. Many opted to stay back and were joined by their families. There was also an influx of traders mainly from Gujarat, who had never been indentured servants.[4] After India became independent, along with business entrepreneurs, there has been a growing presence of Indian professionals like doctors, educationists and engineers in Africa. While the preferred destination appears to have been the English-speaking states in the early years, with time, their numbers have begun to increase in the Francophone states as well. The result is that today there are over 2,000,000 people of Indian origin in Africa, some of whom have been there for over six generations. These people of Indian origin (PIO) can and often do serve as vital links between their adopted states and their home country, India.[5]

The decades following the independence of India, which came earlier, and the states of sub-Saharan Africa were marked by warm relations, highlighted by the fact that both India and Africa had been under colonial rule and had faced the racism and exploitation that went with colonial governance; therefore, there was a great commonality of interests on issues that concerned what came to be known as the Third World, which was itself characterized by underdevelopment and often neo-colonial patrimonialism. Mahatma Gandhi was a cult figure in South Africa, where he had first stood up against British rule, and therefore India had a special place in the minds of African leaders who had themselves struggled against colonialism. According to Tanzania's first President, Julius Nyrere, "Gandhi argued a moral case" and his success "shook the British Empire".[6] Moreover, India's first Prime Minister, Jawaharlal Nehru, was a visionary, who had thought of a common anti-imperialist struggle involving the people of South and Southeast Asia, Latin America and Africa as far back as 1927 when he had actively participated in the Brussels Congress of Oppressed People.[7] Even before India became independent, he had organized the Asian Relations Conference in 1946, and later had been a prime mover behind the Bandung Summit of Asian and African States (1955), which was the precursor of the Non-Aligned Movement (NAM) that was formed in 1961. Nehru along with President Nasser of Egypt and President Tito of Yugoslavia are credited as the founding members, but other leaders like president Nkrumah of Ghana and other African leaders were also crucial to its formation because the continental union of African nations that was formed shortly after, the Organization of African Unity (OAU) became an institutional member of the NAM. The ideological affinity between NAM and Africa was evident in the anti-colonial, anti-racist, anti-apartheid agenda of NAM. Much of the vision of NAM can be attributed to Nehru, who said, "For too long we of Asia have been petitioners in the Western courts and chancelleries. That story must belong to the past. We propose to stand on our own feet and to cooperate with all who are prepared to cooperate with us".[8] The NAM began the AFRICA Fund in 1986 to help frontline states facing difficult problems as a result of continued pressure by white minority regimes. India's initial contribution to this Fund amounted to Rs. 500 million, and this included Rs. 25 million given by private and individual donors.[9] This is significant because India was itself a developing country and could not spare funds of this volume at the time.[10] Cooperation in this area led to many resolutions being passed at the United Nations (UN) General Assembly against apartheid and in favour of the people struggling against racism and colonialism in its different forms. India in fact, accorded diplomatic status to the African National Congress (ANC) of South Africa in 1967 and the South West African People's Organization (SWAPO) of South West Africa/Namibia in 1985.[11]

While the NAM denoted ideological non-alignment from the two power blocs of the Cold War, many countries actually leant towards their particular patrons and were thus only nominally non-aligned. Perhaps a closer affinity between India and African states can be found on developmental issues since both faced similar challenges of being on the periphery of economic decision-making because of the long history of colonialism. Inequality in the terms of international trade, which was seen as largely stemming from the patterns set by the industrialized North during colonial times, was largely blamed for the economic marginalization of the South during the 1960s and 1970s and such thinking led to the formation of the Group of 77 countries (G-77) and the demand for a New International Economic order (NIEO). According to Julius Nyrere, speaking at the fourth ministerial meeting of the G-77, "It was practical experience of the fact that legal independence did not mean economic freedom which made most of us think of cooperating with others similarly placed".[12] Out of such thinking arose the concept of South-South cooperation, a term that has now got much currency in current-day India-Africa relations. However, at the time, India was almost as poverty stricken as many African countries and faced challenges of development of its own. So even though there was much talk of economic cooperation between countries of the South to break dependency on the North, this was easier said than done. India's trade, like that of African countries was directed towards developed countries because of lack of industrialization, which meant a lack of demand for its products among developing countries, which were also exporting similar primary products. Further, India, again like many African countries, decided on a protectionist policy to help its own industrialization, 'nationalizing' many sectors of its economy. This meant higher tariffs and a decline in the feasibility of South-South cooperation.

However, India could and did cooperate in other areas where it had built up its strength and there was potential for partnership. As early as 1964, India established the Indian

Technical and Economic (ITEC) programme, which has so far trained over 10,000 Africans in Indian institutions in fields varying from agriculture and industry to management and diplomacy. India was also involved in several UN peacekeeping missions in Africa beginning with Congo in the 1960s. At another level, it was quick to share the benefits of its democratization experience when requested. For instance, Sudan's first parliamentary elections were conducted with the assistance and advice of Sukumar Sen, the then Chief Election Commissioner of India. What is important is that because of India's long association with Africa at an ideological as well as a practical level both through institutions like the NAM and the G-77, as well as through voting together on economic, political and issues that involved racism, colonialism and apartheid in the UN General Assembly, as also the delivery of practicable assistance through programmes like ITEC, a lot of goodwill had been built up for India which is now paying dividends.

II

Initially, therefore, India's relations with African countries were mainly political with a focus on decolonization, racial equality and assistance in building nation states which involved participating in UN peacekeeping missions, training African students under programmes like ITEC and generally supporting African causes in the UN General Assembly and the NAM. From the 1990s, there has been a marked change in India's foreign policy approaches, which are paralleled by a major improvement in the country's economic status. India seems to have moved away from Gandhian idealism and Nehruvian non-alignment to a 21st century pragmatism with a view to achieving a great power status. India's GDP (purchasing power parity or PPP) is estimated at $ 4.784 trillion and although the GDP growth rate has come down from an estimated 10.1 percent in 2010 to an estimated 5.4 percent in 2012, it is higher than the average GDP growth rates of most developed countries. Its reserves of foreign exchange and gold amounted to $287.2 billion at the end of 2012 while its stock of direct foreign investment at home amounted to $256.6 billion in the same time period.[13] Power in today's world, as it was in earlier times, is seen in terms of financial standing and growth rates. In its quest for great power status, India has been (a) trying to attract investment from abroad, and (b) looking for investment opportunities abroad, both with the objective of fueling its economic growth. Despite doomsayers, India is now considered to be an emerging economic power with enormous potential. This means that it now has the capacity to invest in other countries and it is in its interests to do so. India also has a vibrant private sector that is keen to invest abroad and collaborate with foreign firms, and again it is in their interests to do so. India's major strength lies in the services sector, it being the second largest exporter of computer and information services after the European Union (EU). At the same time, it has also developed considerable skills in manufacturing as well other sectors like power, energy (conventional as well as alternative energy), mining and agriculture.[14] The net result is that India is no longer at a 'recipient' country – it has much to share with the world. In fact, in order to continue on its growth path, India needs new areas to invest in and attract new trade in goods and services.

Africa too has changed in the last decade or so. It is no longer the continent whose products, mainly primary goods, continued to be exploited by former metropolitan powers and dictators while the huge majority of the population reeled under abject poverty; where any amount of developmental aid disappeared (perhaps to private coffers) without showing any signs of development; where investors were afraid to invest considering the fact that they could see their investments vanish at the next coup. According to the International Monetary Fund (IMF), growth south of the Sahara will surge to 6.1 percent by 2014, well ahead of the global rate of 4 percent. Ivory Coast, the world's largest cocoa producer and Mozambique, the host to the world's biggest gas discovery in the past decade, is expected to lead the growth by 8 percent while Nigeria, Africa's top oil producer till now, is expected to have a GDP growth rate of 7 percent.[15] A World Bank report noted that 25 percent of the countries in Africa, particularly Sierra Leone, Niger, Cote d'Ivoire, Liberia, Ethiopia, Burkina Faso and Rwanda grew at the rate of 7 percent in the past few years, and sub-Saharan Africa minus South Africa (where the growth slowed because of miners' strikes) grew at 5.8 percent, higher than the developing country average of 4.9 percent. Including South Africa, the continent's economic powerhouse, the rate is still at a respectable 4.7 percent.[16] Even the share of people living under $1.25 per day has come down from 58 percent in 1996 to 48.5 percent in 2010,[17] which is certainly better than India's performance in this field.

The point in giving these figures is that African countries too are emerging and the South-South cooperation ideal that had been an almost unachievable *mantra* in the 1970s is now becoming a reality with countries of the global South eager to do business with Africa. Foreign direct investment inflows to sub-Saharan Africa are projected to increase to record levels each year over the next three years, reaching $54 billion by 2015. This compares well with $37.7 billion last year.[18] In fact, the changing fortunes of what had long been considered to be the world's poorest continent, is the point of discussion at many summits including the one held recently by the group that was given the acronym of BRICS by Goldman Sachs economists as the emerging economic powers of the future, and of which India is a member. While all the BRIC emerging powers have shown great interest in trade with African countries, India and China were among the first to engage Africa, in fact, at a time when other countries were lagging far behind. Today India is Africa's fourth largest trade partner after the European Union (EU), China and the US. Bilateral trade amounted to $ 57 billion by 2011 and is projected to hit $90 to $100 billion by 2015, and although this trade is small compared to that of EU-Africa trade, which was $300 billion in 2011, it is growing at a pace second only to the China-Africa trade, that is, it grew at an average of 24.8 percent between 2000 and 2011 (from $4.6 billion in 2000 to $57 billion in 2011).[19] In 2011 India accounted for 5.2% of Africa's global trade, up from 2.9 percent in 2000. It is Nigeria's largest export market, accounting for 10.2 percent of Nigeria's trade. It is also Mauritius' top trading partner and South Africa's fifth largest partner. Africa's share of India's trade has grown as well from 5.2 percent in 2000 to 7.6 percent in 2011.[20]

Both India and African states are emerging from decades of dependence on developed countries and engaging with each other on terms that are more cooperative and not exploitative. While the EU, the US, Japan and individual European countries continue to remain among the largest trade partners of almost all countries of the global South, the equations are changing with China overtaking many of these states in Africa, and India not coming far behind (although it still has a long way to go *vis-à-vis* China, but that discussion is not within the scope of this paper). Moreover, the terms of the new equations are quite novel in that the much talked about South-South cooperation of the 1970s seems to be becoming a reality. The new terms are based on mutual interests. India is interested in Africa's resources just as the rest of the world is;[21]on the other hand, India has expertise in industry, mining, infrastructure building, information technology, pharmaceuticals etc that many countries in Africa seek; it can also provide low-cost solutions to poverty alleviation, and is ready to invest in industrial ventures, jointly or otherwise, that will help in the development of African countries and draw them into the international economy without being exploitative, on terms acceptable to both. South-South cooperation is increasingly being viewed by less developed countries as an alternative to North-South aid, which has mainly come to African countries, particularly in recent decades, with conditions like structural adjustments and political reforms attached, and at times, had been used for political purposes.[22] At the same time, investment from Western industrialized countries had been largely in the extraction industries in Africa and as can be seen by the current development status of African states, had not led to any significant growth, development or building of basic infrastructure. Today's South-South cooperation is of a different nature especially where India is concerned. It is more of a partnership whereby India, of course, benefits, but at the same time, it assists in building capacity and infrastructure and in training Africans in skills that in the long run, will lead to the sustainable development of African states. Political relations remain important, but the economic content of India's engagement with Africa has changed and is welcomed by most African countries. In fact, it is countries like India and China that have helped to draw Africa out of its economic stagnation and helped it to join the merging markets of an increasingly globalized world by providing the initial stimulus through investment, training and increased trade.

III

India is today engaging with Africa at three different levels: bilateral, regional and continental. While bilateral relations have existed between India and many sub-Saharan countries for a long time, these have taken on a bigger economic content with India trying to vie with China, Brazil, the US, the EU and even West Asian and Southeast Asian countries for resources in Sudan, Angola, South Africa as well as in Nigeria, an older partner. What is more significant is its engagement with the various regional organizations that have taken on a new life in Africa: it has acquired observer status in a number of regional organizations in Africa such as the Common Market for Eastern and Southern Africa (COMESA), the Southern African Development Community (SADC) and the Economic Community of West African States (ECOWAS). Entrance to these regional economic forums will open up several states to India that it has had little access to in the past. However, it is its engagement at the continental level that reveals the nature of India's relations with Africa. It institutionalized this relationship in 2008 with the first ever India-Africa Forum Summit that now meets on a regular basis to promote India-Africa relations. At the first summit in 2008, Prime Minister Manmohan Singh announced a number of initiatives that included a duty-free trade preference scheme for 34 African countries as well as grants for projects in information technology (IT), telecommunications, power and railways amounting to $500 million over the next six years as part of the Aid to Africa budget of the Ministry of External Affairs (MEA). India's strategy as it appears from this summit as well as the subsequent one is partnership for mutual benefit, for not only does it wish to enhance trade with Africa but also to empower countries in that continent. Even prior to the India-Africa summits, India had begun the Focus Africa programme in 2002 that focused on sub-Saharan Africa, and particularly seven countries: Ethiopia, Tanzania, Nigeria, South Africa, Mauritius, Kenya and Ghana. These countries account for 69 percent of India's trade in the sub-Saharan region. The programme was expanded in 2003 to include 17 countries with some placed in North Africa. Another programme worth mentioning is the TEAM-9 initiative with eight Francophone African states to set up a mechanism for cooperation in bilateral and sub-regional projects with Lines of Credit (LOC) of $ 500 million for those countries, the objective being to build sustainable partnerships through development of institutional capacity in industry, agriculture and infrastructure. India also became the first Asian country to become a full member of the Africa Capacity Building Foundation (ACBF) and committed $ 1 million to it to build capacity for sustainable development and poverty alleviation. It wrote off debt owed by African countries under the Heavily Indebted Poor Countries (HIPC) Paris initiative and also restructured commercial debts.

To promote trade, which after all is a basic driver of growth, the Indian government in partnership with the Confederation of Indian Industry (CII), the Export-Import Bank (EXIM Bank) and the African Development Bank launched the India-Africa Project Partnership Conclave in 2005 to serve as a forum for decision makers and heads of industry in India and Africa. The ninth meeting of the conclave was held in March 2013 and it attracted a record 630 registered delegates from 41 African countries and discussed a host of issues including 475 projects worth $64 billion.[23] Bilateral trade between the two sides has grown from $4.6 billion in 2000 when these conclaves began, to $60 billion in 2011-12, the target being $90-100 billion by 2015, as mentioned earlier. According to a CII-WTO report, overall trade between India and Africa grew at 32.4 percent between 2005 and 2011.[24] It is interesting that the main force behind the expanding India-Africa trade is the Indian private sector. Vedanta Resources has invested more than $750 million in Zambian copper mines, and the Parliament of Liberia has ratified a 25-year deal allowing Arcelor Mittal to launch a $1 billion iron ore mining project. In fact, Vedanta has invested $4 billion in Africa's mining sector in the last nine years. Tata Steel has invested $850 million in a ferro-chrome project in

Richards Bay, South Africa. In 2007 the Indian Farmers Fertilizer Cooperative signed a Memorandum of Understanding with the Senegalese government to revive a phosphoric acid plant belonging to Industries Chimiques de Senegal.[25] In the agricultural sector, Mahindra and Mahindra, the Tata Group, Dabur and other companies have made their mark. African countries are interested in emulating India's 'green revolution' to help them achieve food security and therefore are interested in Indian agricultural methods and farming techniques and this has opened a new arena of trade for small and middle-sized enterprises (SMEs) in both Africa and India. Indian companies are also engaged in ICT, chemicals and the engineering sector. In the power sector Indian companies, such as Bharat Heavy Electricals Limited, Mohan Energy, Kalpataru Transmission and Jyoti Structures, have entered the market. Suzlon Energy, the world's fourth-largest wind turbine maker, plans to invest in the African alternative energy sector in the near future. In the Information Technology (IT) sector, Tata Consultancy Services (TCS), Infosys, Satyam, Bharati Airtel and the government owned Videsh Sanchar Nigam Limited (VSNL) are important players. Indian companies have also entered the real estate sector with Indian tycoon Mukesh Ambani acquiring 10 prime plots for about $35 million in Nairobi recently for commercial and residential development. Indian companies are also present in the automobile (Tata and Mahindra), pharmaceutical (Ranbaxy, Dr. Reddy's, Cipla) and construction (Punj Lloyd, Shahpoorji Pallonji) sectors. It has even entered the financial sector with several state owned banks opening branches in Africa and the State Bank of India acquiring a 51 percent stake in the Indian Overseas International Bank.

Apart from playing a facilitating role, the Indian government is also directly involved in important sectors like hydrocarbons. India, an emerging country has an incremental demand for petroleum and like other countries, wants to diversify its sources. Africa's oil and natural gas resources have been largely untapped, and are now drawing global attention. Around 18 percent of India's oil imports come from Africa (including North Africa). Private companies like Reliance and Essar have invested in Sudan, Nigeria and Madagascar. However, the biggest company is government-owned Oil and Natural Gas Commission Videsh Limited (OVL) which has invested in equity assets in Sudan, Ivory Coast Libya, Egypt, Nigeria, Nigeria–São Tomé and Príncipe Joint Development Area and Gabon.[26] The Indian government and various chambers of commerce began to organize India-Africa Hydrocarbons Conferences to boost trade and cooperation in this area. The 2009 conference identified five main areas of co-operation with African countries: buying more crude oil from Africa, investing more in upstream opportunities on bilateral basis, exploring opportunities to source more liquefied natural gas from Africa, making available India's skills, talent and technology in cost-effective ways for the benefit of Africa and supporting community development programmes in Africa so as to ensure inclusive growth.[27] This suggests that India is not interested only in extracting resources but in infrastructure development and capacity building.

One of the best examples of India's intent is its long-running Indian Technical and Cooperation (ITEC) programme (mentioned earlier) which is actually a Commonwealth programme that began in 1964, but among the chief beneficiaries of which have been Africans. Thousands of African students have been trained under this programme and some of them hold positions of importance in government and industry in Africa. For instance, in Tanzania, 24 percent of government officials have been through this programme and in Botswana, many defence officials have availed of ITEC.[28] In 2008, the slots earmarked for Africa were increased from 1000 to 1600. While ITEC is essentially bilateral in its outreach, its resources have been occasionally used for financing trilateral and regional programmes managed by the Economic Commission for Africa, UNIDO and the Group of 77. Today, the ITEC's activities have expanded to include training and project support to the African Union, Afro-Asian Rural Reconstruction Organization, the Pan-African Parliament and the G-15. ITEC's fastest-growing segment is consultancy and project assistance, which includes preparing feasibility studies and project reports, setting up pilot projects and research centres in the agricultural sector. Another important area of cooperation is vocational training in SMEs and entrepreneurship development in recognition of Africa's need for capacity development. In this context, the ITEC has taken over a United Nations Development Programme (UNDP) project to train elderly women in solar electricity.[29]

Capacity building is in the forefront of India's relations with Africa. In this context, it is necessary to mention the Pan African e-Network Project which was inaugurated by President A.P.J. Kalam in 2007 and the second phase of which was launched in 2010. The basic objective of the Pan-African e-Network project is to assist Africa in capacity building by way of imparting quality education to 10,000 students in Africa over a 5-year period in various disciplines from some of the best Indian universities/educational institutions. Besides, this programme is designed to provide Tele-Medicine services by way of online medical consultation to the medical practioners at the Patient End Location in Africa by Indian medical specialists in various disciplines/ specialties selected by African Union for its member states.[30] Regular tele-medicine and tele-education services have already begun and 2000 African students have been enrolled in various disciplines in five top Indian universities through its services. Tele-medicine has also facilitated consultations with doctors in super-specialty hospitals in India on a need basis. Moreover, regular Continued Medical Education (CME) sessions have been started with effect from April 2009 from 11 Indian Super-Specialty Hospitals. The e-network project is also equipped to support e-governance, e-commerce, infotainment, resource mapping and meteorological and other services in the African countries, besides providing VVIP connectivity among the Heads of State of the African countries through a highly secure closed satellite network.

India is also a leading manufacturer of cheap generic drugs, especially those that are used to fight tropical diseases like malaria, cholera and tuberculosis. It is the biggest supplier of low-cost anti-retroviral drugs to fight HIV/AIDS in sub-Saharan Africa, where this dreaded disease has wrought havoc. It has also invested in a farming initiative in post-conflict Mozambique, biofuels in Western Africa and the textile industry in East Africa – these are attempts to put local resources to the best use for local benefit.[31] At a more practical level, India's partnership plans include training local workers at the local level thus contributing to the building up of human capital. For example, while India is getting an entry into Angola's diamond trade, it has promised to open an institute for jewelry manufacture as well as a diamond cutting and polishing centre in Angola. Again, while Angola has offered a 30 percent stake to India in its upcoming Liberto oil refinery, India has offered to set up a centre of excellence in petroleum technology in Angola as well as to construct a gas based 300 MW plant and rebuild its railway infrastructure and financial sector. Angola's leading diamond company, Endiama, will also tie up with Tata Motors to manufacture its own commercial vehicles.

The new vibrant relationship is not one-sided. For instance, Mauritius has emerged as the largest African offshore investor in India. African companies are gradually entering into joint venture enterprises in India. For instance, Mumbai's international airport is being modernized in a million dollar joint venture between India's GVK Group and the Airports Company of South Africa. In fact, the balance of trade is currently in favour of Africa. According to a recent report of the CII and WTO bilateral trade between India and Africa grew at a much faster rate of 32.4 percent compared to overall China-Africa trade that rose by 27 percent during 2008-2011.[32] While India's exports to Africa grew at a rate of 23.1 percent between 2005 and 2011, India emerged as the fastest growing export market for Africa, growing by 41.8 percent in the same period. The rapid increase in trade is due to the traction gained with commodity exports from Africa to India (mainly petroleum and natural gas) and the technology export from India to Africa. India has signed trade agreements with 19 African countries which give each other most favoured nation status with regard to customs formalities and issue of licenses.[33]

India is of course, interested in trade with Africa and in increasing its import of Africa's resources, just like other countries. However, it should be noted that its interest is not merely in extracting these resources for itself at the expense of the country where the resource exists. It should be emphasized that India believes in partnership, and that has led it to invest quite heavily (one must remember that India is still a developing country with enough developmental problems of its own) in building infrastructure in Africa like roads, airports, the pan-African e-network etc, and in training African personnel and not bringing in its own. In the long run, the specific African country where this investment is going, will benefit and will become economically sustainable. The relationship is based more on cooperation for sustained mutual benefit, and is therefore different from that of other investors in Africa.

Although economic relations are at the centre of the emerging India-Africa partnership, India's relationship with Africa is not limited only to the realm of commerce. Cooperation at other levels is being pursued through new and emerging multilateral forums that have yet to reach criticality but have shown a good beginning. These include the India-Brazil-South Africa (IBSA) Dialogue Forum, the Indian Ocean Rim Association for Regional Cooperation (IORARC), the Asia-Africa Summit, the Group of 33 (G-33) bloc of developing countries in the World Trade Organization (WTO) and now, the Brazil-Russia- India-China-South Africa forum or BRICS, of which South Africa has become a new member. In the WTO, developing countries have put united pressure on the North on issues like unfair agricultural subsidies that provide unfair advantage to developed countries' agricultural commodities. In the UN, both AU countries and the Group of 4 (G-4) want reforms of the Security Council. While they have so far hindered each others' efforts, the closer contact that is developing may help to bring them together under a common platform. India is a member of the African Union Partners Group (AUPG) which meets regularly at Addis Ababa and is therefore in a position to come closer to the African leadership at the continental level.

Both India and Africa have realized the necessity to carry the relationship forward beyond trade, economic cooperation and political platitudes, because both the African continent and India face similar geopolitical and security challenges. For instance, 90 percent of India's trade volume and 70 percent of its trade value comes by sea. Maritime security is therefore of utmost importance. This affects Africa as well since its commodity trade is carried solely via the oceans surrounding it. The growing menace of piracy is a challenge that has led India to enhance maritime cooperation with Africa, resulting in the deployment of the Indian Navy on the East African coast, from the Gulf of Aden to the Mozambique Channel. India established its first overseas surveillance facility in Madagascar in July 2007. It also reached defence agreements with several countries on the Indian Ocean rim – Mauritius, Madagascar, Seychelles, Kenya, Mozambique and Tanzania – and stepped up joint military exercises with states in the region. It also held a joint naval exercise with South Africa and Brazil under an IBSA initiative in May 2008 off Cape Town. It, moreover, held joint patrols off the coast of Mozambique during the AU summit of 2003 and the World Economic Forum in 2004. India is uniquely placed geostrategically and is a regional military power with outreach potential. The Indian Army has trained officers from many African countries under the ITEC programme. It has also sent training teams to countries like Botswana, Zambia and Lesotho. As part of its defence cooperation efforts, it has supplied a small amount of conventional arms for African patrol crafts to countries like Mauritius and Guinea Bissau and light helicopters to Namibia. It also imports some weaponry from South Africa. In fact, its defence engagement with Africa is not merely at a bilateral level, but with the AU. The AU's requirement for training and capacity building of their nascent standby brigade, which will be the base of the AU's future peacekeeping activities are being discussed with India. The aim is to examine how far the Indian experience can be shared with Africa.[34] Cooperation in maritime and other security initiatives with willing African countries and the African Union is expected to be beneficial to both.

IV

It may be noted, however, that both India and the countries of Africa are developing countries. As such, there are many constraints even now to a smooth relationship. Among the two most important constraints in the growth of bilateral and multilateral trade pinpointed by a recent CII-WTO report are the lack of a proper financing mechanism and poor infrastructure facilities.[35] African traders are concerned about poor access to Indian buyers and trade finance, while transport and logistics costs and poor business environments are cited as major difficulties by Indian traders. Private enterprises like Bharti Airtel have also complained about the lack of skills in Africa, something that they have to build locally, until which time Indian expertise has to be imported, adding to the costs of operation.[36] One reason why the trade relationship has not become even more vibrant and has not spread to other areas apart from mainly resource sourcing is that India's trade is still directed mainly towards the North, being a developing country itself. This is true of African countries as well since the EU is Africa's largest trading partner. It will take time for South-South cooperation to really take off, as the South finds more complementariness with other countries of the South; but this is slowly happening.

However, India and African countries need to take a reality check on their respective internal problems. India, as mentioned, is a developing country itself and faces many issues of growth and development, not the least of which is poverty, a huge population, unemployment, inadequate infrastructure and corruption that siphons off funds for personal gain. These are matched by other threats like terrorism, unstable neighbours, some of whom are nuclear-armed, insurgencies that emerge from growing inequalities but are fueled by ideologies that have external sources and succor. As such, India's budget is heavily tilted towards solving its own internal issues, and can spare little for capacity building outside its borders. It is commendable that it still does so. African countries, on the other hand, are democratizing and face the problems of democratization in regions that had known little or no democracy earlier. These include inclusiveness in a population that is not used to it and can be easily manipulated, slide backs towards authoritarian rule, corruption, nepotism, graft etc. These issues will, by themselves make investors wary about investing lest their initial investments, let alone profits, get lost. However, the AU is trying to institutionalize good governance and the prospects of growth and development as well as international censure may go some way in improving the environment for trade and commerce.

India also faces a major challenge from other actors in Africa and this includes not only China but the EU, France, the US, emerging Southeast and West Asian countries apart from countries of Latin America, particularly Brazil and Mexico.[37] While Southeast Asian, Latin American and West Asian countries are not the major players in Africa (except for Brazil, which is Africa's sixth largest trading partner), the EU and the US have far more money power than India has and have been present on the continent for a long time. Moreover, they are also changing their strategies of engagement focusing on Africa's development as part of their agenda, much as India and China have been doing over the past decade. However, it is China that is India's biggest rival *vis-à-vis* projects, agendas and resource needs. China is Africa's second largest trade partner after the EU with bilateral trade amounting to $90 billion in 2009. The towering new African Union headquarters in Addis Ababa was a $200m gift from Beijing and a clear testimony of China's intention, and ability, to engage with individual states as well as an entire continent. China is more or less interested in the same sectors that India is interested in, and has successfully signed agreements with several countries. It has been willing to buy stakes in Africa which are considered to be less profitable or 'too difficult' by the West, and as a result, established a presence in countries like Sudan from the mid-1990s when the country was mired in the North-South civil war, and was buying 50-60 percent of Sudan's oil exports by 2005 when that war was brought to a close by the Comprehensive Peace Agreement. The state-owned China National Offshore Oil Corporation (CNOOC) is also active in Equatorial New Guinea, Chad, Gabon, Angola and Nigeria. It is also deeply interested in the other mineral resources of Africa like copper, uranium, cobalt, gold etc. Apart from buying the Chambezi copper mines in Zambia, it has invested in copper and cobalt mines in the Democratic Republic of Congo and has built roads to facilitate exports.[38] It is also competing with India in the telecom sector – an area of strength for India. Its ZTE Corporation, which manufactures telecom equipment, has set up shop in Mali, Congo, Kenya and Nigeria, to mention a few. It also competes with India in the automobile sector, and further, has a head-start in the manufacturing sector. China has a huge presence in Africa – it has 900 projects, and 800 companies are operating in various countries. It has sent 16,000 medical personnel to Africa, offered scholarships to 20,000 African students, and trained a large number of African professionals. Although India became a regional member of the African Development Bank two years before China (in 1982), China now holds more shares in the bank and has greater voting power, and recently, when the bank chose to hold its first board meeting in an Asian country, they decided on Shanghai and not Mumbai.[39] Moreover, China has learnt the art of symbolic diplomacy, something that is appreciated by Africans. Its Forum on China-Africa Cooperation (FOCAC) attracts many more African heads of state than India's conclaves or other summits, and this is partly because of the care that China takes to demonstrate Africa's importance to China. This is borne out by the fact that President Hu Jintao visited 14 African countries in three years and there were numerous visits by other important officials. Compared to China, India's high-level contact with

Africa has been minimal. Supplementing its symbolic diplomacy, China has been building or refurbishing public infrastructure like stadiums, government buildings etc, and giving this effort a high level of publicity.

India also faces some other challenges in Africa. India has a large Diaspora in Africa, many of whom went as indentured labour but did well later and established themselves at a higher level than the host community, thus creating friction between people of Indian origin and Africans in some countries and in certain times. Although Indians are generally viewed as enterprising and the Diaspora has created good feelings towards their home country, there is a long history of labour problems between Indians and Africans in countries like Kenya and Uganda. New areas of disharmony have also been emerging with India's growing presence. For instance, Indian steelworkers were abducted in Nigeria over a pay dispute with union members in October 2007.

Moreover, if India wishes to strengthen its relationship with Africa, it should pay more attention to its public diplomacy in Africa. At present there are only five Indian embassies in sub-Saharan Africa, with 15 High Commissions in 12 countries and six Consulates in five countries. In total, only 19 of the 48 sub-Saharan states are covered by Indian diplomatic missions with West Africa being largely neglected. A more vibrant relationship requires at least more consulates in every region if not every country for quick access to information regarding India.

V

India's relationship with African countries in general and Africa as a whole has undergone a sea change since the 1990s when India was yet to be seen as an emerging nation and African states were struggling with authoritarian regimes, coups, post-war issues of resettlement and structural adjustment problems that further muddied the waters. Today, India is looking forward to a $100 million bilateral trade relationship in two years time, with the balance of trade in favour of Africa. A study from Ernst & Young found that in the period from 2007 to 2012, India invested in 237 new projects on the African continent, beating China's 152. In fact, three Western countries — the United States, the United Kingdom and France — were the only ones to surpass India in this regard. The dollar values tell a different story; India's $27.3 billion of FDI into Africa last year was no match for China's $119.7 billion.[40] But India's apparent eagerness to pursue new projects speaks of its quickly expanding role on the continent.

The fact is that India is an emerging power and needs resources. Africa is close to India, about 2000 miles across the Indian Ocean. Countries of East and Southern Africa have historically attracted trade and migration from India, and even today, these countries are in the forefront when it comes to trade. Both India and Africa had much in common as India and Africa were trying to throw of the yoke of European imperialism and racism, and later during the Cold War years, survive in an unequal environment where African countries and India were at an economic and political disadvantage *vis-à-vis* the North in terms of power relations. There is much in common even now between India and Africa since both are emerging from the periphery and the waves of globalization are drawing them closer. Further, while India needs resources to feed and care for its burgeoning population, African countries need infrastructure building and capacity development for sustainable growth. Indian companies are increasingly active in such oil-rich regions as Cote d'Ivoire, Libya, Egypt, Angola and Gabon. Indian private companies and public sector units already have oil investments in Mozambique and investments in the gas sector in Kenya and Tanzania. India is also involved in building critical rail and road infrastructure in Ethiopia, Djibouti and Uganda. Africa is also becoming a key destination for Indian investments in the software, telecom, and financial sectors. Besides trade, India also provides development assistance to Africa, largely on an equal partnership basis. This is distinct from the assistance given by the OECD/Development Assistance Countries or the Chinese model, which attaches investments to loans. In 2012, India consolidated its efforts to set up the Development Partnership Agreement (DPA), its own international aid agency. The new agency, under the Ministry of External Affairs, will focus an initial corpus of US$15 billion to streamline projects in more than 60 countries around the world. African leaders at a recent AU summit agreed to explore new funding alternatives and move away from dependence on donor partners. This too can signal a greater role for India in Africa.[41]

Thus, the two sides are well matched to help each other economically and even on the political front on issues like climate change, reform of the United Nations and matters related to trade at the WTO. India's foreign policy strategy in Africa is therefore one of promoting mutual benefits. According to Vice President Hamid Ansari, "Our approach is different. ... The Indian approach is not just to give the fish, it is to teach how to fish".[42] India, in its capacity as a partner in development, is therefore playing the role of a key driver of growth in Africa and will continue to do so in years to come.

REFERENCE

1 Dr. Manmohan Singh, PM's Opening Statement at the India-Africa Summit, April 8, 2008, Government of India, available at mindia.nic.in/speech-details.php?nodeid=643, accessed 1 June 2013.

2 Abulaziz Y. Lodhi, "Bantu Origins of the Sidis of India", 2008-10-29, Issue 404, http://pambazuka.org/en/category/comment/51594,

accessed on May 5, 2009.

3 W.H. Ingrams, *Zanzibar: Its History and Its People,* New York, Cass & Co., 1931, p. 43, and Reginald Coupland, *East Africa and Its Invaders,* Oxford University Press, 1938, p. 16. Coupland believes that the coconut palm was introduced by 'Hindus', since there is mention of 'nauplios' or 'narglios' in *Periplus,* which is apparently derived from the Indian word, 'naryal'.

4 For a study of the people of Indian origin in Africa, see, Government of India, Report of the High Level Committee on the Indian Diaspora, available at http://indiandiaspora.nic.in/diaspora.pdf./chapter7.pdf., accessed on December 13, 2008.

5 See Prime Minister's Address at the Pravasi Bharatiya Divas, January 7, 2007, at the Prime Minister's official website, http://pmindia.nic.in/speech/content.asp?id=485. Accessed on February 15, 2009.

6 Ikaweba Bunting, "The Heart of Africa Interview with Julius Nyrere on Anti-Colonialism", *New International Magazine,* Issue 309, January-February 1999, reproduced in www.hartford-hwp.com/archives/30/049.htm, accessed on May 13, 2009.

7 For the views and ideas of Jawaharlal Nehru, see S. Gopal and Uma Iyengar, eds., *The Essential Writings of Jawaharlal Nehru,* Oxford University Press, 2003. A good account of his early years as Prime Minister is given in Michael Brecher, *Nehru: A Political Biography,* Oxford University Press, 1959.

8 Cited in "Non-alignment was Coined by Nehru in 1954", *The Times of India,* New Delhi, September 18, 2006.

9 Government of India, Ministry of External Affairs, *Annual Report, 1993,* New Delhi, 1993, p. 59.

10 For Nehru's views on Africa, see *Nehru and Africa,* Nehru Centenary Volume, Oxford University Press, November 14, 1989. See also the ANC website, http://www.anc.org.za/ancdocs/history/solidarity/nehru-africa.html. Accessed on April 15, 2009.

11 Indian National Congress, *India and the African Liberation Struggle,* New Delhi, 1976, pp. 92-96.

12 The speech can be found in Phillippe Braillard and Mohammad-Reza Djalili, *The Third World and International Relations,* Lynne Reiner, Colorado, 1986.

13 India Economy 2013: Source: 2013 CIA World Factbook and Other Sources, Theodora.cm available at http://www.theodora.com/wfbcurrent/india/india_economy.html, accessed 24 June 2013.

14 See Tushar Poddar and Eva Yi, "India's Rising Growth Potential", Global Economics Paper No. 152, Goldman Sachs, New York, January 22, 2007, available at http://www.usindiafriendship.net/viewpoint/India_Rising_Growth_Potential.pdf, accessed on January 30, 2009. See also the U.S. National Intelligence Commission unclassified report, *Global Trends 2025: A Transformed World*, available at www.dni.gov/nic/PDF_2025/2025_Global_Trends_Final_Report.pdf, accessed on December 20, 2008.

15 David Smith, "IMF: Africa's Economic Growth Surging South of Sahara", *The Guardian*, 17 April 2013, available at http://www.guardian.co.uk/global-development/2013/apr/17/imf-africa-economic-growth-surging, accessed 24 June 2013.

16 The World Bank, "As Africa's New Wealth Grows, Poverty Must Come Down", April 15, 2013, available at http://www.worldbank.org/en/news/feature/2013/04/15/as-africa-s-new-wealth-grows-poverty-must-come-down, accessed 24 June 2013.

17 Ibid.

18 Smith, n. 14.

19 Standard Chartered Bank, "Africa-India Trade and Investment – Playing to Strengths", 8 August 2012, p.3, available at http://www.standardchartered.com/en/resources/global-en/pdf/Research/Africa-India_trade_and_investment_Playing_to_strengths.pdf, accessed 1 June 2013.

20 Ibid.

21 Jehangir Engineer and Aruna Parimi, "Africa: Great Potential", in V.S. Sheth, ed., *India-Africa Relations: Emerging Policy and Development Perspective*, Academic Excellence, Delhi, 2008.

22 Sanjukta Bhattacharya, "Engaging Africa: India's Interests in the African Continent, Past and Present", in Fantu Cheru and Cyril Obi, eds., *The Rise of China and India in Africa* London, Zed Books, 2010, pp., 63-76.

23 India Africa Connect, India-Africa Project Partnership 9th CII- EXIM BANK Conclave, available at http://indiaafricaconnect.in/index.php?param=news/5787/india-africa-project/141, accessed 4 July 2013.

24 Cited in Murli Krishnan, "Indian Investment in Africa Soars", *DW*, 15th July 2013, available at http://www.dw.de/indian-investment-in-africa-soars/a-16951164, accessed 16 July 2013.

25 Ruchita Beri, "Evolving India-Africa Relations: Continuity and Change", Occasional Paper No. 76, South African Institute of

International Affairs, February 2011, available at http://dspace.cigilibrary.org/jspui/bitstream/123456789/30796/1/saia_sop_76_beri_20110222.pdf?1, accessed 4 July 2013.

26 Government of India, Ministry of Petroleum, India Hydrocarbons Vision 2025, available at http://petroleum.nic.in/vision.doc. Accessed 16 July 2013.

27 Beri, n. 24, p. 8.

28 Manish Chand, "Skills development: The ITEC Way", Public Diplomacy Division, Ministry of External Affairs, Two Billion Dreams: Celebrating India-Africa Friendship, available at http://2billiondreams.in/index.php?param=chapterdetails/10, accessed 16 July 2013.

29 Ibid.

30 Pan African e-Network Project, Inauguration of Pan African e-Network Project (Phase II), available at http://www.panafricanenetwork.com/, accessed 12 June 2013.

31 Also see, Ruchita Beri, "India's Africa policy in the Post-Cold War Era: An Assessment", *Strategic Analysis,* Vol. 27, No. 2, April-June 2003, pp. 216-32.

32 Nayanima Basu, "India-Africa Trade Grew Faster than China-Africa", *Business Standard,* New Delhi, July 9, 2013.

33 Government of India, Ministry of Commerce and Industry, department of Commerce, texts of agreements available at http://commerce.nic.in/trade/international_ta_indaf.asp, accessed 4 July 2013.

34 Ministry of External Affairs, Government of India, Report: "India-African Union Relations", available at http://meaindia.nic.in/staticfile/India-AU-March-12.pdf, accessed 4 July 2013.

35 "Major Constraints to Trade between India and Africa", *The Hindu,* Chennai, July 9, 2013.

36 Indian Defence Forum, "Bharti to replicate India business model in Africa", available at http://defenceforumindia.com/forum/foreign-relations/32662-india-africa-relations-4.html, accessed 1 June 2013.

37 Sanjukta Banerji Bhattacharya, "The Other Powers in the Continent", *Africa Quarterly,* New Delhi, Vol. 51, No. 3-4, Aug 2011-Jan 2012, pp 28-41.

38 For an interesting Chinese account of China's interests in Africa, see Jian Junbo, "China in Africa: From Capitalism to Colonialism", *Asia Times (online),* January 5, 2007, available at http://

www.atimes.com/atimes/China/IA05Ad01.html, accessed on February 13, 2009. The author notes that "Though China is not a colonialist, it is a successful capitalist in Africa... Of course, we cannot be blind to the possibility of China becoming a colonizing power some day. The day might come when African national economic systems have become so dependent on Chinese investments and export commodities that their domestic and foreign policies would in effect be decided by Beijing." The author, it should be pointed out, is a lecturer at Fudan University, Shanghai, China.

39 Sudha Ramchandran, "India Pushes People Power in Africa", *Asia Times (online)*, July 7, 2007, available at http://www.atimes.com/atimes/South_Asia/IG13Dfo3.html, accessed on February 13, 2009.

40 Jacey Fortin, "Creeping Tiger: India's Presence In Africa Grows, Even As China Steals The Spotlight", *International Business Times*, June 27, 2013, available at http://www.ibtimes.com/creeping-tiger-indias-presence-africa-grows-even-china-steals-spotlight-1324989, accessed 13 July 2013.

41 Anirudh Menon, "Time to scale up relations between India and Africa", 2 July 2013, available at http://blogs.lse.ac.uk/africaatlse/2013/07/02/time-to-scale-up-relations-between-india-and-africa/, accessed 4 July 2013.

42 Fortin, n. 40.

9

Indo-China Relations in the Era of Soft Power

Amit Kumar Gupta

Burden of history should not distract nations from present opportunities. It's heartening to see leadership on both sides look more closely at cooperation in the economic arena despite their competing geo-political interests. (Sunil Mittal 2010)

The aforesaid statement made by Sunil Mittal (Chairman and Managing Director of Bharti Group) is a truism that summarizes the actuality of the nature of Indo – China relations. The first statement speaks of the fact that all has not been well between India and China in their near history. The following statement draws attention to the fact that both India and China have cast aside their differences of the past and are cooperating in the field of economics. However, competition concerning geo-political interest still exists between the two.

As a matter of fact, both India and China are major civilizations having a global impact, for the reason that together they have a combined population of 2.5 billion, which represents more than a third of the world's humanity. This enriches both India and China in terms of human resources and potential. Not begetting much surprise thus, both countries are emerging economic super power houses, with amazing growth rates. The Chinese economy today is the second largest in the world while India is ranked third in terms of Purchasing Power Parity (PPP) calculations (Table 1)

Table 1. Top 10 Countries: Economy

Rank	Country	GDP (Purchasing Power Parity) (Billion $)
1	United States	15,290
2	China	11,440
3	India	4,515
4	Japan	4,497
5	Germany	3,139
6	Russia	2,414
7	Brazil	2,324
8	United Kingdom	2,290
9	France	2,246
10	Italy	1,871

Note: Figures are January 01, 2012 estimated.

Source: index mundi, at, http://www.indexmundi.com/g/r.aspx?v=65&t=10

Original Source: CIA World Factbook, at, https://www.cia.gov/library/publications/the-world-factbook/

If both the countries are able to maintain their economic growth rate, they are prophesied not just to overtake the United States in terms of ranking, but also would conceivably wipe out poverty within a few decades. Moreover, the duos are political, technological and military heavy weights in their regions. (Lam Peng, 2009) India and China thus herald a new Asian Century that would dramatically alter the structure of world politics. Thus and so, it becomes all the more important to comprehend the nature of bilateral relations between the two Asian giants.

In a little over six decades of their formal existence and the establishment of diplomatic relations between the two, an intriguing fact that has been evident has been that their relationship has witnessed both, the phase of intimacy; that was expressed by a phrase 'Hindi-Chini Bhai-Bhai' (India and China are brothers), and the phase of acrimony, when their armies confronted each other in the years 1962, 1967 and 1987. This period was farcically articulated by the phrase 'Hindi-Chini Bye-Bye'. However, though circumstances began to change post-1988, when Rajiv Gandhi the then Prime Minister of India visited China and there on the duo have put aside their differences to give way for stronger diplomatic and economic cooperation. Nonetheless issues of dissention still persist, which occasionally creep up only to be hushed-up politically.

BACKGROUND: THE HISTORICAL RELATIONSHIP

India and China, the two ancient civilizations had relatively little political contact before the 1950's, inasmuch as the scope of interaction between the two was limited by the barrier of the Himalayas. However, the barrier was not opaque enough to stop the duo from maintaining cultural and trade relations. Written records of commercial contacts between India and China dates back to 2nd century B.C. Such contacts at the level of people to people through commerce got a boost with the advent of Buddhism into China from India in the first century A.D. Later, a Chinese monk, Fa Xian (Fa-Hsien), visited India in 402 A.D. for 10 years, and after his return translated many Sanskrit, Buddhist texts into Chinese. His record of journeys Fo Guo Ji (Record of Buddhist Kingdoms) is an important historical source of the Indo-Chinese relationship that existed during the period. Similarly, Kumarajiva, a renowned scholar in Vedas as well as Buddhist Sutras, was said to be born of a Chinese mother and an Indian father. His translations of Sanskrit Sutras into Chinese are valued even today. Likewise, in the 5th Century AD Bodhidharma, a South Indian monk, became the first founder of the Shaolin Monastery in China. In the 7th Century A.D. during Harsha Vardhana's reign Xuan Zang (Hiuen Tsang) visited India in search of Buddhist scriptures. His journey became part of traditional Chinese lore, which was narrated in a book called 'A Journey to the West'. (Embassy of India 2013)

Evidence of historical cultural ties between the two regions (though mostly one way – India to China) can be established by, various grottoes and temple sites still found and preserved in China. Some of the sites in China are named as under: (Embassy of India 2013)

Grottoes

- Dunhuang
- Xinjiang
- Luoyang
- Dazu
- Datong

Temples

- Five Pagoda Temple (Wuta Si), Beijing
- White Horse Temple (Baima Si), Luoyang
- Big and Little Goose Pagodas, Xi'an
- Famen Si, Fufeng
- Shaolin Temple
- Kong Xiang Temple, Sanmenxia
- Kaiyuan Temple, Quanzhou

In addition to these grottoes and temples there are various memorials and museums in China which hold ancient Indian scriptures and artifacts, which lay evidence to the large scale cultural ties between the two regions.

Trade relations between the two countries were carried on via the *Silk Road* (viz., Nathula pass and Jelepla Pass), whereby the Chinese imported Indian Jades and exported rich silk to India. Evidence of which can be found in *Chanakya*'s renowned work *Arthashastra* (4th Century A.D.), which refers to Chinese *silk* as 'cinamsuka' (Chinese silk dress) and 'cinapatta' (Chinese silk bundle). (Chung Tan 1998). However, with the decline of Buddhism in India and spread of colonialism (British rule) in both the countries, resulted in diminished cultural exchanges between the two. Nevertheless, people of both the countries revived old friendship, especially during their respective struggles for freedom. Some of the landmark events of this period are Kang Youwei's stay in India (1890s), Tagore's visit to China (1924), setting up of Cheena Bhawan in Viswabharati University by Professor Tan Yunshan under Tagore's guidance (1937), sending of the Aid China Medical Mission, which included Dr. Dwarakanath Kotnis, by the Indian National Congress (1938), and Xu Beihong's visit to Shantiniketan (1939-40). (Embassy of India 2013)

Post-Indian independence in 1947 and the establishment of Communist China in 1949, saw the resumption of diplomatic ties between the two countries, with India being the first non-communist country to have recognized China in 1950. Here on, the early fifties and the 'Hindi-Chini Bhai Bhai' phase of 1950s witnessed a further strengthening of these ties, which however, was set to decline until the later half of 1980's.

The contemporary relations between India and China can be understood better under the following heads.

POLITICAL RELATIONS

With the establishment of new governments in each of the countries in 1947 (India) and 1949 (China) respectively, the first formal diplomatic relationship was established between the duo in 1950, which was initiated with the establishment of an Indian Embassy in China (the first non-communist country to do so). In the same vein the two countries jointly signed an agreement on cooperation based on the principles of Panchsheel. Here Panchsheel refers to the five principles of peaceful co-existence, which are as enumerated below:

1. Mutual respect for each other's territorial integrity and sovereignty;
2. Mutual non-aggression;
3. Mutual non-interference in each other's internal affairs;
4. Equality and mutual benefit; and
5. Peaceful co-existence

Subsequent to the agreement, numerous political visits were exchanged between the two countries. This phase of intimacy was expressed by the phrase 'Hindi-Chini Bhai Bhai' (India and China are brothers). However, things started changing for the worse, after a revolt broke out in Tibet, as the Chinese had started to doubt the Indian role in the revolt and consequently a war broke out in 1962 between India and China, over disputed territories of Aksai Chin, Arunachal Pradesh and few other smaller territories along the Indo-China border. The Indians received a crushing defeat in the war and henceforth the relation between the two suffered a setback.

The two nations however, restored their ambassadorial relationship in 1975. Atal Bihari Vajpayee the then external Minister of India during the Janata government visited China in February 1979, and attempted to better the relations between the two. This visit was reciprocated by the Chinese Foreign Minister Huang Hua, when he paid a return visit to India in June, 1981. However, the true impetus to improving the relationship between the two regions was received in

December 1988, when India's Prime Minister Rajiv Gandhi visited China. During this visit, both sides agreed to develop bilateral relations for which to fructify, a Joint Economic Group (JEG) and a Joint Working Group (JWG) was sought to be established that would seek improvement in economic ties and a fair, reasonable and a mutually acceptable solution to the boundary dispute. Following suit, the Chinese Premier Li Peng visited India in December 1991. And again in reciprocation India's Prime Minister Narasimha Rao visited China in September 1993. Through this visit an attempt was made to reach an agreement on the Maintenance of Peace and Tranquility along the Line of Actual Control (LAC) in the India-China Border Area. (Khanna 2010, Ministry of External Affairs 2012)

In May 1992, it was for the first time that an Indian head of state, President R. Venkataraman paid a State visit to China, following which China's head of state, President Jiang Zemin reciprocated and paid a visit to India in 1996. This was also the first ever visit of a Chinese head of state to India. During the visit various Confidence Building Measures (CBMs) were agreed upon so as to promote cooperation and trust. Ensuing these measures of cooperation, the relation between the two again soured momentarily when India gate crashed into the nuclear club, after testing five nuclear bombs at Pokhran in 1998. Relations could be normalized only after Jaswant Singh, the then External Affairs Minister of India paid a visit to China in June 1999 and reiterated that neither of the countries are threat to each other. Following this visit, high level exchanges and visits of officials and ministers to each other's regions has been a dominant feature in the bilateral relations of both India and China. And during each of these visits numerous measures have been taken so as to short out the differences and strengthen their cooperation. Some of which include; (Ministry of External Affairs 2012)

- The Declaration on Principles for Relations and Comprehensive Cooperation, which was the first ever comprehensive document on development of bilateral relations signed at the highest level between India and China in the year 2003.
- In the same year India and China also concluded a border trade protocol, so as to add a border crossing between Sikkim and Tibet Autonomous Region. The crossing point on the Indian side is at Nathu La, perched at an altitude of around 14,500 feet. This route was officially opened for trade on July 6, 2006.
- In November 2006, during Chinese President Hu Jintao's visit to India the two countries issued a Joint Declaration that contained a ten-pronged strategy to intensify cooperation in all areas so as to bolster the India-China Strategic and Cooperative Partnership.
- In the year 2008, during Prime Minister Manmohan Singh's visit to China, a joint document entitled 'A Shared Vision for the 21st Century of the Republic of India and the People's Republic of China' was issued, which outlined common positions on a number of international and bilateral issues.
- In December 2010, during Chinese Premier Wen Jiabao's visit to India six agreements on cultural exchange, green technologies, media exchanges, hydrological data, and banking were signed and also a Joint Communiqué was released.
- Also during the visit, a bilateral trade target of 100 billion US dollars was set to be reached by 2015.
- Year 2011 was declared as the 'Year of India-China exchange'.
- Also in the year 2011 a hotline between the Indian Prime Minister and the Chinese Premier was established.

- The year 2012 was announced as the 'Year of India-China Friendship and Cooperation'.
- The two countries have also instituted dialogue mechanisms on issues relating to counter-terrorism, policy planning and security, besides strategic dialogue and regular consultations.
- Over and above, there has also been close cooperation in areas as diverse as water resources, judiciary, science & technology, audit, personnel, finance, labour etc.
- Exchanges of officials and ministers at the government, Parliamentary and Party levels have also expanded over the years.
- Both the countries are also cooperating in various regional organizations, with BRICS being the latest of them all.

ECONOMIC RELATIONS

As specified above India and China have stepped up functional cooperation in all areas, though economic relation remains at the core of all its interactions. Both the countries have granted each other the status of the 'Most Favored Nation', so as to boost economic ties. China is currently India's one of the largest trade-in-goods partner. The volume of trade between the two countries, as was merely 270 million USD in 1990, has galloped upwards to touch a mark of 66.47 billion USD in the year 2012. And now a bilateral trade target of 100 billion US dollars has been set, which is to be reached by 2015. (Varma 2013). The figures showcase a stupendous amount of growth in the economic ties between the two countries, also while considering the fact that India and China had officially resumed trade just in 1978.

However, ground realities disclose that trade relations between India and China has not been stress free. Indian authorities very regularly express their concern on the heavy trade deficit with China, as India exports much lesser than what it imports from China. As a consequence, Indian markets are flooded with Chinese goods. Thus, one finds India indulging in trade protection measures against Chinese products, for which the Chinese are very concerned. In fact the Chinese claim that India has used antidumping measures against China more than the United States has done against it. Moreover, India is yet to declare China a market economy. Considering these facts, many argue that if trade friction continues between India and China, it could become a source of major contention. (Rosenfield 2010)

CULTURAL RELATIONS

As noted earlier, India and China shared a rich historical connection in the past. However, cultural ties dwindled with the spread of colonialism in the area. Nonetheless, post-1947 and post-1949, when they both began their journey as independent sovereign nations, attempts were made to revive the cultural ties between the two regions. Consequently, in the year 1955, the first Indian cultural delegation headed by the then Deputy Minister of External Affairs Mr. A. K. Chanda visited China, who with his team was warmly received by the Chinese leaders and the people of the region. The trip was considered to be very successful. However, this cooperation in the field of culture could not be continued for long, considering the political and military tensions that emerged during the 1960s and 70s. However, a point hereto note is, regardless of the snapped ties during this period, Indian Bollywood movies such as 'Do Bigha Zameen', 'Awara', 'Sree 420' and 'Noorie' struck an emotional chord in the hearts and minds of the Chinese people. It is also said that Bollywood stars like Raj Kapoor and Nargis left a lasting impression on the Chinese during that period of bitter relations between the two regions. (Ministry of External Affairs 2012)

And during the 1980s, with the resumption of political relations between the two countries, the cultural ties too showed signs of improvement. In 1986, a film delegation from India visited China under the Cultural Exchange Programme, and in May 1988, the broad contours of the India-China cultural cooperation was laid down in the Agreement on Cultural Cooperation. Such an agreement was revived in December 2010, and thus the last 30 years have witnessed a remarkable progress in the Indo-China cultural relations. The nature of cultural exchanges between the two countries includes exchanges of visits of performing artists, officials, writers, archivists and archaeologists, organizing cultural festivals, film festivals and exchanges in the field of mass media, youth affairs and sports. The momentum of cultural ties between the two regions is set as is evident from the following list of cultural events that was organized in the year 2011: (Ministry of External Affairs 2012)

- Celebration of Vishwa Hindi Diwas in Beijing, January 10, 2011.
- 62nd Republic Day Celebration in China, January 26, 2011.
- Book release ceremony at Culture Wing, Embassy of India- 'Rising Elephant' by Professor Ma Jiali- March 10, 2011
- Book release ceremony of 'India That You May Not Know' by Prof. Wang Shuying-Culture Wing- April 27, 2011
- 150th Anniversary of Rabindranath Tagore celebrated in China, 7th May, 2011.
- Tagore Evening at Culture Wing, Embassy of India, Beijing, 08 May, 2011.
- India Day at Peking University, 22nd May, 2011.
- Buddhism: Mapping Asia's History and Culture, Beijing, 18-20 June, 2011.

- 'Evening Prayers at the bank of Ganges'- a Cultural program organized at the National Center for Performing Arts (NCPA) - July 3, 2011.
- Odissi Performance by Padma Shree Ms. Ranjana Gauhar at National Centre for Performing Arts (NCPA), Beijing on 10 July 2011.
- Odissi Recital by ICCR Troupe led by Padma Shree Ms. Ranjana Gauhar at the Beijing Music Conservatory on 11 July 2011.
- Felicitation ceremony for students of Tagore International School, New Delhi, at Culture Wing, Embassy of India, 5 August 2011.
- Independence Day Celebrations at Indian Embassy, China, August 15, 2011.
- International Yoga Conference, Beijing, 26th August 2011.
- Hindi Diwas Celebration at Culture Center, Embassy of India.
- Indian Youth Delegation's visit to China, 21 Sep- 29 Sep2011.
- 'Bollywood Love Story', a musical program held at Central Conservatory of Music, Beijing, 22 September, 2011.
- 142nd Gandhi Jayanti Celebrations on 2nd October 2011, Embassy of India, Beijing.
- Lecture by Prof Tansen Sen 'India, China and the West: Thoughts on Colonial Period', Singapore, 10th October, 2011.
- Lecture by Nobel Laureate Prof. Amartya Sen 'Higher Education in History- Asia and Europe', 15 October 2011, held at 100 Years Auditorium, Peking University, Beijing.
- Diwali Celebrations for young Indian and Chinese

school children 'Diwali Milan Ceremony', held at Culture Wing, Embassy of India on 23 October 2011.

- Embassy of India hosts Indian Tea Tasting Ceremony at Culture Wing on 28 October 2011.
- 2011 Beijing Foreign Language Festival and Chaoyang Foreign Language Carnival, October 2011.
- Deepawali Celebrations held at Embassy of India Lawns, Beijing, on 29th October 2011.
- 'The future of India-China Cultural exchanges', an Interactive Session with a prestigious panel of Indian artists and literary personalities held at Indian Cultural Center on November 9, 2011.
- Indian Movie Festival, Beijing, 29th November to 4th December, 2011.
- 'Folklore in Kalahandi' Talk by Dr. Mahendra Kumar Mishra, held at Indian Culture Center on 15th December, 2011.
- Inauguration of painting exhibition of Mrs. Anjula Sharma, Beijing, 18 December 2011.
- Buddhist Photography Exhibition, Sanya (China), 19-20 December, 2011.

CONCLUSION

The list of cultural activities and the ever expanding political and economic ties between the two countries highlights the robust nature of their improving relationship. And one very dominant reason for this improvement has been the increasing faith of these two nations on the use of 'soft power' (power based on intangible influences, such as culture, values, knowledge, ideology and the like). As soft power today is considered to be one of the most important tool at the hands of the nation to enhance its intangible standing in the international platform. The cultural activities, the exchange programmes, people to people contacts are all tools at the hands of soft power. One can thus verbalize that India and China are making very efficient use of their soft power resources so as to strengthen their ties and put an end to all their issues of contention.

REFERENCES

1. Chung Tan, 1998, 'A Sino-Indian Perspective for India-China Understanding', IGNCA, (Online Web), Accessed June 05, 2013, URL: *http://ignca.nic.in/ks_41019.htm*
2. Embassy of India, 2013, 'India-China Bilateral Relations: Historical Ties', (Online Web), Accessed May 25, 2013, URL: *http://www.indianembassy.org.cn/DynamicContent. aspx?MenuId=1&SubMenuId=0*
3. Index mundi, 2012'Country Comparison: GDP (Purchasing Power Parity)', (Online Web), Accessed June 07, 2013, URL: *http://www.indexmundi.com/g/r.aspx?v=65&t=10*
4. Jacob Jabin T., 2012, 'India's China Policy: Time to Overcome Political Drift', S. Rajaratnam School of International Studies, Nanyang Technological University, Singapore, (Online Web), Accessed June 04, 2013, URL: *http://www.rsis.edu.sg/publications/policy_papers/Time%20to%20Overcome%20Political%20Drift.pdf*
5. Khanna, V.N., 2010, *Foreign Policy of India,* Vikas Publishing House PVT LTD, New Delhi.
6. Lam Peng Er and Lim Tai Wei, 2009, 'The Rise of China and India: A New Asian drama', World Scientific, Singapore.
7. MEA (Ministry of External Affairs), 2012, 'India-China Bilateral Relations', (Online Web), Accessed May 25, 2013, URL: *http://www.mea.gov.in/Portal/ForeignRelation/China-January-2012.pdf*
8. Rosenfield Julia M., 2010, 'Exploring the China-India Relationship', Roundtable Report, CAN China Studies, (Online Web), Accessed June 25, 2013, URL: *http://www.cna.org/sites/default/files/research/D00234594.A1%20Exploring%20the%20China-India%20Relationship.pdf*
9. Sunil Mittal, 2010, 'Growing Beyond Geopolitics', in *India China Ties: 60 Years 60 Thoughts,* Embassy of India, Beijing
10. Varma KJM, 25th May 2013, 'Top Commerce Team to Visit China to Discuss Trade Deficit', *The New Indian Express,* Chennai.

10

India-Japan Relations on a Roll: Evolving Strategic and Security Issues

Mohammed Badrul Alam

This chapter shows that India and Japan are acutely aware of the need for strategic and security cooperation between the two countries for ensuring order, stability and equilibrium among the region's great powers. Both the countries recognise that India-Japan cooperation and the process of engagement cannot be sustained on sheer expediency, episodic and transactional basis but has to be firmly rooted in shared values in both security and strategic terms. In view of the economic opportunities and geo-strategic compulsions between India and Japan, one hopes that the same momentum would be carried forward in 2013 and beyond toward a new paradigm of mutual benefit.

Framing the relationship within the broad Realist theoretical discourse of International Relations, one can surmise the following:

- "No nation can have a sure guide as to what it must

do and what it need not do in foreign policy without accepting the national interest as that guide. ...Universal moral action cannot be applied to the action of states" (Hans J. Morgenthau, 1951)

- "The State's interests provides the spring of action" (Kenneth Waltz, 1979)
- "States seek power and they calculate their interests in terms of power" (Robert Keohane, 1986)
- "The international system is anarchic. The most basic motives driving states is survival" (John Mearsheimer, 1994)
- "States are motivated primarily by national interests" (Robert Gilpin, 1996)
- "Japan and India , as the two largest democracies in Asia share universal values such as freedom, democracy and rule of law" (Prime ministers, Shinzo Abe and Dr.Manmohan Singh, 2013)

Power in the most generic term refers to the ability of influencing and articulating the behaviour of other states in order to achieve favorable outcome a state desires through attraction, inducement or coercion. Various national governments have at different times utilized their economic and military muscle in realizing and enhancing their primary goals by increasing their raw power potential. The currency of power and security objectives are clearly evident in the 21st century globalised world with multiple transnational connectivity and changing contours of power. One can argue that India's power has been enhanced in Asia Pacific in general and in context to Japan in particular. In this context, foreign policy of India, like that of any other country, is shaped and influenced by geopolitics, geography, history, cultural parameters, and most importantly vital national interests. The changing economic, military and strategic environment in and around South Asia, South East Asia and

East Asia has had its repercussions with India trying to reach out for new avenues for exercising greater mobility and flexibility in the regional sector for the conduct of its foreign policy. In this context, on one important issue, namely, the issue of nuclear proliferation as well as related security issues had its impact on India-Japan relations with profound policy ramifications.

ISSUE OF NUCLEAR PROLIFERATION AND RELATED SECURITY ISSUES

In view of the painful experience of being the only country in the world so far where nuclear bombs have been used to devastating effect, Japan has been overtly sensitive to any issues related to nuclear proliferation.

When India and Pakistan went for nuclear tests in May 1998, it was a rude shock to Japan's sensibilities. Along with other western countries and in particular the G-8 nations, Japan imposed severe economic sanctions on both India and Pakistan and accused them of flagrant violations of the letter and spirit of nuclear disarmament.

Japan, toward the end of 1999, provided indication in subtle terms to go soft on the continuance of economic sanctions on India. In an interview with ***Daily Asahi Shimbun***, Vice-minister Ichita Yamamoto expressed his satisfaction with New Delhi's "positive and forward-looking stance regarding signing CTBT and Japan's inching towards ending economic sanctions against India."(1)

In the aftermath of the terrorist incidents of September 11, 2001, both India and Japan came closer in cooperating in various facets of security perimeter affecting Central Asia, South Asia, South East Asia and East Asia. India had actively supported anti-terrorist stand taken by Japan and had lauded Japan's decision to send S.D.F (Self-Defense Force) units to the Arabian Sea and the Indian Ocean regions. India had also provided landing, refueling and docking facilities to

Japanese fighter jets and ships.

In the foreseeable future in terms of security cooperation, Japan and India, are likely to have confined themselves to:

- Energy Security
- Maritime Security
- Enhanced contacts between the Armed Forces of the India and Japan

In all these three security fields, as Subash Kapilla analyses, (2) the operative principle should be that spheres of initiatives and cooperation are restricted to the bilateral context of Japan-India relations. The aim of Japan-India strategic cooperation should not be viewed to target containing China but moderating and engaging proactively China's approaches to Asian and East Asian Security to the extent possible under 'congagement'. Some observations from Kapilla are worth repeating, namely:

- Without getting overtly drawn into a United States-China strategic confrontation, countries such as Japan and India will be well advised to operate in close cooperation and in sync with each other and which could hopefully provide necessary counter-ballast for ensuring peace and stability in the Asia-Pacific
- With Japan and India opting for strategic cooperation, the third big Asian power i.e. China would consequently afford much needed strategic space to these two powers and thereby paving the way for a balanced Asian Security.

Recognising that India and Japan have large Exclusive Economic Zones and maritime interests (including safe passage or Japanese oil tankers plying from the Persian Gulf to Strait of Malacca through Arabian Sea, Indian Ocean and Bay of Bengal under protection from Indian Navy and its Coast Guards) there is a need for enhance cooperation in capacity building, technical assistance and information and data sharing between their respective agencies and undertake anti-piracy measures in the high seas. Annually about 50,000 ships, more than a quarter of world's maritime cargo shipment and about one half of entire trade volumes of Japan, China and South Korea navigate through the strategic Malacca-Singapore Strait. Considering only the tanker shipments, about 50 per cent of world's tankers and about 85 per cent of oil tankers navigating from the Middle East and Gulf region to the Northeast Asia go through Indian Ocean and Malacca-Singapore Strait. Trilateral Maritime Partnership of India-Japan-US, in this regard, can shoulder responsibilities as the core responsible parties of a voluntary 'Maritime Security Coalition' covering the Broad SLOC (Sea Lines of Communication) of the 'East-West Expanded Asia' in the Indo-Pacific region. The security of SLOCs in the Indo-Pacific region is a significant factor for the economy and the stabilisation of the region as a whole. The regional economy has developed with and is largely dependent on the maritime transportation using secured SLOCs. Especially vital oil resources that are indispensable for existence and prosperity of the regional littoral countries including India and Japan are largely dependent on the security of the SLOCs, connecting Indian Ocean, Malacca-Singapore Strait, South China Sea and East China Sea.(3)

Similarly, regular exchange visits between the two Coast Guards through meetings of heads of Coast Guards, mutual visits of Coast Guard ships and holding of combined exercises are very important for both India and Japan in strengthening their respective security perimeters. In this context, the signing of a Memorandum on Cooperation between the Coast Guards was welcomed. Coming into force of the Regional Cooperation Agreement on Combating Piracy and Armed Robbery against Ships in Asia (ReCAAP) and reaffirming to enhance cooperation in respect of anti-piracy countermeasures under its framework are welcome measures in this direction.

Japan and India condemn terrorism in all its forms and manifestations and stress that there can be no justification whatsoever for any act of terrorism. They share the view that international community must further intensify all out efforts and cooperation to fight this menacing threat to global peace and security. In this context, the two countries have pledged to work in unison through the India-Japan Joint Working Group on Counter Terrorism. Both Japan and India have also called upon all Member States of the UN to work towards the expeditious adoption of a Comprehensive Convention on International Terrorism. (4)

EVENTS AND TRENDS

In contemporary times, from the time of Yoshiro Mori as Prime minister, subsequent Japanese prime ministers in the recent past have shown real enthusiasm and made tangible efforts for the improvement of relationship with India.

After the mutual warmth in the 1950s during the Nehru era, India and Japan drifted apart during the Cold War. (5) Shinzo Abe during his landmark August 2007 visit to India, however, traced his personal affinity towards India to the sentimental visit of his grandfather and prime minister of Japan, Nobusuke Kishi, who arrived in India during 1957 to a friendly reception from Jawaharlal Nehru. Abe reciprocated this great gesture by inviting Prime minister Dr. Manmohan Singh to Tokyo in December 2006 and in arranging a speech made by Dr.Singh to members of Japanese Diet and a rare audience with the Japanese emperor. Subsequently, Dr. Singh made official visits to Japan in 2008 and 2010 as well geared toward advancement of strategic and economic partnership between India and Japan.

Second, Indian political elite has increasingly looked to Japan as it steered Japan towards a new proactive role and has looked at India as a hard power of 'coercion', soft power of 'attraction' and cultural super power of 'inducement' in Asia and the world. New generation of leaders in Tokyo believed that Japan should shed its defensive posture about its imperial past and become a "normal" power. From Abe to Noda, each of the Prime ministers was also pressing ahead with Koizumi's agenda of unshackling Japan from its post Second World War political limitations and constitutional inhibitions on taking new, visible security responsibilities in Asia and beyond.

Third, the rise of China in recent years has compelled Japan to re-evaluate its own long-term options in Asia that many expect would inevitably become Sino-centric for maximising Chinese national interests. As Japan, much like the United States, hedges its bets against the rise of China including its assertiveness on matters related to South China Sea and Senkaku/Diaoyu island, political and security cooperation with India has become imperative of Japan's new grand strategic calculus. However, Japan's new emphasis on a "global and strategic partnership" with India by no means implies that the two want to ally against China. In an age of rapid economic integration in Asia, China is already the largest trading partner of Japan and is set to acquire a similar status with India. The focus of both New Delhi and Tokyo is on widening the window of flexibility and opportunity in their conduct of foreign and security policies in Asia rather than seek an impossible containment of China that would provide no benefits to any party either in the short term or long term.

Fourth, while China will remain the key partner for Japan, Tokyo under Shinzo Abe is inclined to invest and enter into another important economic relationship for a possible multi-polar Asia. As a consequence, India has overtaken

China as the largest recipient of Japan's overseas development assistance. As Japan has fallen behind China and Korea in taking advantage of India's economic reforms, Abe has highlighted the need for engaging India and its emerging economy.

Finally, for the first time in the last sixty years, Abe has injected the notion of shared and complementary political values into the bilateral discourse between the two countries. Despite being two major working democracies in the world, the common vision to democracy has never figured in India-Japan relationship. With a firm commitment to openness and constructive engagement, the Indo-US nuclear deal, for example, promises to change New Delhi's standing in the global nuclear order and with Japan providing a helping hand to harness India tap nuclear energy in its civilian sector. The US-India nuclear deal, which fundamentally transformed the nuclear export regime, also provided a major condition under which Japan could engage with India. Not only did the deal signal Washington's commitment to India but also the near inevitability of Japanese involvement in India's potential nuclear energy industry due to the structure of nuclear conglomerates. A wave of deals from 2006, including tie-ups between Toshiba and Westinghouse, Mitsubishi Heavy Industries and Areva, and Hitachi and GE, consolidated Japan's leading edge within the industry, holding a considerable amount of leverage and leeway in the form of expertise, technology, and process-management ability.(6)

As Asia, the largest continent, undergoes major transformation in terms of power configurations, India and Japan are acutely aware of the need for political and security cooperation between the two countries for ensuring order, stability and equilibrium among the region's great powers. There are, however, limitations to enhanced defense cooperation; one concerns disagreements over the value of the Proliferation Security Initiative (PSI), and a second pertains to explicit arms sales between Japan and India. On the former issue, while both share a strong commitment and vision in pursuing goals leading to disarmament and non-proliferation objectives as partners seeking a peaceful nuclear weapon free world, their means differ. India rejects the initiative as an extension and perpetuation of existing US-led military alliances in Asia-Pacific region while Japan has been a strong supporter since its inception. And, despite high demand in India for high-quality search-and-rescue seaplanes as well as infrastructure for military ports (India is currently the world's largest importer of arms), even after the relaxation and easing of Japan's arms export controls in December 2011, it is uncertain whether or not this will extend to trade with India.(7)

Both the countries recognise that India-Japan cooperation and process of engagement cannot be sustained on sheer expediency but has to be firmly rooted in shared values in both economic and strategic terms. That precisely is why Dr. Manmohan Singh and Yoshihiko Noda found it so important to emphasize nourishment of democracy and liberal democratic values as the future bilateral political glue between the two Asian powers. In May 2013, Prime Minister of Japan, Shinzo Abe and Prime Minister of India, Dr. Manmohan Singh held the Annual Bilateral Summit in Tokyo. They discussed several important bilateral as well as regional and global issues. Both sides reaffirmed that Japan and India as partners share common values and strategic interests and have made a strong commitment to develop the Strategic and Global Partnership further for the deepening of their bilateral relations as well as peace and prosperity of the region and the world. The two Prime Ministers also noted the successful outcomes achieved during the "2 plus 2" dialogue, the Foreign Secretary level Dialogue, the Foreign Office Consultations, the Defence

Policy Dialogue, the Trilateral Dialogue between India, Japan and the United States, as well as other key interactions and engagements on various areas including cyber terrorism, counter-terrorism and economic partnership and the launch of the bilateral Maritime Affairs Dialogue. Both sides have also expressed their commitment to continue to work to prepare the ground for India to become a full member in the international export control regimes: the Nuclear Suppliers Group, the Missile Technology Control Regime, the Australia Group and the Wassenaar Arrangement and to accelerate the negotiations of an Agreement for Cooperation in the Peaceful Uses of Nuclear Energy towards an early conclusion.(8). In view of economic opportunities and geo-strategic compulsions between India and Japan, one hopes that under Japan's current Prime minister Shinzo Abe's stewardship, the same momentum would be carried forward in 2014 and beyond toward a new paradigm of mutual benefit on a win-win proposition.

FOOTNOTES

1. ***India Today***, New Delhi, November 15, 1999, "Japan urges Pakistan to restore democracy, sign CTBT", http://www.india-today.com/intoday/newsarchives/99/11/15/n45.shtml, see, Miyashita, Akitoshi and Yoichiro Sato(eds.), *Japanese Foreign Policy in Asia and the Pacific*, New York: Palgrave Publications, 2001, also, see, Sanjana Joshi, *Changing Japan: Opportunities and Challenges for India*, Delhi: Shipra Publications, 2008
2. Dr.Subash Kapilla, "Japan-India Strategic Dialogue: A Misnomer", South Asia Analysis Group, Paper No. 2187, 29.03.2007, see, also, *The Japan Times*, February 15, 2012, http://www.japantimes.co.jp/text/nb20120215d1.html,
3. Hideaki Kaneda, "Web of Maritime Security Coalition Bilateral, Trilateral and Multilateral", *Defense and Security Alert*, Delhi, May 13, also, available at, http://www.dsalert.org/strategic-partnership-india-japan-vietnam/588-web-of-maritime-security-coalition-bilateral-trilateral-and-multilateral
4. from, Rediff.com, December 15, 2006, " India, Japan to establish Strategic Partnership, http://www.rediff.com/news/2006/dec/

15ind.htm, also, see, Brahma Chellaney, " India-Japan Relationship: Shard Values to Shared Interests", *The Economic Times,* Delhi, December 29, 2011

5. C. Raja Mohan, "Visit of the Rising Ties", *The Indian Express,* New Delhi, December 14, 2006, http://www.indianexpress.com/story/18476.html, see, Panda, Rajaram and Yoo Fukazawa(eds.), *India and Japan: Blossoming of a New Understanding,* New Delhi: Lancer Books, 2004, also, see, Dharmdasani, M.D, *Indo-Japan Relations: Challenges and Opportunities,* New Delhi: Kanishka Publishers, 2004, see, Jithin George, "India-Japan Relations at 60: Setting the Stage for Kizuna", Institute of Peace and Conflict Studies, Delhi, Article No.3561, 20 January 2012, http://www.ipcs.org/article/india/india-japan-relations-at-60-setting-the-stage-for-kizuna-3561.html
6. See, Victoria Tuke, "Expanding Strategic Horizons: Japan's Foreign Policy towards India", March 25, 2013, also, available at http://www.tokyofoundation.org/en/articles/2013/expanding-strategic-horizons
7. See, Victoria Tuke, No.5, ibid
8. .Ibid, C.Raja Mohan, No.27, also, see, http://www.mofa.go.jp/region/asia-paci/india/pmv0912/joint.html , see, http://www.mea.gov.in/bilateral-documents.htm?dtl/21755/Joint+Statement+ on+Prime+Minis ters+visit+to+Japan+Strengthening+the+Strategic+and+Global+Partnership+betwe en+India+and+Japan+beyond+the+60th+ Anniversary+of+Diplomatic+Relations, also, see, http://www.rediff.com/news/slide-show/slide-show-1-pm-abe-script-next-level-of-indo-japan-strategy/20130529.htm

REFERENCES

C. Raja Mohan, "Visit of the Rising Ties", The *Indian Express,* New Delhi, December 14, 2006.

Dharmdasani, M.D, *Indo-Japan Relations: Challenges and Opportunities,* New Delhi: Kanishka Publishers, 2004.

Drifte, Reinhard, *Japan's Foreign Policy in the 1990s: From Economic Super Power to What Power?,* London: Macmillan Press, 1996.

Jain, Purnendra C.(ed.) *Distant Neighbours: Japan and South Asia,* New Delhi: Sterling Publishers, 1996.

Keshavan, K.V(ed.), *Building a Global Partnership: Fifty Years of Indo-Japanese Relations,* New Delhi: Lancer Books, 2002.

Lim Hua Sing, *Japan's Role in Asia: Mutual Development and Ruthless Compeition,* Singapore: Eastern University Press, 2003.

Masako Fukuda, "India Blasts Fire up Resistance to Nuclear Weapons in Japan", *Nikkei Weekly*, 18 May 1998, p.1.

Mattoo, Amitabh, "India's Strategic and Foreign Policy Perceptions", in Keshavan, K.V(ed.), *Building a Global Partnership: Fifty Years of Indo-Japanese Relations*, New Delhi: Lancer Books, 2002.

Miyashita, Akitoshi and Yoichiro Sato (eds.), *Japanese Foreign Policy in Asia and the Pacific*, New York: Palgrave Publications, 2001.

Murthy, P.A.Narasimha, *India and Japan: Dimensions of their Relations*, New Delhi: Lancer Books, 1993.

Panda, Rajaram, *Japan and the Third World: Political and Economic Interactions 1980s-1990s*, New Delhi: Lancer Books, 1994.

Panda, Rajaram and Kazuo Ando (eds.), *India and Japan Multi-dimensional Perspectives*, New Delhi: Lancer Books, 1997.

Panda, Rajaram and Yoo Fukazawa (eds.), *India and Japan: Blossoming of a New Understanding*, New Delhi: Lancer Books, 2004.

Rajesh Kapoor, "Dawn of a New Era in India-Japan Relations", Institute of Peace and Conflict Studies, New Delhi, Article No.2177, 4 January 2007.

Rukmani Gupta, "PMs Japan Visit", Institute of Peace and Conflict Studies, New Delhi, Article No.2185, 9 January 2007.

Dr.Subash Kapilla, "Japan-India Strategic Dialogue: A Misnomer", South Asia Analysis Group, Paper No. 2187, 29.03.2007.

Wolf Mendel, *Japan's Asia Policy: Regional Security and Global Interests*, New York: Routledge, 1995.

11

India, South East Asia and India's Look East Policy

Dr. Biswajit Mohapatra

South East Asia is one of the fastest developing regions in the world today and enjoys the enviable reputation of being business and investment friendly while the north eastern has the potential to emerge as a strategic base for foreign and domestic investors, given the calmness that has been restored in the both political and societal terms. Some of the sectors which offer very strong opportunities for mutual cooperation have been identified as, infrastructure, energy, oil and gas, mining, manufacturing, agriculture and agro- processing, healthcare, information and communication technologies and hospitality, which enjoy a strong demand both within the region ,sub-region and also worldwide.

The year 1991 truly is a memorable period as, along with the launching of New Economic Reforms Policy, India also launched a major foreign policy initiative, viz., *Look East*

Policy, which is regarded not only as a major shift in the context of India's foreign policy, since it demonstrated a kind of confidence never seen before and also strong determination of the country to play an important role befitting its image on the global stage. It was also evident that in the rapidly changing economic and strategic arena concerning Asia and our own neighbourhood, India truly realized the opportunity of scaling up its economic growth as a whole and to develop a region which had been neglected heretofore besides strengthening its ties with the countries of South East Asian region.

While some commentators hailed it as a strategic shift, others chose to describe it as an attempt at reviving India's many centuries old historical links ,which it shared with the South East Asian Countries ,in the field of commerce, culture and communications. The present thaw in the bilateral relationship between India and China also acted as a booster for the SE Asian countries to warm up to India's overtures in this respect. Some have even gone very far to point out that the ASEAN member countries were the first to have realized the inherent economic gains that could accrue to them in this change of course of India's economic policies and the burgeoning size of the domestic market. While others have pointed out that this policy can be said to be primarily aimed at the need of balancing China's fast growing expansion along with kick starting India's economic engagement in Southeast Asia, it also addresses its domestic concerns in the north eastern region.

RISE OF ECONOMIC IDIOM IN LOOK EAST POLICY

In India's Look East policy, one can easily find the diplomatic realism of former Prime Minister P.V. Narasimha Rao, in the launching of this initiative, particularly at a time when India was faced with a national crisis in the 1990s. Against this background, India pursued this policy for India's long-term engagement with key regional powers. As was expected, such diplomacy extended beyond the economic realm as India's strategic calculations were also evident. This policy as such was based on economic realism driven by political will and also was meant to confront the challenge of harmonizing a sort of pacifist principle with a pragmatic policy.

It is now well known that the so called talk about building up Asian solidarity among the countries in Asia, in the late 1940s and early 1950s, could not materialize due to the severe and perceptible impact of the Cold War politics on the region, besides the tense relationship seen between India and China. These factors didn't help in the establishment of a conducive environment for any kind of commercial cooperation among the Asian countries and forced the countries to look outwards for the required trade linkages.

With the rapid changes coming up in the geopolitics of the region, marked by significant rate of growth in the economies of the Asia in the last few decades and increasing integration among them, an Asian economic miracle, viz., the success of Japan, South Korea, Southeast Asia, and China and albeit late participation of India since 1991, recording an average growth of over 6% and India becoming the fourth largest economy in the world in terms of purchasing power parity, the emphasis on the idea of attainment of peaceful development rather than the involvement in any kind of geopolitical conflict ,inevitably got strengthened in the region.[1] This changed climate again raised the unfulfilled Asian solidarity amongst the Asian neighbours, encouraging them to launch vigorous initiatives for increased economic cooperation within the great continent in a remarkable way.

This remarkable transformation was very lucidly underlined by the then External Affairs Minister, Yashwant Sinha, in his speech, titled, 'Resurgent India in

Asia' at *Harvard University, on* September 29, 2003. While dwelling upon India's new initiatives in Asia He said," In the past, India's engagement with much of Asia, including Southeast and East Asia, was built on an idealistic conception of Asian brotherhood, based on shared experiences of colonialism and of cultural ties. "The rhythm of the region today is determined, however, as much by trade, investment and production as by history and culture. That is what motivates our decade-old Look East policy. Asia mattered only verbally in the past articulation of Indian foreign policy. It now is a throbbing commercial reality behind India's diplomacy."[2]

The North eastern region ,with its 99 per cent of the outer boundaries, sharing the borders with foreign countries is as such of very crucial and vital geographical importance as this part of the country , was very rightly believed to have played a very important role in the multiple aspects of security, trade, commerce and connectivity being planned under this new policy venture. As such connecting India to South East Asia through the North Eastern Region of India (NER) was a significant objective of this initiative. The North Eastern Region is an important focal point in many respects, which is closely intertwined with the achievement of many *Look East Policy* objectives.

Given the fact that the region's strategic location and untapped natural resources has promises for abundant economic growth for the region and the country as a whole, the problem of insurgency and conflicts in the region were believed, can be overcome as the Look East Policy would make available various avenues for faster economic development for the people in the region. The development of India's Northeastern states and the need to curb insurgency activities along the border with Myanmar were accorded high priority with the strong belief that the economies of India, China and the ASEAN could be centered on the states of the region. This region retains a high prospect to play a contributory role in propelling the economies of the sub-continent and the ASEAN countries simultaneously.

INDIA'S LOOK EAST POLICY- PHASE ONE

Yashwant Sinha said, "The first phase (1991-1997) of India's 'Look East' policy was ASEAN-centered and focused primarily on trade and investment linkages. The new phase of this policy is characterized by an expanded definition of 'East', extending from Australia to East Asia, with ASEAN at its core. The new phase also marks a shift from trade to wider economic and security issues, including joint efforts to protect the sea-lanes and coordinate counter-terrorism activities. Asia's challenge lies in its immense political, economic and social diversity, as also the seemingly unique dynamics of its different regions. A cooperative future global order will inevitably require full Asian participation. With its increasing weight in world economy, Asia holds the key to collective global prosperity and security."

In the earlier times, when the then Indian Prime Minister, Shri Narasimha Rao had outlined India's Look East policy a decade ago, it was regarded by many as tentative and was greeted with some kind of scepticism both within the country and in the Southeast Asian region, the reason being that during the Cold War years, India and ASEAN had moved apart, and as the Look East Policy initiative now is aimed at restoring vigorous economic ties between the two. With the rapid unfolding of India's economic reforms, the initiatives to integrate the country's economy with the region saw a steady rise, particularly in the last two decades. The rapid expansion of India's relations with the region can be very well gauged from the fact that the Trade between India and ASEAN multiplied fourfold — from $ 3.1 billion in 1991 to about $ 12 billion by 2002, motivating the then

Indian Prime Minister Shri A.V.Bajpai to set the target of up to $ 30 billion by the year 2007. Trade with ASEAN countries was a mere $2.5 billion in 1993 when this policy was initiated and in 2010-11 it is estimated to cross $45 billion.

The determination of entering into Free Trade Agreements with the ASEAN as a whole and with Thailand and Singapore came to be seen as instruments of India's strategic shift in its policy towards Asia. In the words of Shri Sinha, the intensification of such economic linkages with ASEAN, has quietly led India into a second phase of its Look East policy. While the Phase one of the policy was characterized by trade and investment linkages, the Phase two can be seen particularly marked by "arrangements for FTAs and establishment of institutional economic linkages between the countries of the region and India."

INDIA'S LOOK EAST POLICY-PHASE TWO

The pursuit of physical connectivity to Southeast Asia received added importance under the phase two of India's Look East policy,. With fast realization amongst the policy makers that the region is an integral part of India's extended neighbourhood, improved trade with Southeast Asia received its much deserved attention. With this, establishment of air and land links to East and Southeast Asia also has been given due priority in the phase two of the policy. As immediately after the 1997 financial crisis, the Phase two of Look East Policy was launched, it has focused upon building up 'arrangements for Free Trade Agreements (FTAs) and establishment of institutional linkages between the countries of the region and India. This second part is more significant as within the context of Look East Policy, India has also developed closer relations with CLMB countries (Cambodia, Laos, Myanmar and Brunei) by November 2000. It's seen that India's relations with the countries of Southeast Asia greatly got strengthened especially after President Clinton's visit to the region in 2000, which also had brought about dramatic improvement in the Indo-US ties. India also took the lead for the institution of the India-ASEAN Summit two years after, i.e., in 2004. In a significant move, India is now engaged actively in building transport corridors to the region, which inter alia, included the trilateral highway project involving Myanmar and Thailand and the proposed rail link between New Delhi and Hanoi, which is being hailed as a part of its new road diplomacy.

It is true that the Look East policy in phase two has the potential to enable India to break out of the political confines of the subcontinent, which had severely restrained India's grand strategic options. The Look East policy allowed India as such to transcend the existing political barriers between the Indian subcontinent and Southeast Asian region. As an added incentive ,a new economic grouping called BIMSTEC, was formed bringing together the five nations of the Subcontinent (Bangladesh, Bhutan, India, Nepal and Sri Lanka) together with two countries from Southeast Asia, Myanmar and Thailand, with the sole aim of promoting regional cooperation amongst them, helping both India and other SAARC countries to engage in economic cooperation in the subcontinent ,which they had been deprived of so far despite their collective need and recognized potential for rapid economic growth.

If we analyze the various new features that have come to mean definitive points in the Phase two of India's Look East policy, one easily sees that there is an an expansion in the larger geographical scope of this policy initiative — from that of the initial focus on merely the Southeast Asian region, it now included East Asia and South Pacific. The Phase two also came to be marked by an expanded definition of 'East', "stretching from Australia to China and East Asia with ASEAN as its core." With the new focused initiative, while

South Korea has emerged as a major economic partner of India; the economic ties with Japan came to receive added emphasis, and the Sino-Indian linkages, got more strengthened, over the last few years as with Australia and the South Pacific, which were recognized as potential trade areas which need to be pursued more vigorously.

Beginning from 1991, with exchange of several high level political visits, the policy showed initial success as ASEAN made India its Sectoral Dialogue Partner (SDP) in 1992. To begin with, both India and ASEAN focused on four areas, where the potential for cooperation was realized to be high, such as trade, investment, tourism and human resource development including science and technology. After Four years thereafter, ASEAN accepted India as its Full Dialogue Partner (FDP), together with China and Russia, after trade and investment relations showed impressive result from 1993 to 1995. Thereafter the regional body also invited India to join the ASEAN-drive Regional Forum, where annual review of issues relating to regional peace and security is undertaken.

The movement away from exclusive focus on economic issues in phases one to a broader agenda in phase two, involved security cooperation, including joint operations to protect sea lanes and pooling resources in the war against terrorism. The military contacts and joint exercises that existed between India and the ASEAN countries now had the possibility of getting expanded into full-fledged defence cooperation. With this India not only undertook initiatives to have regular access to ports in Southeast Asia, its defence ties now included countries like Japan, South Korea and China, with whom it had little contact on issues of defence and security. Never before in the history of India, one had seen it engaged in such multi-directional defence diplomacy in Asia.

In the phase two of India's Look East policy, the pursuit of physical connectivity to Southeast Asia received added importance. With the realization that the region is very much a part of India's extended neighbourhood, improved trade with Southeast Asia became the focal point. And as such establishment of air and land links to East and Southeast Asia has now become an integral part of the phase two of the policy. Immediately after the 1997 financial crisis, the Phase two of Look East Policy was launched and as such it focused upon building up 'arrangements for Free Trade Agreements (FTAs) and establishment of institutional linkages between the countries of the region and India. This second part is more significant as within the context of Look East Policy, India developed closer relations with CLMB countries (Cambodia, Laos, Myanmar and Brunei) by November 2000. It's seen that India's relations with the countries of Southeast Asia greatly got strengthened especially after President Clinton's visit to the region in 2000, which also had brought about dramatic improvement in the Indo-US ties. India also took the lead for the institution of the India-ASEAN Summit two years after, i.e., in 2004. In a significant move, India is now engaged actively in building transport corridors to the region, which inter alia, included the trilateral highway project involving Myanmar and Thailand and the proposed rail link between New Delhi and Hanoi, which is being hailed as a part of its new road diplomacy.

It is true that the Look East policy in phase two has the potential to enable India to break out of the political confines of the subcontinent, which had severely restrained India's grand strategic options. The Look East policy allowed India as such to transcend the existing political barriers between the Indian subcontinent and Southeast Asian region. As an added incentive ,a new economic grouping called BIMSTEC, got formed bringing together the five nations of the

Subcontinent (Bangladesh, Bhutan, India, Nepal and Sri Lanka) together with two countries from Southeast Asia, Myanmar and Thailand, with the sole aim of promoting regional cooperation amongst them, helping both India and other SAARC countries to engage in economic cooperation in the subcontinent ,which they had been deprived of so far despite their collective need and recognized potential for rapid economic growth.

The Look East Policy at the time of its launch had raised high hopes of fast economic development and alleviation of poverty amongst the people in the region because of the potentialities which were hidden behind such initiative. In this context, it was thought that with the gradual implementation of the Look East Policy, some of India's biggest challenges and the region's development obstacles, e.g., the outstanding political issues concerning insurgency and statehood, lack of political stability and high degree of unemployment in the region can be overcome. Therefore the major challenge that faces the policy makers and the political establishment today is how can India confront these challenges and realize the available opportunities of creating an environment congenial for infrastructure development and investments to enable the region to facilitate international trade and commerce between India and the ASEAN countries and which would no more downgrade the importance of the North-east as a development region and also combine the potential of the region along with the national support in the realization of India's Look East policy.

CHINA AND INDIA-SOUTH EAST ASIA RELATIONS

It has often been pointed out by analysts that India's Look East policy has been driven, at least in part, by some form of ineluctable rivalry with China. It has to be remembered that though competition between countries is a kind of reality, such competition also holds out the chance for collaboration when there is synergy in their relations. But the warmth that is seen in the relations between India and these ASEAN countries and their mutual eagerness for strengthening ties with India, though points out to the success of this policy in terms of its strategic achievements and economic returns yet is fraught with tensions as the success of India's diplomatic overtures has unnerved the other regional power active in the region and in the rest of the world. The growing strength of these has created some kind of an unease for China as it feels India's Look East diplomacy, is nothing more than that of an euphemism for a "contain China policy", and also as an attempt by the leadership of the United States to leverage it for its own strategic interests. Its believed the success of India forced China, what's called as 'String of Pearls', in the Indian Ocean, to checkmate India's growing influence over the ASEAN countries.

It has been held that India's Look East Policy, Phase Two is not driven by any fear of China nor India's desire to become a frontline state against it and that there exists scope for Sino –Indian cooperation, with the ASEAN negotiating free trade arrangements with China, Japan, South Korea and India. Yet New Delhi's completion of negotiation over the framework agreement on free trade between India and the ASEAN, within a year after, a successful milestone for Indian commercial diplomacy, was seen as a remarkable achievement. The setting up of a FTA with ASEAN has been commented as "attempts by India to counterbalance the increased Chinese influence within the association."[3] Bötscher Johanna, further argued that this situation merely supports the often held view that China and India are in competition with each other in Asia and also though China has been India's largest trading partner beginning from the year 2008, there has been no attempt for an India China Free Trade Agreement, for which China has been goading India, as it believes, "would result in the biggest free trade region in the world."[4]

India has always avoided any reference to China being the reason for deepening of ties with the ASEAN countries over trade and investment and has always rationalized it in terms of complementarities in their economic structure."The combination of our geographical proximity, economic complementarities and human resources create a huge potential, which needs to be optimally exploited."[4] Even in the Sixth Indian -ASEAN Summit, Prime Minister Manmohan Singh emphasized that "India was determined to take the FTA process forward, because we are convinced that it's a win-win situation for both of us"[5].

Even S.M.Krishna, India's External Affairs Minister, explicitly rejected the idea that the China factor may play an important role in Indian policies towards the ASEAN.he was quoted in Jakarta Post, "Under our Look East Policy, we have committed to developing relations with ASEAN .We have our own approach to ASEAN .This is now ay related to China."[6] It is said that "India does not want to explicitly admit that with its Look East Policy, it is following a counter-balancing strategy towards its northern neighbour."[7] One week before the conclusion of the FTA with ASEAN, PM Manmohan Singh pointed out that "India could not risk to be excluded from free trade with ASEAN because it would surrender significant benefits to those countries that already have an FTA with the association. He further said India could not be seen to be lagging behind."[8] The Indian Ambassador to Thailand, Pinak raja Chakravarty ,while addressing a seminar held forth, "The process of integration that is undertaken through FTA is not just economic,[9] but is closely tied to the shape the evolving regional security architecture may take in the future. "

INDIA ASEAN RELATIONS AND CHINA

It's well known that the ASEAN states regard China more as a threat than a potential partner. Firstly, the ASEAN states were concerned mainly with political and military threats from the north.[10] Indeed, this was also one of the primary reasons for the formation of ASEAN in 1967, i.e., to counter the spread of communism in the region.[11] With China's emergence as one of the most competitive producers of many products in the world, ASEAN started to perceive China more as an economic threat. Due to the remarkable similarity in their industrial structures: both specializing in labor-intensive products and both concentrating on the US, EU and Japan as their major exporting markets.[12] Forging Closer ASEAN-China Economic Relations in The Twenty-First Century, A Report Submitted by the

The ASEAN countries believed that China could increase its exports during the last two decades of the twentieth century only at the expense of its neighbors in Southeast Asia. With China becoming a major exporter, the ASEAN countries who were China's neighbors to its south came to be deprived of FDI, as the investors felt with wage levels in China so much low, to invest in China rather than the ASEAN countries.

China doesn't want to miss any opportunity to seize the leadership role in Asia, hence it has locked its horns with India, it realizes that it would be quite some time before China could challenge the military dominance of the US in Asian region. Hence China has to pursue the strategy of achieving economic integration with the ASEAN and other economies in Asia, for achieving its political strategy through economic means.

With improvement of India United States relations and the consequent signing of India US strategic Partnership, China feels that some kind of axis is in operation in the region and it may be targeted by them in the near future. But if India has to address its domestic concerns and particularly in the development of India's northeastern states and the need for curbing insurgency activities along the border with Myanmar, a close Chinese ally, India needs to develop a strategy to build an international environment conducive to the goal of China's peaceful rise rather than to be perceived by it, to have a possible role in a US led containment of China, which will be to our peril.

"We see our partnership with ASEAN not merely as a reaffirmation of ties with neighbouring countries or as an instrument of economic development, but also as an integral part of our vision of a stable, secure and prosperous Asia and its surrounding Indian Ocean and Pacific regions."[13]

"While each one of us has a unique and rich heritage, there are abiding linkages of culture and custom, of art and religion and of civilization, all of which create a sense of unity in the diversity and pluralism in our region. In addition, given that together we constitute a community of 1.8 billion people, representing one-fourth of humanity, with a combined GDP of 3.8 trillion U.S. dollars, it is only natural that India should attach the highest priority to its relationship with ASEAN."[14]

"In addition, given that together we constitute a community of 1.8 billion people, representing one-fourth of humanity, with a combined GDP of 3.8 trillion U.S. dollars, it is only natural that India should attach the highest priority to its relationship with ASEAN.

We see our partnership with ASEAN not merely as a reaffirmation of ties with neighbouring countries or as an instrument of economic development, but also as an integral part of our vision of a stable, secure and prosperous Asia and its surrounding Indian Ocean and Pacific regions."[15]

REFERENCES

1 William H. Overholt, *Asia, America, and the Transformation of Geopolitics*, Published by Cambridge University Press. 2008

2 http//www.meaindia.nic.in/ speech/2003/9/harvardlecture29ss01.htm,accessed on 15th March 2013

3 Bötscher Johanna, A Neorealist Assessment of India S Look East Policy, Published by GRIN Verlag,2011,pp70

4 Prime Minister A B Vajpai's interview reported in Financial Times,October9th 2003

5 Prime Minister Manmohan Singh's speech at Sixth Indian-ASEAN Summit Meeting held in Singapore,21st November 2007

6 Jakarta Post,22nd January,2010

7 Anindya Batabyal, "Balancing China in Asia, A Realist. Assessment of India's Look East Strategy," China Report 42, no. 2 ,2006

8 IPS,August 8th 2009

9 Bangkok Post ,august 16th,2010

10 The Three Ages of ASEAN, Lecture delivered by Rodolfo C. Severino, Secretary-General of ASEAN at the ARCO Forum of Public Affairs, Kennedy School of Government, Harvard University, 3 October 2002, available at http://www.aseansec.org/12310.htm.,accessed on 15th March 2013

11 Ibid

12 Forging Closer ASEAN-China Economic Relations in The Twenty-First Century, A Report Submitted by the ASEAN-China Expert Group on Economic Cooperation, October 2001, at p.15, available at http://www.aseansec.org/newdata/asean_chi.pdf.,accessed on 15 March 2013

13 PM Man Mohan Singh's opening statement at Plenary Session of India-ASEAN Commemorative Summit, http://pmindia.nic.in/speech-details.php?nodeid=1259, accessed on 10th April 2013

14 Ibid

15 Ibid

REFERENCES:

Sanjib Baruah (2004), 'Between South and Southeast Asia Northeast India and Look East Policy', Ceniseas Paper 4, Guwahati.

India (2004), *Economic Survey*, Delhi.

India (1997), Transforming the North East, High Level Committee Report, Planning Commission, New Delhi.

Sushil Khanna (2002), 'Trade and Investment in South Asia Sub Region: Barriers and Opportunities', IIM Calcutta, mimeo.

NCAER (2004), *East India: Human Development Report*, New Delhi, OUP.

B.G. Verghese (2001), 'Unfinished Business in the Northeast: Pointers Towards Restructuring, Reconciliation and Resurgence', Seventh Kamal Kumari Memorial Lecture, http://www.freeindiamedia.com/economy/19_june_economy.htm

John Walley (1996), 'Why Do Countries Seek Regional Trade Arrangements', NBER Working Paper 5552, Washington.

World Bank (2001), *Forging Subregional Links in Transportation and Logistics in South Asia*, Washington.

SECTION-III :
INDIA AND THE MUSLIM WORLD

12

India's Relationship with West Asia

Prasanta Kumar Pradhan

The relationship between India and the countries of West Asia are historic and both have enjoyed warm ties since a very long time. India's relationship with the region has gone through many ups and downs at different periods of history. Immediately after the independence, India supported the Palestinian cause and built up strong ties with the socialist regimes like Egypt, Syria and Iraq. India's strong support for the Palestinian cause did not allow a strong India-Israel relationship. At the same time, India's relationship with the Gulf monarchies suffered as they remained allied to the West and India remained non-aligned. It is only in the beginning of the 1990s that India built up diplomatic ties with Israel and the relationship with the Gulf countries has strengthened significantly. India's strong democratic roots, growing economy, rising international stature are some of the reasons which draw the countries of the region towards it. As a result India's engagements with the region is becoming steady and stronger day by day.

India has several interests in the region. The region is the primary source of India's energy needs. India's trade with the region is growing rapidly with countries like Saudi Arabia and UAE among the top five trade partners for India. There are around 6.5 million Indians living in the region. India's security is closely linked to the security of the India's 'extended neighbourhood'- the Gulf region. The threats of terrorism and piracy are important issues which need cooperation and collaboration with the countries of the region.

The region remains politically divided over several issues among themselves and it poses several challenges for India to pursue its interests in the region. At present there are three major players in the region: the Saudi Arabia led Gulf Cooperation Council (GCC), Iran and Israel. Unfortunately, none of them enjoy cordial relationship among themselves for several reasons. Thus, India's relationship with one does not go well with another. India has interests with all the countries. Thus it becomes important for India to calibrate its policies carefully. The emergence of protests in the Arab streets against their rulers known as the 'Arab Spring' has further complicated the political situation of the region and has added to the existing uncertainty. While the region continues to boil amidst regime changes and continuing protests, India is watching the developments carefully.

INDIA AND THE GCC

The relationship between India and the Gulf Cooperation Council[1] (GCC) has grown since the formation of the organisation in 1981. For India, its relationship with the GCC represents its varied interests in the economic, strategic and political fields. In recent times, both India and the GCC have been looking for new areas of cooperation and are trying to improve their relationship. Although there have been a number of irritants, the interests of both the parties have kept the relationship going at a steady pace.[2]

India's relationship with the Gulf countries has been based on mutual trade and business, and this continues to grow. Gulf region has been a lucrative market for Indian manufactured goods like textiles, spices, food products, and lately, electrical goods and machineries, and information technology products. At present, according to the Department of Commerce, Government of India, India's total bilateral trade with the GCC is US$ 145 billion. The growth in trade can be gauzed from the fact that the total trade with the GCC has gone up from US$ 5.55 billion in 2000-01 to over US $ 145 billion in 2011-12.[3]

As part of the efforts to further enhance bilateral economic ties the first GCC–India Industrial Conference was held in Mumbai in February 2004, which was attended by the then GCC Secretary General Abdulrahman bin Hamad Al Attiyah and industry ministers of all the GCC countries. The leaders discussed ways and means to promote economic cooperation between India and the GCC. The conference focused on trade, investment, industrial and technological cooperation and issued a 'Mumbai Declaration'.[4] In August 2004, India and the GCC signed a framework Agreement on Economic Cooperation. Later, in November of the same year, a three-member GCC negotiating team visited India and held discussions on a broad range of issues, including the possibility of initiating negotiations towards a free trade agreement (FTA) and non-tariff barriers affecting Indian exports to the region.[5] The second conference was held in Oman in March 2006. The third conference in May 2007 decided to facilitate and expedite projects in the field of agriculture and food processing, which was identified as a new sector with significant opportunities for trade and investment. The GCC states agreed to receive and facilitate the visits of Indian agro-processing companies, and India was to reciprocate.[66] Press release, Department of Commerce, Ministry of Commerce and Industry, Government of India, May 30, 2007, available at http://commerce.nic.in/pressrelease/pressrelease_detail.asp?

Both India and the GCC countries are keeping close watch on the developments and making endeavours to further their trade by establishing joint bilateral commissions. At present, India has such bilateral arrangements with all the GCC countries. Figures indicate that in recent years, India's bilateral trade with the GCC countries has been increasing at a faster rate than the rest of the countries such as Iran, Iraq and Yemen.

The GCC countries are an important source of India's energy needs which is important for the growth of Indian economy. Among the GCC countries, Saudi Arabia is the top supplier of oil to India supplying 30.41 MMT in 2011-12, followed Kuwait, (17.91 MMT) and UAE (14.36 MMT).[7] Similarly, Qatar is the largest exporter of natural gas to India supplying 13.3 billion cubic metre of liquefied natural gas in 2011.[8]

Further, about six million strong Indian community constitute the largest expatriate workforce in the GCC countries. They constitute a natural link between India and the region. Indian workers are generally preferred over others because they are considered to be hard working, sincere, efficient, low paid and law abiding.[9] India also benefits from the foreign exchange received from such migrant workers who send a good amount of their earnings to their families back home. Remittances received from them constitute a significant portion of India's foreign exchange receipts. According to the World Bank statistics, in 2012, India received US$ 29.69 billion as remittances from the GCC countries. The amount constitutes 47 percent of the total remittances to India, out of the US$ 63 billion received from all over the world in the same year.[10]

But robustness of trade and business has not been reflected in the political field between India and the GCC as the political relationship has not been so warm. It is only in the recent years that some understanding at the political level has been arrived by both sides. It is important for India and the GCC countries as well to achieve political understanding between them. Such an understanding would be fruitful not only to further their economic interaction but also in the security and strategic fields. Issues such as terrorism, piracy, money laundering, criminal activities, illegal supply of arms etc are some of the critical issues that affect both India and the GCC countries. Dealing with these important issues requires the active cooperation both for which understanding and trust is necessary.

Saudi Arabia is the largest and most powerful country in the GCC. India has been trying to strengthen its relationship with Saudi Arabia; and the kingdom has also been reciprocating. King Abdullah's visit to India in 2006 as the chief guest at the Republic Day celebrations is important for many reasons. King Abdullah is only the second Saudi king to visit India after King Saud in 1955. Apart from signing the Delhi Declaration and some other bilateral agreements, the visit was important as it seems to have given a fresh start to the relationship. As per the Delhi Declaration, both sides agreed to strengthen ties by deepening cooperation in energy, trade, science and technology, education and health, and political cooperation to promote regional and international peace. A number of ministerial visits from both sides have followed the king's visit. In February–March 2010, Manmohan Singh visited Riyadh, reviewed the implementation of the Delhi Declaration with King Abdullah and further consolidated ties by signing the Riyadh Declaration. In the Riyadh Declaration, the two leaders condemned terrorism and extremism, agreed to enhance cooperation for the exchange of information relating to terrorist activities, money laundering, narcotics, arms and human trafficking, and to develop joint strategies for combating these threats. They lauded the existing cooperation in defence fields and agreed to further strengthen this cooperation to realise their common interests. Both leaders also agreed to develop a broad-based economic partnership for developing infrastructure, energy and for enhancing bilateral trade. The Riyadh Declaration has been termed 'a new era of strategic partnership' by both countries. Manmohan Singh urged Saudi Arabia to forge a comprehensive energy partnership with India. The Saudi side assured the Indian prime minister of the Kingdom's desire and readiness to provide India with its present and future oil needs. Undoubtedly, the two high-level visits have given a boost to the relationship and have helped in laying a solid foundation for the future. However, it is necessary to keep the momentum going and to continue working on issues that benefit both countries.[11]

The Gulf countries expect India to play an active role in the region and join the Gulf security architecture to ward off any threat to them. India, on the other hand, does not have the required resources nor the political will to undertake such activities in the region. To play such an active role India needs to completely restructure its foreign policy towards the Gulf region. India, clearly, is very well aware of its own limitations before it would venture into the Gulf. For India, its 'extended neighbourhood' is a region where it can rely on increasing economic activities, get the necessary support for dealing with terrorism, piracy and other security related issues and receive active political and diplomatic support in the international forums. On its part, India is also ready to cooperate with the Gulf countries over all these issues. But it seems, at present, India is unprepared to move beyond and play any kind of a mediatory role in the region or join the regional security architecture. Playing any proactive role in the region must be followed by establishment of strong ties characterised by a convincing political understanding and strategic partnership. Otherwise it will result in rejection and unnecessary political backlash which would be detrimental for the relationship.

INDIA AND IRAN

Despite the historical and civilisational ties, India-Iran relationship has not been a solid one. Though both the countries are important players in their respective regions, several political and strategic issues have not allowed the relationship to strengthen. In the recent times, the relationship has been eroded since the emergence of Iranian nuclear controversy. The nuclear issue came up when both the countries were coming closer to each other with a couple of high level bilateral visits and signing of a defence cooperation agreement in 2001. The visit of former Prime Minister Atal Bihari Vajpayee's visit in 2001 to Iran gave a boost to the Indo-Iranian bilateral ties in the recent times. Also, the visit of former Iranian President Mohammad Khatami in 2003 gave a further impetus to the India-Iran relations. But the bonhomie could not continue for long and the controversy over the Iranian nuclear issue emerged as a hurdle in the way. The relationship has been affected as India has voted against Iran at the International Atomic Energy Agency (IAEA). India has also asked Iran to clarify doubts about its suspected nuclear programme while supporting Iran's right under the nuclear Non Proliferation Treaty (NPT) to use nuclear energy for peaceful purposes. On its part, Iran is of the view that India has come under the pressure of the USA, Europe and the GCC and has compromised its independent foreign policy and affected its relationship with Iran. The misunderstanding that has crept into the relationship over the nuclear issue has been reflected in the irregular high level visits between the two countries. Though interactions at the ministerial level continue, top level visits have been affected. Iranian President Mahmoud Ahmadinejad visited India in 2008 while Prime Minister Manmohan Singh visited Iran in 2012 to attend the 16th Nonaligned Movement (NAM) summit in Tehran.

Though political and diplomatic ties between India and Iran have suffered because of the regional and international political dynamics, relations in the economic front have been positive and healthy. Iran is an important source of energy for India. At present Iran is the third largest exporter of oil to India. Indian oil import from Iran has suffered in recent times because of the payment problems to which Iran alleges that India has come under the pressure of the USA and the EU to cut oil imports so as to further tighten the sanctions on Iran. The bilateral total trade between India and Iran, at present, stands at US$ 15.9 billion.[12]

Apart from the trade and economic ties, Iran is a strategically important country for India. India looks at Iran as a connecting route to Central Asia. India is also helping Iran to build the Chabahar port which will further strengthen connectivity which would help India to connect with Afghanistan. Thus for several important reasons, Iran is an important country for India and thus India should carefully calibrate its policies while dealing with Iran.

INDIA AND ISRAEL

In the years following India's independence, India-Israel ties could not strengthen because of India's unwavering support for the Palestinian cause. Also, the changing international political situation, the Cold War and the domestic political compulsions were some other important factors which did not allow India-Israel relationship to normalise.[13] India-Israel relations began to take root with the establishment of full diplomatic relations in 1992. Since then the relationship has been moving in an upward direction. Both countries have found mutual interests with each other and there is some convergence of interests between the two. The threat and challenge of Islamic terrorism has played an important role in bringing both countries together.

Economy, agriculture, science and technology, and defence are among the key sectors where cooperation between the two countries is increasing. The bilateral total trade between the two countries in the year 2012-13 is US$ 6 billion.[14] The bilateral trade is getting diversified and both the countries are negotiating for a Free Trade Agreement. Around two-thirds of the total Israeli exports to India are hi-tech products.[15]

Israel has been a major source of arms for India. Living in a hostile neighbourhood, India has looked for arms to deal with countries like Pakistan and China. Israel has been, since 1992, a reliable partner for India. In a span of two decades Israel has emerged as an important defence partner for India. The approximate total value of the weapons supplied by Israel to India over the past decade is estimated at around $10 billion.[16] In the near future, it seems highly likely that India would continue to engage Israel for weapons.

Apart from cooperation in defence field, joining hands to fight terrorism is a mutual area of interest for both India and Israel. Both the countries face the threat of Islamic terrorism emanating from their respective neighbourhood. While India faces such threats from Pakistan, Israel faces countries such as Syria and Iran who it alleges as supporting various terrorist groups targeting Israel. The common threat of terrorism has drawn both the countries closer. This has led to cooperation in the fields of intelligence sharing on terrorist groups. Israel is also providing crucial logistical support to India to deal with terrorism.[17]

Also there are a number of areas where both the countries have agreed to cooperate such as telecommunication, agriculture, space, information technology and so on.

INDIA'S BALANCING ACT

As reflected in the above sections that India has huge interests with all the three major players in the region. All the regional players also acknowledge India as an emerging power with a strong economy and an established democracy in the world. The nature of regional politics in West Asia is such that there exist deep rivalries among themselves. For instance, in the Gulf region, Saudi Arabia and Iran have deep political, ideological and strategic rivalries. None of these two countries recognise Israel; and Iran-Israel relationship, in particular, has touched a new low since the last decade. In such a situation in becomes difficult for India to pursue its interests in the region. India's strong ties with one do not go well with others. For instance, both Saudi Arabia and Iran accuse India of softening its stand Palestine issue since India developed ties with Israel. They take special note of India-Israel arms trade in particular. Though India has reiterated its undiluted support for the Palestinians, they remain somehow unconvinced.

Thus, India needs to tread carefully in the region as present interests are huge and there lies even more long term opportunities for the future. Saudi Arabia and other GCC countries are important for India for its energy security, trade, presence of India community; Israel is an important source of weapons for India along with growing trade and cooperation in science and technology; and Iran is a major source of India's energy, an important trade partner and geo-strategically important in the region. the principal challenge for India is to craft an approach to maintain equilibrium between the technology-cum-strategic relationship between all the major powers of the region.[18] Thus, it becomes imperative for India to deal with all the three major regional players.

INDIA AND ARAB SPRING

The emergence of the protests in the Arab streets against their rulers, known as the 'Arab Spring', has brought significant changes in to the political and strategic horizon of the region. The protests have removed long serving authoritarian leaders like Ben Ali of Tunisia, Hosni Mubarak of Egypt, Ali Abdullah Saleh of Yemen and Muhammad Gaddafi of Libya were thrown out of power. The situation in Syria continues to deteriorate day by day in the fight between the regime's forces and opposition. It reported that more than 100,000 people have been killed and large number of people are displaced. Besides, popular protests were also held in the countries like Bahrain, Saudi Arabia, Jordan, Morocco, Iraq etc. This led to changes in the enormous political changes in the region.

The sudden change in the political scenario in the region with popular protests and regime changes has led to shift in the regional balance of power in the volatile West Asian region. India has a number of vital interests in the region such as energy security, trade and commerce, safety of the India community living in the region and so on. Any change in the political and security situation in the region will impact India's interests. In the region, India's interactions are mostly concentrated in the Gulf region. Bahrain was the only country which witnessed somewhat serious protests than other Gulf neighbours. But the protests in Bahrain were quelled with the help of the Saudi and UAE forces who entered Bahrain under the umbrella of the Peninsula Shield Force. Thus, India's interests were not that seriously affected as the situation in the Gulf region was effectively controlled by the authorities. But, still there are a number of in which

India has been affected by the changing situation.

Firstly, like all other oil importing countries of the world, India has been affected by the immediate rise in oil prices that followed the protests. India is a major importer of oil from the Gulf region which caters around two-thirds of India's energy requirements. Thus, the rise of oil prices has impacted the Indian economy as it is largely dependent on the oil imports.

Secondly, the protests have implications for the Indians who are working in the region. The countries of the Gulf region have adopted nationalisation programmes intended to absorb their own educated youths in the job market in order to reduce dissatisfaction among them. Saudi Arabia has begun its *Nitaqat* programme in order to clean up the illegal foreign workers. Other GCC countries are also mulling over the idea of nationalising their work forces. If such programmes are taken up seriously then it will also affect the Indians who are currently working in those countries. Though till now the situation is not that critical, a nervousness is definitely present there.

Thirdly, the protests have raised the important issue of safety of the Indians living in the region. For India, it will be a herculean task to evacuate its citizens and bring them back to India or move them to any other safer place. India had to move immediately to evacuate its citizens from countries like Libya and Egypt where comparatively less number of Indians work and live. For any such task to be undertaken in the Gulf region will require huge manpower and material support.

Fourthly, the situation has created a prolonged political uncertainty and heightened tension in the volatile region. Tensions between Iran and Saudi Arabia has further worsened echoing the fears of a protracted Shia-Sunni conflict in the wider west Asian region. The situation still continues to unfold and tension continue in several parts of the region. The overthrow of Mohammed Morsi by the Army in Egypt is a case in point which shows that the situation is still not stable even after the Mubarak regime is overthrown. Thus, in such a fluid situation it becomes difficult for India to pursue its national interests. The fluid situation proves to be more testing for India's foreign policy in the region.

CONCLUSION

India's growing interests and rising regional and global profile call for strengthening ties with the region. For this India needs to engage deeply with the countries of the region. This would mean adding further political and strategic content in to the already vibrant trade and business ties. There is a need for exchange of bilateral high level visits and engaging the countries in deeper security cooperation. Though several challenges remain on the way, India's interests in the Gulf and the common bilateral issues of concern between India and the region is an opportunity for both to further cooperation.

It is in India's interest to engage with the region politically and diplomatically. In the world scenario, India desires to be a major world power and, therefore, it needs to engage its extended neighbourhood more productively. Active support from these neighbours will not only provide India the much-needed political and diplomatic standing, but will also contribute to improve India's image in rest of the Muslim world. Building a cordial relationship with the region will be a very useful platform to begin that process.

The region is going through a difficult phase of change and transformation. The Arab Spring has brought to the fore the vulnerabilities of the Arab Gulf monarchies. Iran is in the midst of its nuclear controversy which does not look like being resolved anytime in the near future. Iraq is facing several challenges internally and making efforts to keep the internal security situation under control. There is growing uncertainty in Egypt after Mohamed Morsi has been overthrown by the Army. Similarly, the situation in Syria is becoming worse day by day. Yemen is going through the transition process with the threat of secession. Thus, the region is going through such a churning at a time when India's interests there are increasing rapidly.

India, undoubtedly, is concerned about the situation unfolding in the region, but it has chosen to remain non-intervening. India, understandably, is playing very cautiously in the region as it does not want to spoil the political and diplomatic capital it has accumulated in the region over several decades of engagement. India, on its part, does not want to be seen as a big neighbouring country exercising power in the region. Rather India views West Asia as a region where it can establish friendly ties with the countries, seek their cooperation on mutual issues of concern, which would give boost to its own economic and political clout in the region and beyond.

REFERENCES

1 The Gulf Cooperation Council consists of six Arab Gulf countries – Bahrain, Kuwait, Oman, Qatar, Saudi Arabia and UAE.

2 See Prasanta Kumar Pradhan, "India and Gulf Cooperation Council: Time to Look Beyond Business", *Strategic Analysis*, Vol. 34, No. 3, 2010, pp. 409-419.

3 Export-Import Data Bank, Department of Commerce, Ministry of Commerce and Industry, Government of India.

4 Ministry of External Affairs, Government of India, at http://meaindia.nic.in/onmouse/gcc1.pdf

5 Ibid.

6 Press release, Department of Commerce, Ministry of Commerce and Industry, Government of India, May 30, 2007, available at http://commerce.nic.in/pressrelease/pressrelease_detail.asp?id=2062

7 Export-Import Data Bank, Department of Commerce, Ministry of Commerce and Industry, Government of India.

8 BP Statistical Review of World Energy, June 2012.

9 Prakash C. Jain, "An 'Incipient' Diaspora: Indians in the Gulf Region", in Prakash C. Jain (ed.), *Indian Diaspora in West Asia: A Reader*, Manohar Publishers, New Delhi, 2007, pp. 198–199.

10 "Gulf remittances 2012: Which countries sent money where?", *Arabian Business*, 13 May, 2013, available at http://www.arabianbusiness.com/photos/gulf-remittances-2012-which-countries-sent-money-where—501228.html?img=2, accessed on 20 May 2013.

11 For a discussion on India-Saudi Arabia relationship see Prasanta Kumar Pradhan, "India's Relationship with Saudi Arabia: Forging a Strategic Partnership", *Strategic Analysis*, Vol. 37, No. 2, 2013, pp. 231-241.

12 Export-Import data Bank, Department of Commerce, Ministry of Commerce and Industry, Government of India.

13 P. R. Kumaraswamy, *India's Israel Policy*, Magnum Books Pvt. Ltd., New Delhi, 2010, p.183.

14 Export-Import data Bank, Department of Commerce, Ministry of Commerce and Industry, Government of India.

15 "India, Israel negotiating FTA", *The Hindu*, July 24, 2013.

16 Efraim Inbar and Alvite Singh Ningthoujam, "Indo-Israeli Defence Cooperation in the Twenty-First Century", Mideast Security and Policy Studies No. 93, The Begin-Sadat Centre for Strategic Studies, Bar-Ilan University, Ramat Gan, Israel, January 2012, p. 6.

17 Harsh V. Pant, *Contemporary Debates in Indian Foreign and Security Policy, India Negotiates its Rise in the International System*, Palgrave Macmillan, New York, 2008, p. 135.

18 Hamid Ansari, "West Asia: The Imperative to Comprehend the Directions of Change" in Rajendra M. Abhyankar (ed.) *West Asia and the Region*, Academic Foundation, New Delhi, 2008, p.76.

13

India-Iran Economic and Trade Relations: Prospects and Challenges

M Mahtab Alam Rizvi

INTRODUCTION

In a bid to overcome challenges posed by the United States (US) and the European Union (EU) in the form of economic sanctions against Tehran, India has been exploring for ways to increase economic and trade relations with Iran. The recent visit of Indian External Affairs Minister, Salman Khurshid to Iran has once again brought to focus India's changing role in the West Asian region where it has important stakes. The recent visit indicate that India is committed to maintain strong economic and trade ties with Iran. Both countries are also committed for joint exploration and joint investment in infrastructure to enhance bilateral trade. Recently India also agreed to participate in the upgradation of the Chabahar port and invest around US $100 million[1] in the project in the initial stage.

Trade relations between India and Iran have witnessed a significant increase during the last decade, with India's total trade with Iran growing from US$ 1.185 billion in 2003-04 to US$ 14.95 billion in 2012-13.[2] This buoyant trend has been maintained by both growth in India's exports to and imports from Iran. The exports to Iran have increased from US$ 918.11 million in 2003-04 to US$ 3.35 billion in 2012-13. India's imports to Iran have also increased as well. In 2003-04, India's import from Iran was 266.82 million only however, it increased by 11.6 billion in 2012-13[3] due to huge oil imports by India from Iran. Though, the trade balance is in favour of Iran due to huge oil imports by India from the Islamic Republic. In order to correct this imbalance the focus of India's trade with Iran needs to be shifted to investment and joint ventures. India should also focus on enhancing trade in commodities, manufacturing as well as in services. However, despite huge growth in bilateral trade between India and Iran, the total trade has been declining in recent year. One of the reasons in declining of total trade between the two countries is the US and the EU economic sanctions against Iran (reflected in table below). According to ministry of commerce (Government of India) Iran is India's eighteenth largest trading partner, with a share of 1.89 per cent of India's total trade in 2012-13. During the year 2011-12 growth rate of bilateral trade was 28 per cent between the two countries.[4] In light of current development it is argued that the time is ideal for upgrading the India-Iran trade relationship substantially in the coming years based on shared complementarities and improved political ties. In this context, this chapter explores the contours and prospects for improving trade relations between India and Iran.

India-Iran Bilateral Trade

(Figures in US $ Million)

	2008-09	2009-10	2010-11	2011-12	2012-13
India's Exports to Iran	2,534.01	1,853.17	2,492.90	2,411.33	3,351.07
India's Imports from Iran	12,376.77	11,540.85	10,928.21	13,556.71	11,603.79
Total Trade	14,910.78	13,394.01	13,421.12	15,968.03	14,954.86
% Growth		-10.17	0.20	18.98	-6.35

(*Source:* Government of India, Ministry of Commerce & Industry)

BACKGROUND

Iran's economy is based on oil, which provides the majority of government revenues of around 80 per cent. Price controls, subsidies, and other rigidities weigh down grade the economy, undermining the capability for private-sector-led growth. Private sector activity is only confined to small-scale workshops, farming, and services. However, in December 2010, president, Mahmoud Ahmadinejad implemented a law (after approval of the parliament) known as Targeted Subsidies Law (TSL) to reduce state subsidies on food and energy. This was the significant economic reform since the government implemented gasoline rationing in 2007. Over a five-year period the bill will phase out subsidies that previously cost Tehran US$ 60-$ 100 billion annually[5] and mainly helped Iran's upper and middle classes. Due to expansionary fiscal and monetary policies, government mismanagement, the US and the EU sanctions, and a depreciating currency are fueling inflation, and GDP growth remains stagnant. Iran also continues to experience from double-digit unemployment and underemployment. Even in recently held presidential election, June 14, 2013, the main agendas of the all presidential candidates including Hassan Rohani (who won the presidential race) were high inflation rate and growing unemployment. The official inflation rate of the country hit 32.6 per cent in June 2013.[6]

India's economic and trade relations with Iran are not new, it's started from civilization period. The Indus people, and their ancestors, had trade links with Iran. India imported silver, copper, turquoise and lapis lazuli from Persia in return for ivory. India exported spices such as black pepper to Iran. The grape, introduced from Persia with the almond and walnut, was cultivated in the Hindukush and western Himalayas. Bam, in south-east Iran, was a major commercial and trading town on the well-known Spice Road, a major tributary of the Silk Road that connected trade routes from India through Iran to Central Asia and China.

JOINT MECHANISM TO BOOST BILATERAL TRADE

India and Iran which enjoy civilisational and cultural linkages are trying to strengthen their relations in various sectors including economic, trade and energy. Business delegations have played a significant role in consolidating business ties between the two countries. Recently in May 2012, an Iranian delegation visited India and signed agreements to purchase shipment of rice, sugar and soyabean from India. Both countries also agreed to strengthen their annual trade to US$ 24 billion in the medium term from US$ 16 billion now.

One of the means by which both countries are enhancing their bilateral trade is the Joint Business Council (JBC), set up by the Indian Chambers of Commerce and Industry and the Iran Chamber of Commerce, Industries, and Mines.[7] Both India and Iran hold Joint Business Council meetings regularly. The 10th meeting of the JBC was organized by the Federation of Indian Chambers of Commerce & Industry (FICCI) in New Delhi on November 13, 2009. Iran Chamber of Commerce, Industry & Mines president Mohammad A Nahavandian told during meeting with Indian delegation that the time was ripe "to move away from oil to the non-oil sectors such as agricultural machinery, food processing, pharmaceuticals, auto and auto components, telecommunications, mining, physical infrastructure, IT & ITeS and biotechnology. This is also the time to move from just trade to cooperation in investment and R&D by pooling our assets for the common good of the people of Iran and India."[8] He also proposed to elevate the JBC into a Joint Business Chamber which could be mandated to draw up an action plan to upgrade business relations.

Another means of interaction between India and Iran in economic and trade sectors, is Joint Commission Meeting (JCM). The JCM meeting also helps to remove barriers in the two-way trade and facilitate the flow of investments. The JCM is a forum to review bilateral economic and cultural co-operation between the two countries. Both countries hold regular bilateral talks on economic and trade relations at the JCM Meeting. The 16th JCM was held in New Delhi on July 8-9, 2010. A 30-member delegation of Iran led by Shamseddin Hosseini participated in the meeting. The meeting was co-chaired on the Iranian side by Seyed Shamseddin Hosseini, Minister of Economic Affairs and Finance, of Iran and on the Indian side by the then External Affairs Minister S.M. Krishna. The following MoUs/Agreements were signed during the JCM Meeting:

(i) Air Services Agreement; (ii) Agreement on Transfer of Sentenced Persons; (iii) MoU on Cooperation in New & Renewable Energy; (iv) MoU on Cooperation in Small Scale Industry between National Small Industries Corporation (NSIC) and Iranian Small Industries and Industrial Parks Organisation (ISIPO); (v) Programme of Cooperation on Science & Technology and (vi) MoU on Cooperation between Central Pulp and Paper Research Institute of India (CPPRI) and Gorgan University of Agricultural Science and Natural Resources (GUASNR).[9]

The 17th Joint Commission meeting was held in Tehran on May 4, 2013. The meeting was co-chaired by Iran's foreign minister, Ali Akbar Salehi and Indian External Affairs minister, Salman Khurshid. The meeting was aimed at expanding bilateral ties and mutual co-operation between the two countries. The two sides also agreed to work on a trilateral transit agreement involving India, Iran and Afghanistan.[10] At the meeting the two sides reviewed the progress on the proposed International North-South Transport Corridor (INSTC) which will link Russia with Iran. The JCM was set up in 1983.

However, despite strong historical and cultural linkages between India and Iran, India does not figure in the list of Iran's top trade partners. It has been observed by the two sides that the level of trade was not reflective of the close relations between the two countries and should be strengthened. In this regard, agriculture and pharma products and aeronautics were among the areas identified where cooperation could be enhanced. At the meeting the two sides also observed the importance of enhancing cooperation in expanding trade and banking relations and agreed to study the prospects of joint investment in both countries. Both countries are also agreed to diversify their cooperation in this regard. It's worth to mention here that Iran is a radiant and vibrant market and India look forward to larger engagement by the Indian corporate in various sectors apart from oil and gas. However, recent economic and trade data indicates that India and Iran trade are increasing day to day.

India and Iran are making robust efforts to renew and strengthen the bilateral economic and trade relations. The relationship between the two countries has evolved into a significant partnership in the economic and commercial sphere. At the same time, Indians have emerged as important investors in the Iran, and India as an important export destination for the Iran manufactured goods.[11]

TOP ITEMS OF EXPORTS FROM INDIA

India's exports to Iran have increased by 40 percent over the past year and expected to increase further. India's exports to Iran include petroleum products, rice, cereals, machine tools, automobile parts, steel, metals, primary and semi finished iron, drugs/pharmaceuticals & fine chemicals, processed minerals, manmade yarn & fabrics, tea, organic/ inorganic/agro chemicals, rubber manufactured products, etc.[12]

Rice and textile exports have witnessed the biggest jump. Indian officials hope that a liberalized visa policy for businessmen from both sides is implemented soon and it will enhance the exports. Indian exporters are now allowed to re-export goods to Iran. They only need to add 15 per cent to the value of these goods.[13] During 2001-2010, India's exports to Iran have risen around to ten-fold, from US$ 253.3 million in 2001 to US$ 2.5 billion in 2010. The main reason of India's exports to Iran increased during this period was; rise in exports of inorganic chemicals, cereals, iron and steel and articles of iron or steel to Iran. India's exports basket to Iran is dominated by inorganic chemicals, articles of iron or steel and cereals, with these three items accounting for a significant 50.6 per cent of India's total exports to Iran in 2010.[14]

Recently, the head of the Federation of Indian Export Organizations, Rafeeque Ahmed said that the latest measures to liberalize trade with Iran will result in sizeable growth in exports this year. India's exports amounted to less than US$ 3 billion last year, while its oil imports totaled about US$ 11 billion. India presently exports mostly agricultural products such as rice. Ahmed says it now hopes to diversify into new areas such as textiles, machinery and consumer goods. Ahmed also stated "We feel that certain chemicals, automobile parts, some light engineering items, and home needs can exports to Iran." He added "With this facility they can set up projects... And there are companies in India which are capable of it, but they had to import certain parts from outside. That can be done now."[15]

TOP ITEMS OF IMPORTS BY INDIA

India's imports from Iran include crude oil, urea, Petroleum products, Saffron, Dry Fruits. India's imports from Iran is dominated by crude oil. In 2010, Iran was the third largest source of imports of mineral fuels for India, accounting for 8.2 per cent of India's total imports of mineral fuels. In 2012 Iran was also second largest supplier of crude oil to India. However, due to the US and EU sanctions, Iran position is replaced by Iraq. Iran is also a major source for India's imports of plastics and articles thereof, as well as fertilizers, ores slag and ash.[16]

INVESTMENTS

India and Iran are in the process of finalizing a Bilateral Investment Promotion & Protection Agreement (BIPPA) and a Double Taxation Avoidance Agreement (DTAA). Recently, India had announced several investments in Iran. These include a railway project from Chabahar to Bam that has a free trade industrial zone. This is potentially a big investment for India at a time Iran needs friends and is likely to reward those who stand by it. The Chinese and Russians have similarly invested in Iran. Similarly, the Zaranj-Delaram road that India is helping to build links up with Afghanistan and is important for the Indian geo-strategic perspective.[17] India is one of the largest foreign investors in Iran's oil and gas industry. China is now Iran's leading trading partner and is undertaking massive investments in Iran, quickly capturing the space vacated by western companies due to economic sanctions. Where China's economic engagement with Iran is rapidly growing, India's presence is shrinking, as firms such as Reliance Industries have, partially under western pressure, withdrawn from Iran and others have dropped their plans to make investments.

FOREIGN INVESTMENT LAW

The Iranian government passed the Foreign Investment Promotion and Protection Act (FIPPA) in October 2002. FIPPA overhauled and consolidated various older laws that had loosely regulated foreign investment. The FIPPA prohibit foreign dominance in Iranian industry. Article 2 (d) of FIPPA says that the foreign share of the market may not exceed more than 25 per cent in any one sector or 35 per cent in an individual industry. However, these ratios do not affect to foreign investment for the production of goods and services for export purposes, other than for crude oil.[18]

ENERGY

India-Iran economic and commercial ties have traditionally been buoyed by Indian import of Iranian crude oil. The significance of Iran's energy resources has also to be perceived in the context of India's growing demand for energy. Recently on May 31, 2012, Indian and Iranian foreign ministers emphasized their closeness in the different sectors including trade and energy. Iranian foreign minister, Ali Akbar Salehi stated that Iran is a crucial trade partner for India and also a major source of energy supplies. The then Indian foreign minister S.M. Krishna also said that Iran remained India's important source for oil given the growing domestic demand for crude.[19] Both countries are also working for setting up a number of projects, which include the IPI gas pipeline project, a long term supply of 5 million tons of LNG, development of the Farsi oil and gas blocks, South Pars gas field and LNG project.[20]

However, the recent tougher economic sanctions

imposed by the US and the EU on the Iranian oil and financial sectors have led to increased isolation of Iran from the international community. Iran used to be India's second largest supplier of oil but now has come down to the sixth position. Now Iraq has become the second largest supplier of oil after Saudi Arabia. India imported 16.083 million tonnes of oil in 2010-2011 and 14.689 million tonnes of oil during 2011-2012 from Iran.[21] Despite tremendous pressure by the US and the EU, and a significant reduction in oil imports from Iran in 2012, Indian officials have clearly indicated that they are not willing to stop trade relations altogether with Iran.

INFRASTRUCTURE

Iran is one of the important players in the West Asian region. Given Iran's potential to play a significant role in the region, its importance for India is undeniable. Iran is not only a gateway for India to Central Asia, but India and Iran share an interest in the stability of Central Asian countries. Iran can also provide an alternative route for trade with the Central Asian states (CAS). More importantly, its potential to play a pivotal role in a number of regional configurations, mainly in the Persian Gulf, Afghanistan and the Caspian Basin area, enhances its significance for India. Both countries have observer status in the Shanghai Cooperation Organisation (SCO). Due to strategic importance of Iran for India and India importance for Iran, both are working for the setting up for number of projects including the International North-South Transport Corridor (INSTC) project, the Chabahar container terminal project and Chabahar-Zaranj railway project.

The INSTC was established in September 2000 by India, Iran and Russia in order to promote transportation cooperation among the members. Later Azerbaijan, Armenia, Kazakhstan, Kyrgyz, Tajikistan, Turkey, Ukraine, Belarus,

Oman, Syria and Bulgaria joined the corridor. The INSTC connects India to Central Asian Republics (CARs) through Iran, and will also reduce the logistics of moving goods and diminish travel time and transport costs. This corridor also connects India Ocean and Persian Gulf to the Caspian Sea via Iran, and then is connected to St. Petersburg (Russia) and North European via Russia. Recently on May 30, 2012, a high level experts meeting held in New Delhi. The experts emphasized for coordination among member states and also discussed about a dry run, proposed for the next year (2013), conducted from Mumbai to Russia via Bandar Abbas and the Caspian Sea. To resolve operational issues, the experts also proposed to set up an INSTC Operational Authority. The INSTC could play a pivotal role in developing practical policy options to improve connectivity in the region. The INSTC is making strides towards achieving a new framework. The unique feature of the project is that it has the capacity to incorporate other interested states, including countries of the Caucasus, Central Asia, and Eastern Europe.

The primary step towards trade enhancement between India and Iran, was signing of Memorandum of understanding between the two countries over the development of Chabahar Port and transhipment facility at Bandar Abbas. The Chabahar Port in Iran along with a railway link offers India direct access to Afghanistan and the CARs. Through this project Islamic Republic of Iran will also enable to access Central Asian countries including Afghanistan. The Chabahar port has been jointly financed by India and Iran. A highway between Zaranj and Delaram (Zaranj-Delaram Highway) is also being built with financial support from India. Zaranj-Delaram Highway will connect Herat and Kabul via Mazar-e-Sharif in the North and Kandahar in the South. This would permit Indian goods to move into Afghanistan via Delaram and beyond.

POTENTIAL AREAS FOR BILATERAL TRADE

To improve bilateral economic and trade relations with Iran, India should focus on the following areas:[22]

- Identification of major items in Iran's import basket, and share of India in each product line.
- Selection of potential items, based on low share of India in Iran's import basket of major commodities. This would entail identification of potential export items under each product category, up to 6-digit HS Commodity code.

The potential items of exports to Iran would include:[23]

- Machinery & instruments(HS-84)
- Iron and steel (HS-72)
- Electrical, electronic equipment (HS-85)
- Vehicles other than railway (HS-87)
- Plastic and articles (HS-39)
- Mineral fuels & oils (HS-27)
- Optical, photo and medical apparatus (HS- 90)
- Pharmaceutical products(HS-30)
- Residues, wastes of food industry (HS- 23)
- Sugar and sugar confectionery (HS-17)
- Misc. chemical products(HS-38)
- Aluminium and articles(HS-76)
- Edible fruits (HS-8)
- Oilseed (HS-12)

SANCTIONS AND ITS IMPACT ON BILATERAL TRADE

Iran nuclear programme and economic sanctions on Iran have had its impact on the India-Iran bilateral trade as well. India's surprise vote against Iran in the International Atomic Energy Agency (IAEA) governing board in September 2005, and again in February and March 2006 has led to mistrust between the two countries. On September 24, 2005, the IAEA adopted a resolution that found Iran to be in contravention with its NPT safeguards agreement. Experts believe that India voted against Iran under the US pressure. David Mulford, US ambassador to India said on January 25, 2006 that if India chose not to side with the US on the IAEA vote, the future of the Indo-US nuclear deal could be adversely affected because it would not be passed by the US Congress.[24] However, India's official stand on this has been that while it backs Iran's peaceful use of nuclear energy, as a member of the Non-Proliferation Treaty (NPT) Tehran must observe its obligations under the treaty, and must take the international community's and the IAEA's views into consideration. The continuity of India's official position on Iran's nuclear programme was reflected in Prime Minister Manmohan Singh's statement during the Ninth India-EU Summit on September 29, 2008, making it clear that India will not support Iran's nuclear weapons ambitions. However, in a balancing act, Manmohan Singh also mentioned that Iran as a signatory of the NPT was entitled to all that is needed to develop its civil nuclear programme, for which it must undertake all its obligations.[25] Despite New Delhi's repeated explanations, this issue remains a major challenge between India and Iran bilateral relations.

The recent US and the EU sanctions on the Iranian oil and financial sectors also impacted bilateral trade relations between the two countries. However, the US recently renewed six-month waivers on sanctions for India, China and seven other countries in exchange for their agreement to reduce oil purchases from Iran. Iran has also agreed to take payments for oil it sells to India entirely in rupees to get-out the US and western sanctions. India has been, since July 2011, paying in euros to clear 55 percent of its purchases of Iranian oil through Ankara- based Halk bank. The remaining 45 percent due amount was remitted in rupees in accounts Iranian oil company opened in Kolkata-based UCO Bank. Payments in euro through Turkey stopped from February 6, 2013 but the rupee payments for 45 percent of the purchases continued through UCO Bank. India had in 2012-13 imported 13.14 million tons of crude oil from Iran.[26] Iran can use the revenue accumulated in UCO Bank account to purchase "permissible" services and goods, such as food, medicine and basic medical equipment. Iranians have already accumulated US$ 5-6 billion[27] in the UCO Bank account and ways are being explored to observe how Tehran can utilise that revenue either by increasing import of food grains or tools and machinery including cars and tractors.

CONCLUSION

It has been observed from the above discussion that India's trade relations with Iran has witnessed a robust trend in recent years. Iran will continue to be a strategic partner for India even as New Delhi underscores the need for Tehran to come clean on its nuclear programme. Increasing trade and economic relations between India and Iran will no doubt have a spillover effect in the political and security arenas. With improvement in political ties between the two sides, it appears that the situation is ideal for taking the India-Iran trade relationship to a higher orbit. A large number of Agreements and MoUs have been signed in the last few years covering wide ranging areas. India being a US$ 100 billion market is very relevant to Iran. It is not simply the import of crude oil and gas by India that underpins India-Iran economic relations but also the trade in other petro-products and fertilizers and manufactured goods. With the likelihood of US involvement with the region decreasing and muted economic growth in Europe in the next two decades, Iran will be looking forward to a higher level of trade and economic relationship with India. India needs to leverage its geographical proximity, economic and cultural relationship going back thousands of years, and economic complementarities to enhance its trade and economic ties with Iran. There are a host of issues on which the two countries can cooperate to each other such as INSTC, Chabahar Port, economic and trade.

However, despite India's historical and cultural linkages with Iran, India is not exploiting the opportunities presented by the Islamic Republic, especially in the economic and trade sectors. The global economic crisis and the US and EU economic sanctions on Iran have had its impact on the India-Iran bilateral trade as well. It can be concluded that in the light of current developments, the swiftly-changing international milieu and the associated strategic concerns, have forced the two countries to reorient their foreign policies toward each other. However, much still needs to be done to give the bilateral relationship a long-term strategic direction. It not only will strengthen Indo-Iran relations but also benefit the people from both countries.

REFERENCES

1 Harsh V Pant, "India-Iran relations: A tangled web", May 14, 2013, available at http://www.rediff.com/news/column/india-iran-relations-a-tangled-web/20130514.htm (accessed on June 30, 2013)

2 Government of India, Ministry of Commerce and Industry, Department of Commerce, 2013, available at http://commerce.nic.in/eidb/iecnt.asp (accessed on 7 April 2013)

3 Ibid.

4 Ibid.

5 India-Iran Economic Relations, FICCI, 2013, available at http://www.ficci.com/international/75186/Project_docs/India-Iran-Economic—Relations.pdf (accessed on July 11, 2013)

6 "Iran's Inflation Rate Rises To 32.6%", *Middle East Economic Survey*, June 28, 2013, available at http://www.mees.com/en/articles/7928-irans-inflation-rate-rises-to-32-dot-6-percent (accessed on June 28, 2013).

7 Government of India, Ministry of External Affairs, May 2004, available at www.mea.gov.in, (accessed on February 03, 2013).

8 The *Financial Express*, November 14, 2009. See also http://www.mea.gov.in/mystart.php?id=50044479

9 Government of India, Ministry of External Affairs available at http://www.mea.gov.in/mystart.php?id=50044479 (accessed on June 29, 2013).

10 "Salman Khurshid in Tehran; India, Iran decide to give major push to bilateral ties", *Times of India,* May 4, 2013, available at http://articles.timesofindia.indiatimes.com/2013-05-04/india/39026313_1_two-sides-salmankhurshid-indian-cultural-centre (accessed on July 30, 2013)

11 India-Iran Economic Relations, FICCI, 2013, available at http://www.ficci.com/international/75186/Project_docs/India-Iran-Economic—Relations.pdf (accessed on July 11, 2013).

12 Ibid.

13 "Iran, India boost trade ties", *Press TV,* July 6, 2013, available at http://www.presstv.ir/detail/2013/07/06/312454/iran-india-boost-trade-ties/ (accessed on July 13, 2013)

14 "Potential for Enhancing India's Trade with Iran: a Brief Analysis", Working Paper No. 18, Export-Import Bank of India, July 2012, p.12.

15 Anjana Pasricha, "India Takes Steps to Boost Trade With Iran", *Voice of America,* June 15, 2013, available athttp://www.voanews.com/content/india-trade-iran/1682636.html (accessed on July 16, 2013)

16 "Potential for Enhancing India's Trade with Iran: a Brief Analysis", Working Paper No. 18, Export-Import Bank of India, July 2012, p.12.

17 "A tightrope walk with Iran", *Indian Express,* June 13, 2013, available at http://newindianexpress.com/opinion/A-tightrope-walk-with-Iran/2013/06/13/article1631836.ece (accessed on July 20, 2013).

18 "Potential for Enhancing India's Trade with Iran: a Brief Analysis", Working Paper No. 18, Export-Import Bank of India, July 2012, p.48.

19 "Iran remains an important source of oil for India: Krishna", The *Hindu Businessline,* May 31, 2012, available at http://www.thehindubusinessline.com/industry-and-economy/article3477010.ece, (accessed on February 03, 2013).

20 "Potential for Enhancing India's Trade with Iran: a Brief Analysis", Working Paper No. 18, Export-Import Bank of India, July 2012, p. 13.

21 Department of Commerce, Export Import Data Bank Country Wise all commodities available at http://commerce.nic.in/eidb/Icntcom.asp (accessed on May 12, 2013).

22 "Potential for Enhancing India's Trade with Iran: a Brief Analysis", Working Paper No. 18, Export-Import Bank of India, July 2012, pp. 14, 15.

23 Ibid.

24 "US warns India over Iran stance", January 25, 2006, *BBC News*, available at http://news.bbc.co.uk/2/hi/south_asia/4647956.stm (accessed on 12 April 2009).

25 "India won't support Iran's N-Weapon ambition: PM", *Sify News*, September 29, 2008, available at http://www.sify.com/news/india-wont-support-iran-s-n-weapon-ambitions-pm-news-national-jegwuEfeijd.html (accessed on January 21, 2011).

26 "Iran agrees to receive all oil payments from India in rupees", *Mehr News Agency*, July 15, 2013, available at http://old.mehrnews.com/en/newsdetail.aspx?NewsID=1824970 (accessed on July 23, 2013)

27 "Iran agrees to receive all oil payments from India in rupees", *Mehr News Agency*, July 15, 2013, available at http://old.mehrnews.com/en/newsdetail.aspx?NewsID=1824970 (accessed on July 23, 2013)

14

India's Role in Afghanistan since 9/11: An Analysis

Reyaz Ahmad Ganaie

INTRODUCTION

As the deadline of the complete withdrawal of U.S troops from Afghanistan approaches, a military victory against Taliban remains elusive. Even the much hyped U.S-led effort to enter into reconciliation with the 'moderate' or 'good' Taliban has failed miserably. Thus, a Post-ISAF (International Security Assistance Force) Afghanistan presents a scenario full of political and economic concerns which will largely be left unattended by U.S and its allies who seem to be in a hurry to disengage from the war torn country. One would like to see that such disengagement does not lead to same repercussions as did happen previously when U.S abandoned Afghanistan following the withdrawal of Soviet Troops way back in 1989.

The main challenges confronted by Hamid Karzai led

Government at present include the building up of a strong and capable Afghan National Army; consolidation of nascent democratic processes throughout the country; and most importantly, negating the Taliban influence[1], thus securing Afghanistan from plunging into a renewed internecine conflict. India in the capacity of a large aid donor and a potent regional ally has contributed considerably in order to meet these challenges. However, such broad based engagement is not only necessitated by humanitarian concerns per se but the geo-strategic location of Afghanistan in the region embodies a number of strategic interests for India.

Although the reconstruction efforts undertaken by India have received appreciation from all stakeholders, the expanding India's presence within Afghanistan has been resented by Islamabad as a conscious step intended to encircle Pakistan.[2] Initially, U.S allowed for a limited Indian involvement in Afghanistan confining its engagement to humanitarian assistance and infrastructure related activities. However, lately, a discernible shift in the U.S policy, seeking a larger role for India points towards the possibility that India may step into the role of, as Leon Panetta once remarked, "the net provider of security from Indian Ocean to Afghanistan and beyond".[3] While the situation inside Afghanistan remains in a flux, India has to strike a proper balance in its policy thus sustaining the momentum of the reconstruction process and more importantly, capitalising on the position it has been able to gain in order to secure its vital interests in the region without antagonizing other regional neighbours particularly Pakistan.

INDIA'S ENGAGEMENT IN AFGHANISTAN: AN OVERVIEW

India has always enjoyed excellent diplomatic ties with all Afghan governments, starting from King Zahir Shah's tenure to the successive regimes including those that were hoisted on the country following the Soviet invasion in December 1979. The advent of Taliban in 1996 resulted in complete rupture in Indo-Afghan relations as Taliban shared close liaison with Pakistan's military and Intelligence establishment. What left India worse off in the coming years was the Indian decision to enter into a working relationship with Northern Alliance which stood opposite to the Taliban. Following the ouster of Taliban in late 2001 by the U.S led coalition in response to the 9/11 Attacks, India was swift in renewing its diplomatic ties with Afghanistan. Immediately after Karzai took the reins of Afghanistan, India's Minister for External Affairs, Jaswant Singh, flew to Kabul to participate in Interim Government's inauguration and to re-open the Indian embassy, which closed on the eve of the Taliban's seizure of Kabul in 1996.[4] Since then India's relations with Afghanistan have improved considerably for a number of factors facilitated such a renewal of diplomatic ties. First, India kept its post 9/11 Afghan policy completely in sync with the principles mandated under the Bonn Agreement of 2001. Second, unlike Pakistan, Indo-Afghan relations are not hampered by the existence of a contiguous and contested border. Third, India was able to garner official support from the Kabul government, as many members of the Northern Alliance which India supported in the mid-1990s, became members of the Interim Government or held influential provincial posts.[5]

Avoiding any sort of military engagement, India adopted the "Soft Power Approach" towards Afghanistan sticking to civilian issues rather than military matters. With the inception of the Interim Government led by Hamid Karzai, Prime Minister A.B. Vajpayee immediately announced a U.S $100 million in reconstruction aid to Afghanistan. Since 2001, India has already pledged $2 billion on various projects, emerging as the fifth largest bilateral donor to Afghanistan. India's assistance was largely directed towards education, health and infrastructure related activities. Specifically, India has been till now successful in constructing a 218-Km long highway linking the town of Zaranj near the Iranian border to Delaram in the northeast Afghanistan despite periodic attacks on Border Roads Organisation (BRO) personnel. Furthermore, India has accomplished the task of constructing Afghanistan's new parliament building and the construction of Salma Dam project in Herat from which a power transmission line to Kabul has also been set up. Moreover, India has successfully renovated the damaged Indira Gandhi Institute of Child Health and has regularly dispatched teams of doctors to Herat, Mazar-e-Sharif and Kandahar to attend to the massive medical needs of Afghanistan. India has also granted 500 scholarships annually to Afghan students under the auspices of Indian Council of Cultural Relations (ICCR).

While the war in Afghanistan seems nowhere near the end, India's civilian centric policies have gained wide currency and appreciation at official level and among local populace as well. President Karzai has time and again reiterated his government's admiration for India's policies in Afghanistan. Since 2001, several high level official visits from both countries have strengthened the case for closer and enhanced cooperation between the two countries. For instance, India and Afghanistan signed a Preferential Trade Agreement (PTA) in 2003, aimed at removing all obstacles in the way of increasing mutual trade and commerce. This agreement made India one of the major trading partners of Afghanistan and its fifth largest source of imports. Similarly, in 2005 when Indian Prime Minister Manmohan Singh met Afghan President Hamid Karzai in Kabul they agreed on expanding bilateral cooperation to wide ranging areas including development, defence, education, energy, trade, combating terrorism and working towards greater economic and cultural integration of South Asia. On October 4, 2011,

India and Afghanistan signed a milestone agreement on "strategic partnership" that included, inter-alia, provision for both security and economic cooperation, training and equipping of Afghan National Security Forces, provision of economic aid and assistance, development of mining and energy production, and establishment of 'strategic dialogue' between their national security advisers to provide a framework for cooperation in the area of national security.[6] The recent dialogue between Indian Prime Minister Manmohan Singh and Afghan President Hamid Karzai in November 2012 in New Delhi provided further impetus to the bilateral partnership. Both leaders agreed on the need for deepening economic cooperation in areas ranging from agriculture, small business to mining and infrastructure. Hamid Karzai in a bid to woo Indian investors remarked "We would like to welcome you on red carpet and others on grey carpet. If you don't arrive on the red carpet it will get dusty. Therefore, do hurry up and take advantage of the opportunities in Afghanistan".[7]

INDIA'S INTERESTS IN AFGHANISTAN

Afghanistan is host to a number of vital and strategic interests for India. It is around these interests that India has vigorously pursued a pro-active Afghan policy and has expanded its diplomatic energy in the recent years. The continued Indian assistance aid to Afghanistan is aimed at preserving these interests and work towards their fulfilment.

CONTAINING PAKISTAN'S INFLUENCE

Typically, India's interests in Afghanistan have been viewed through the prism of Indo-Pak rivalry. This rivalry has largely been driven by real or imagined security threats and has plotted Afghanistan as a field for both countries to gain power and influence in the country.[8] Limiting Pakistan's influence and ensuring that any regime around the order of

Taliban is not allowed to gain foothold inside Afghanistan remains the top priority for Indian policy makers.

On the one hand, India views good relations with Afghanistan as a means to check the terrorist threat looming large from the Af-Pak region and is also interested in retaining Afghanistan as a friendly state from which it has the capacity to monitor Pakistan and even cultivate assets to influence activities in Pakistan.[9] While on the other, Pakistan has suffered from historic paranoia of being trapped in a pincer movement should India be able to gain political and military space inside Afghanistan. Therefore, a friendly political dispensation in Kabul, often referred to as strategic depth, is viewed by Pakistan as essential to escape the strategic dilemma of being caught between a powerful adversary in India in the east and an irredentist Afghanistan with claims on the Pashtun dominated areas in the west.[10] In response, Pakistan alleges that Indian intelligence personnel particularly RAW (Research Analysis Wing) officials in connivance with Afghan intelligence are actively instigating Baluch separatism inside Pakistan and also supporting TTP (Tehreek-i-Taliban Pakistan). As Christine Fair argues, while these mutual recriminations are nearly impossible to verify yet it can be said that Pakistan's most sweeping claims are ill founded while at the same time Indian claims to complete innocence are also unlikely to be true.[11]

India's interests in Afghanistan stand in sharp contrast with those of Pakistan's and are virtually antithetical. India is also concerned by the limits put on its activities and presence by U.S on account of security threat perceived by Pakistan which have considerably constrained the ability of the former to contribute towards stabilisation in Afghanistan. India strongly believes that U.S should not give any undue concessions and disproportionate importance to Pakistan and its military, often seen by the west as indispensible to

Afghan peace process as India fears about the close ties that Pakistan shares with Taliban. Any move by U.S aimed at giving more space to Pakistan's military, India contends, is going to jeopardise the entire effort of ushering Afghanistan into a stable and democratic state. It is in this backdrop that a robust Indo-Pak rivalry manifests itself inside Afghanistan. However, any attempt by either of the two states to completely sideline the other is surely going to be detrimental to the security of the entire region in general and to the rebuilding process of Afghanistan in particular.

EXPANDING REGIONAL INFLUENCE

Explaining how India defines its strategic space, C.Raja Mohan argues that India's grand strategy:

> ...divides the world into three concentric circles. In the first, which encompasses the immediate neighbourhood, India has sought primacy and a veto over the actions of outside powers. In the second, which encompasses the so-called extended neighbourhood stretching across Asia and the Indian Ocean littoral, India has sought to balance the influence of other powers and prevent them from undercutting its interests. In the third, which includes the entire global stage, India has tried to take its place as one of the great powers, a key player in international peace and security.[12]

It can be deduced from this explanation that India is quite keen in projecting itself as a major regional player and at the same time trying to carve out a significant role for itself at the global level as well. India's aid assistance and reconstruction effort in Afghanistan are to be viewed through this paradigm. India, given its formidable economic and military profile, wants to consolidate itself as a prominent regional power willing to take responsibility for ensuring security in the region. It was towards this end that India kept its Afghan policy largely in sync with the U.S approach so as to gain wider recognition to take on such a role.

CONTAINING ISLAMIST EXTREMISM

One of the serious security concerns that India faces in Afghanistan is the prospect of return of Taliban and its overall impact on the religious fundamentalism in the region. Taliban's symbiotic relationship with Pakistan's military and intelligence establishment further compounds the problem for India.[13] Given Taliban's anti-India rhetoric, India would like to see the consolidation of democracy in Afghanistan besides denying any political or military space to Taliban and other such fundamentalist groups. This will not only ensure the safety and security of Indian personnel working on infrastructural projects in Afghanistan but also cut off Afghanistan as a training ground for Pakistan based terrorist outfits operating inside Kashmir. The return of Taliban in whatever form will not only pose a security challenge to India inside Afghanistan only but also lead to increased insurgency in Indian administered Kashmir which has seen a considerable decline in the recent years. India's support to Northern Alliance and its refusal for any negotiations with Taliban are a part of this objective.[14]

TAPING ENERGY RESOURCES

Stability in Afghanistan remains an indispensible necessity for India in many ways. It will not only guarantee India with the opportunity of taping vast oil and natural gas reserves in Afghanistan but also create a viable route for transporting energy from Central Asian states to Indian markets.[15] Afghanistan considered as the traditional gateway to Central Asian states which are known for their abundant energy and hydrocarbon reserves thus holds pivotal importance for India particularly in a scenario where the demand for oil and hydrocarbons are on an ever high note. Moreover, Afghanistan's oil reserves have hitherto been left largely untapped which may likely create an avenue for enhanced investment in the country.

POLICY OPTIONS FOR INDIA

As the date of withdrawal of the international forces draws nearer, alternate policy options are being charted out in India which can best withstand the challenges that a post-U.S Afghanistan is likely going to pose. While the primary objective for India still remains to facilitate Afghanistan's pursuit towards democracy, a number of factors have lately come to impede India's ability to contribute towards this end. These include the continued animosity of the resurgent Taliban baked by an inimical Pakistan; India's restricted involvement as dictated by the west, the growing narco-trafficking sustaining the Taliban movement, and a widening trust deficit between India and other like-minded regional players arising from their perception that it is no longer an autonomous player, but merely a U.S camp follower.[16] Given this shrunken and limited strategic space, India needs to strike a proper balance in its Afghan policy keeping in view its immediate and long term interests in the region.

On the one hand, the advocates of soft power strategy argue for the continuation of this approach in Afghanistan as they suggest that it is the only way forward by which India can maintain and keep alive the goodwill gained in the last decade. Furthermore, they argue that at present, until an alternate picture emerges in Afghanistan, both India and U.S are faced by a TINA (There Is No Alternative) factor[17] as there is no other option available to India except supporting Karzai government on the same pattern as it has done in the last decade. However, within the broad framework of soft power strategy, India must distance itself from the west and carve out its own independent narrative on Afghanistan;

implying that India should refrain from making a case for continued western presence and at the same time enhance its assistance not only in economic terms but also by providing military equipment and training to the Afghan armed and security forces. Pleading for extended U.S presence in Afghanistan will not only be unwelcomed by common Afghan masses but will also engender disagreement with Iran who wishes to see an early U.S exit from Afghanistan.

On the other side of the debate are those who contend that although the soft power strategy has helped India in winning 'hearts and minds' in Afghanistan but the policy has not yielded any perceptible strategic gains so far and hence India must consider the option of an increased military presence inside Afghanistan. A significant military presence inside Afghanistan will not only help India to repel any undue Pakistan's interference in Afghanistan but will also alter the geo-strategic landscape in the extended neighbourhood, by expanding India's power projection in Central Asia.[18] Furthermore, an enhanced military presence in Afghanistan will also strategically benefit India by shifting the battleground away from Kashmir and the Indian mainland.[19]

However, this policy option has attracted fierce criticism from different quarters within India. As the critiques of hard power approach argue, that if the U.S forces aided by NATO and ISAF could not eliminate Al-Qaeda and Taliban from Afghanistan, there is least one can expect the feat being achieved by Indian forces on their own. Moreover, Indian military presence is again a strategic move which will utterly be unwelcomed by Afghans who have already seen a lot of foreign troops. Indian government has also indicated its unwillingness in engaging militarily in Afghanistan, the signs of which became manifest when Indian Foreign Office quickly distanced itself from the proposal made by U.S ambassador Timothy Roemer in May 2010 to engage in joint operations in Afghanistan.

Apart from this soft power- hard power debate a more worthwhile option that India has been pushing for is the adoption of a regional approach towards the Afghan quagmire. The rationale behind employing this strategy stems from the fact that India along with other regional neighbours of Afghanistan most notably Iran, Russia, and the Central Asian Republics share commonality of interests on some vital issues in Afghanistan. All these states concur on the need of preventing Taliban from returning to power and combating the spread of narco-trafficking emanating from Afghanistan from entering into their respective territories besides the shared interest in stabilising Afghanistan.[20] These areas of convergence may lead to the formation of a regional forum which may be helpful in channelizing the collective effort of these states in a more efficacious manner towards the rebuilding and reconstruction of Afghanistan. Such an understanding among the regional players will not only smoothen the way for Afghan stabilisation but may cater to the energy needs of these individual states by developing Afghanistan as a transit corridor for transporting Central Asian energy to the energy deficient Indian Subcontinent.

CONCLUSION

The real need for India remains to engage all ethnic groups in Afghanistan so as to gain wider acceptability among common populace as a friendly neighbour. Given the persistent efforts led by Karzai aimed at reconciling with former Taliban fighters[21], India must not rule out the option of engaging with them as well. A modicum of rapprochement and selective engagement with Taliban will certainly send a strong message to Islamabad than sending forces to Afghanistan. As Vishal Chandra argues, terrorism being a non-conventional threat cannot always be countered by conventional means alone; sometimes it requires non-conventional approaches to address it.[22] India needs to cooperate with other regional neighbours to address pressing issues in Afghanistan and back Karzai in his efforts towards rebuilding and reconstruction of the war weary country. India must see to it that Afghanistan does not once again become the breeding ground for religious fundamentalism and therefore must do everything in its capacity to help Afghanistan in its nation building process. A stable and democratic Afghanistan will not only serve India's interests within Afghanistan alone but also limit to a large extent Pakistan's manoeuvring of religious fundamentalism and terrorism as a state policy.

REFERENCES

1 Raghav Sharma, "India and Afghanistan: charting the future," *IPCS Special Report 69*, April 2009, p-2.

2 Summit Ganguly, "India's Role in Afghanistan," January, 2012, p-1. found at: http://www.idos.org/es/ontent/download/.../SUMMIT_GANGULY.pdf

3 Julian E. Barnes, "U.S Seeks Larger Role for India," *The Wall Street Journal*, June 6, 2012 P-9.

4 C. Christine Fair, "Under the Shrinking U.S Security Umbrella: India's Endgame in Afghanistan," *The Washington Quarterly*, p-180.

5 Harsh V. Pant, "The Afghanistan Conflict: India's Changing Role", p-33, found at: http://www.meforum.org/2895/India-Afghanistan.

6 Found at: http://www.Indo-Afg/India,%20Afghanistan%20sign%20strategi%20pat%20-%20WSJ.com.htm.

7 The Hindu, 13 November, 2012.

8 Gautam Mukhopadhaya in Ashley J. Tellis and Aroop Mukharji (eds), "Is a Regional Strategy Viable in Afghanistan," *Carnegie Endowment For International Peace*, 2010, p-27.

9 C. Christine Fair, "India in Afghanistan and Beyond: Opportunities and Constraints," *Century Foundation Report*, 2010, p-8.

10 Riffat Hussain, "Pakistan's Relations with Afghanistan: Continuity and Change," *Strategic Studies*, Vol.4, 2002, p-22. Found at: http://

www.issi.org.pk/journal/2002_files/no_4/article/3a.htm. Accessed on: 3 June , 2011.

11 C. Christine Fair, "India in Afghanistan and Beyond: Opportunities and Constraints," *Century Foundation Report*, 2010, p-13-14.

12 C.Raja Mohan, "India and the Balance of Power," *Foreign Affairs*, Vol: 4, July 2006, p.18.

13 Gautam Mukhopadhaya in Ashley J. Tellis and Aroop Mukharji (eds), "Is a Regional Strategy Viable in Afghanistan," *Carnegie Endowment For International Peace*, 2010, p-27.

14 Raghav Sharma, "India and Afghanistan: charting the future," *IPCS Special Report 69*, April 2009, p-2.

15 Ibid.

16 Satish Chandra, "India's Options in Afghanistan", *Strategic Analysis*, Vol.35:1, January 2011, p-125.

17 Mahendra Ved, "Af-Pak and Indi's Options in Afghanistan," *Strategic Analysis*, Vol.34:5, September 2010, p-687.

18 Sushant K Singh, "A Bigger Military Presence Is Essential," *Pragati: The Indian National Review*, No.17, August 2008, p-12.

19 Ibid.

20 Gautam Mukhopadhaya in Ashley J. Tellis and Aroop Mukharji (eds), "Is a Regional Strategy Viable in Afghanistan," *Carnegie Endowment For International Peace*, 2010, p-33.

21 In the first week of December 2012, Afghan foreign Minister Zalmai Rasool and Hina Rabbani shook hands on a diplomatic deal aimed at releasing Taliban prisoners from Pakistan so that they may come at negotiating table.

22 Vishal Chandra, "India in the Afghan Maze: Search for Options," Strategic Analysis, Vol 35, No.1, January 2011, pp-120-124.

SECTION-IV :

INDIA AND ITS NEIGHBOURS

15

India-Pakistan Relations: The Contemporary Phase

Veena Kukreja

Since the partition of the Indian sub-continent in 1947 the relationship between India and Pakistan has been the most intractable and the most dangerous political stand off in South Asia. India and Pakistan are the major concern of each other's foreign and security policies. They have developed adversarial relations with each other since the partition of the subcontinent. Both countries share bitter memories of three wars, three decades of proxy war and the baggage of a painful co-existence. Indo-Pakistan relations have been nurtured on institutionalized hate and mistrust.

India-Pakistan relations have been full of conflicts and tensions since 1947 including the conflict over Kashmir. Kashmir is the symbol of India-Pakistan conflict. Pakistan's perspective on Kashmir is that it is more of an ideological than a territorial dispute. It sees the Kashmir issue in the light of Mohammad Ali Jinnah's 'two-nation theory' whereas India views Kashmir as a symbol of its secularism and composite nationalism.

During the last 65 years, Indo-Pakistan relations have not gone beyond the framework of mutual suspicion and discord. This perception goes as an input into the decision-making apparatus and policy formulation, and further strengthens the same 'national psyche'. This process is a vicious cycle. It has also promoted the image of the other as an enemy, which in turn has created a mindset of hostility and antagonism at the elite level. Pakistan's establishment is observed with Kashmir and they have strategically developed this obsession for political gains. It also justifies maintaining a large army (Dixit 1995 : 244). Every establishment and government in Pakistan has used Kashmir to its own advantage, as it comes in handy in diverting attention from domestic failures and is useful in stifling people's voices whenever necessary.

It was only under General Zia-ul-Haq's regime that Kashmir acquired the position of being the 'cone issue'. Zia-ul-Haq followed a hot-and-cold diplomacy and to take avenge of Pakistan's humiliating defeat in 1971 Indo-Pakistan War[1] initiated the systematically designed proxy wars in Punjab (1984) and Kashmir (1989). General Zia conceived the 'Operation Topac' in April 1988 and outlined the likely course of Pakistan's action in Kashmir (Operation Topac 1989 : 39-49). The Pakistan Inter Service Intelligence (ISI) enjoying autonomous power in orienting foreign and defence policies of Pakistan, took over the Kashmir issue after the successful Afghan adventure. In 1998, India and Pakistan became overtly nuclear and Kashmir was depicted by the western countries as a nuclear flash-point.

India-Pakistan relations have steadily deteriorated since 1989. Pakistan's continued sponsorship of cross-border terrorism, not only in Jammu and Kashmir but also elsewhere in this country. The Kargil Aggression[2] over the Kashmir issue, in 1999 have only deepened the chasm (Singh : 1999 and Kukreja 2000). Notwithstanding this long history of antagonism the Indian Prime Minister Atal Bihari Vajpayee invited President-cum-General Pervez Musharraf to Agra Summit in July 2001 (Kukreja 2002) despite the Kargil aggressor and continuing cross-order terrorism.

9/11 AND ITS IMPACT ON INDIA-PAKISTAN RELATIONS

The terrorist attacks on the World Trade Centre and Pentagon (Symbols of economic and military might of the sole super power) on 11 September 2001, resulted in a shift in all geo-political dynamics – international, regional, and local. The extraordinary situation in which it was placed forced the US to co-opt Pakistan – the epi-centre of terrorist activities – into its 'crusade' against global terrorism. Pakistan, once again, on account of dictates of geography, became a frontline state against Afghanistan for a second time within a decade.

Pakistan has created and nurtured the Taliban to acquire to much vaunted 'strategic depth' vis-à-vis India and Iran. The US was interested in the Taliban as a possible operational asset against Iran and as the facilitator of oil and gas pipelines from Turkmanistan to Pakistan through Afghanistan.

After the black Tuesday terrorist attacks, the military regime in Islamabad was caught in the biggest dilemma Pakistan has ever faced. The military regime's option were limited to risking US punishment for supporting the Taliban, or seeking strategic dividends by assisting the US. Fearing further global isolation, bankruptcy, even a possible American attack on Pakistan's nuclear facilities, General Musharraf has decided to make a virtue of necessity and has proclaimed support for US moves to target Osama bin Laden and the Taliban leadership.

Pakistan has chosen to side with Washington by offering its unstinted cooperation. However, the spin-offs of Pakistan's U-tern as its Afghan policy included financial dividends in term of lifting of sanctions imposed on it in 1998 by the US, waiver of loans, fresh dose of economic aid plus a more sympathetic view of its position an Kashmir.

General Musharraf seemed eager to persuade his compatriots, especially, the critics, that he faced a virtual Hobson's choice in deciding to go along with the US in the latter's war against terrorism. He utilized a televised address to portray his US friendly act as a 'strategic decision' that was designed to prevent a proactive India from isolating Pakistan on the international scene in the aftermath of the world's worst episode of terrorism. He also specified Pakistan's integrity, the state of economy, the sustainability of its strategic assets of nuclear weapon and missiles, besides the Kashmir issue.

Operation Enduring Freedom in Afghanistan has made little dent in curbing cross-border terrorism in Jammu and Kashmir. In India those who expected that Pakistan, source of cross-border terrorism, would be a prime target of the US war against terror have been disappointed. Large scale terrorist attacks in Jammu and Kashmir and elsewhere in India continued. Moreover, the brutal attack on the Jammu and Kashmir Assembly complex by a suicide squad of Jaish-e-Mohammad (JeM) was launched on 1 October, 2001, even as analysts were predicting a period of relative peace for the state consequent to the forces shifting to Afghanistan. This attack had a direct linkage with Pakistan's volatile situation emanating from *Jihadi* demonstrations against Pakistan's decision to make common cause with US against the Taliban. Having joined the US in its fight against terrorism, General Musharraf needed as rarely before to pacify the *Jihadis* and demonstrate his commitment to Kashmir. Implicit in the attack was a warning to India about joining any global war against terrorism (Kukreja 2003 : 287-88). Pakistan refused to take cognizance of India protest.

In the context of Pakistan supported cross-border terrorism in Jammu and Kashmir, the US did nothing more than listing the Laskhar-e-Taiba (LeT) and the JeM as 'foreign terrorist organization'. In fact, General Pervez Musharraf was considered by the US and his other Western allies as an important bulwark in the anti-terrorist fight, a moderate who needs to be supported and fortified.

In the post-Taliban scenario, General Musharraf has only the Kashmir issue to build domestic support in his favour and divert attention from the foreign policy failures. The 13 December 2001 terrorist attack by JeM on the Indian parliament, located at the heart of the capital's high security zone, substantiates this view. The attack was well-planned, carefully crafted and timed with precise intelligence outputs. This has deeply scarred the collective psyche of the Indian state. It was to convey two strident messages on behalf of Pakistan's Musharraf's regime. The first was that despite the success of the United States – led coalition in the Afghan war, terrorism is alive and well. It had become imperative to send it to raise the morale of terrorists in India and Pakistan which had sunk to their boots following the collapse the Taliban regime. The second message was that the attack was a proof of the fact that the Musharraf regime had not sold out to the US, and its alliance with the latter was meant to safeguard Pakistan's nuclear arsenal and prevent the US from including its cross-border terrorism against India in its anti-terrorist agenda. It was addressed principally to fundamentalist Islamic militias like the LeT, HuM and JeM Pakistan which were fuming over what they considered to be the Musharraf regime's betrayal of the Taliban and Osama bin Laden.

In this context, it is noteworthy that General Musharraf in his speech of 12 January 2002, which was delivered under presence from the UK and the US had committed himself to pushing Pakistan towards Islamic moderation and agreed to stop cross-border terrorism. The whole exercise was part of the war against terrorism, and it had only marginally to do with the Indo-Pakistan border confrontation (Subrahmanyam 2002 : 14).

General Musharraf's so-called 'bold and visionary' speech was in fact clearly addressed to three distinct audiences – people in the West particularly the United States, in his own country and India. He had two messages for the first two. The first was that Pakistan was breaking with Islamic fundamentalism and charting a new path towards becoming a modern, dynamic, Islamic 'welfare state'. The second message was that terrorism, whether domestic or meant for export would be dealt with firmly. All this was aimed to please the western countries, particularly the US, which were deeply concerned over the rise of Islamic fundamentalist in Pakistan and its emergence as a world-wide exporter of terrorism.

However, the message to India was considerably different. General Musharraf even while renouncing terrorism for the Kashmir cause has repeated his usual formula on the Kashmir issue. He talked of Kashmir as being part of every Pakistani's blood. There was hardly anything for India in the speech. He had not changed a comma in the policy Pakistan had been following towards India in the last six and a half decades. He was the same old, rigid and threatening general. General Musharraf employed the same phrase – "we shall continue to give Kashmiris moral and diplomatic help" – which one of his illustrious military predecessor, Zia-ul-Haq used, to camouflage cross-border terrorism (Nayar, 2002 : 11).

The terrorist attack on Indian Parliament prompted New Delhi to undertake 'Operation Parakram', pushing its troops into the forward areas in full mobilization, which pushed India-Pakistan to the edge of another war. For the first time India decided that it was not possible to continue the policy of trying to engage Pakistan even while it was a target of the latter's covert war. Diplomatic interaction were reduced to a minimum, sporting ties were frozen, cross-border transport and overflights were restricted, and dialogues were put on hold. For the next ten months it was an eyeball-to-eyeball confrontation between their armed forces on the India-Pakistan border. In October 2002, India decided to withdraw its troops gradually. Some signs of thaw between the two countries began to surface from April 2003 when the Indian Prime Minister Atal Behari Vajpayee announced in his historic public meeting that he was extending the hand of friendship to Pakistan.

PEACE PROCESS BETWEEN INDIA AND PAKISTAN (2004-2008)

On 22 October 2003, India offered a set of 12 proposals to nurture peace, between India and Pakistan. On November 26, 2003, Pakistan ordered a unilateral ceasefire on the Line of Control (LOC) in Kashmir. A million-dollar question is being asked: why did Pakistan spring a sudden ceasefire surprise? Pakistan has been under tremendous pressure from the US to go in far talks (Lieven 2002: 106). This pressure hinged on the American thinking that tensions between India and Pakistan could escalate to the nuclear level. The US intervention in the aftermath of the Indian military mobilization post-13 December 2001 was apparently instrumental in ending the crisis situation by June 2002. The US effort was geared towards to a commitment from Pakistan that it would end cross-border infiltration permanently, which was evident from the much-publicized speeches that General Musharraf was forced to give during this period (Kumar 2003: 490). This move was in turn expected to extract from India a resolve towards substantive dialogue with Pakistan on various bilateral issues, including the Kashmir issue (Kukreja and Singh 2005 : 262).

The 12th SAARC Summit Conference held in Islamabad on 6 January 2004, was significant, especially in the context of Pakistan's tacit admission on terrorism. It provided India a written commitment from Musharraf that he will not permit any territory under Pakistan's control to be used to support terrorism. Besides, India retained its stand for the need to discuss all issues instead of just focusing on Kashmir, which was Pakistan's core demand.

After six years, in June 2004 India and Pakistan resumed the composite dialogue process that covers eight baskets[3] of issues agreed upon in Male in 1997 between the former Indian Prime Minister I.K. Gujral and the former Pakistan Prime Minister Nawaz Sharif.

The peace process took a step forward via nuclear Confidence-Building Measures (CBMs) after the change of government in New Delhi was in May 2004. The June talks on nuclear CBMs dealt with measures to 'reduce risks relevant to nuclear issues'. The two sides also agreed to improve upon the agreement on the technical parameters on pre-notification of missile testing with more relevant information.

Both countries agreed to start a new rail service between Khokhrapar (Pakistan) and Munnabao (India) in addition to the train service already running between Delhi and Lahore. Bus service in two countries has received a tremendous boost in people to people contacts. Since 1999, the New Delhi-Lahore bus had been the only service running between the two countries. Now, bus services from Srinagar-Muzzaffarabad, Lahore-Amritsar and Nankana Sahib-Amritsar have been added.

The framework for solving the Kashmir problem focused on 'soft' borders encouraging greater movement of people, goods and services across the LOC. In order to enable people on both sides of LOC in Jammu and Kashmir to move freely and trade with one another, cross-LOC CBMs have been put in place and one being strengthened. These include trade and travel on the Srinagar-Muzaffarabad and Poonch-Rawalakot routes across the LOC.

On 25 October, 2004 Musharraf announced proposal to resolve the Kashmir dispute. He proposed identifying regions on both sides of the LOC to the demilitarized and then either making them independent or placing them under Indo-Pakistan joint control or that of the UN. The General's plan has the full backing of the Bush administration, as exemplified by the fact that the US Deputy Secretary of State Richard Armitage in Pakistan on 9 November 2004 endorsed the proposal and found it 'very interesting', and called Musharraf 'forward-thinking'. However, his 'seven-point Kashmir proposal' was geared more to self-protection than solving any issue.

General Musharraf's proposal was merely an attempt to get Kashmir to the centre of negotiations. Talks have been trundling along the tracks of more economic, social and political contacts as a warm-up to tackling more difficult security issues, including reducing troops on Siachen. It could be embracing and domestically contentious for Musharraf if Kashmir gets sidelined. He was trying to placate extremists at home by showing that Islamabad was not diluting its claims on Kashmir as part of a larger settlement.

Four rounds of dialogues were completed between January 2004 and November 2008 with two short interruptions. This contributed to improving relations between India and Pakistan. People-to-people contacts between the two countries increased because the visa rules were somewhat relaxed. Important progress was made on the contentious issues like the Siachen Glacier and Sir Creek boundary. Bus service and trade across the LOC in Kashmir initiated in 2005 and 2008 respectively. This period witnessed growth in bilateral trade by 550 percent between year 2003-04 and 2007-08 from US$ 344.59 million to US$ 2.23 billion.

2008 MUMBAI TERRORIST ATTACKS: PEACE PROCESS SUSPENDED

The ominous shadow of terrorism manifested in 26/11 bloody terrorist attack in Mumbai brought the composite dialogue to an abrupt end. Though earlier terrorist attacks were equally brazen, this one had surpassed them all in its impunity (Bahadur 2011: 355).

India accused Pakistan-based LeT and its counterpart Jamaat-ul-Dawa (JW) of masterminding 2008 Mumbai attack. It also blamed Pakistan's ISI for sponsoring the LeT attack in Mumbai. India's official and non-official circles explored the option of some punitive military action against Pakistan. This option was later dropped.

India maintained that it would not resume. The dialogue with Pakistan until Pakistan does its best to pursue and prosecute those complicit in the crime. Islamabad had no way to escape responsibility. In response to the Indian demand, Pakistan arrested 7 LeT and JD leaders in December 2008. One of them Hafiz Muhammad Saeed, was released by the court. Other six have been in prison since then. Their case is proceeding at very slow pace because the evidence provided by India is considered very weak and insufficient by Pakistan courts. Pakistan's instance on the resumption of the dialogue only means that they seek the dialogue to be held under the shadow of terrorist gun.

RESUMPTION OF PEACE PROCESS (MARCH 2011)

As a result of their meetings in April 2010 in Thimphu on the sidelines of the SAARC Summit, Prime Minister Manmohan Singh and Prime Minister Yusuf Ali Gilani of Pakistan mandated the two Foreign Ministers and Foreign Secretaries to hold discussions on the modalities for restoring trust and confidence in order to pave the way for a comprehensive, sustained and meaningful dialogue on all issues of mutual interest and concern.

DYNAMICS OF THE PEACE PROCESS

India and Pakistan formally announced on 10 February 2011 structured revival of the dialogue process which had been suspended since November 2008 following the 26/11 terror attacks. On 25 March Prime Minister Manmohan Singh invited Pakistan's President and Prime Minister to watch the India-Pakistan cricket World Cup semi-final match at Mohali. A day after the Indian Prime Minister's invitation, the Government of India unilaterally decided to increase the period of stay persons visiting to Jammu and Kashmir and Pakistan occupied Kashmir to six months with multiple entries (*The Asian Age*, 27 March 2011).

The latest phase of the dialogue between India and Pakistan began when the Interior/Home Secretaries of Pakistan and India met in New Delhi on March 28-29, 2011, and discussed issues ranging from the 26/11 terror attacks and cross-border terrorism to smuggling of narcotics, flow of counterfeit Indian currency notes, release of prisoners etc. They agreed, among other things, to establish 'terror hotline' between Islamabad and Delhi for communicating quickly on terrorist threats. Indian and Pakistani prime ministers also held a 'wide-ranging conversation' on 30 March and decided to take forward their recently started dialogue.

The two-day deliberations on 27-28 April between the commerce secretaries ended with setting of time table for addressing the 'identified doables'. This included Pakistan granting Most Favoured Nation (MFN) status to India and moving to a negative list approach to tariff lines, and New Delhi becoming more amenable to addressing Islamabad's concern regarding the flow of Pakistani goods into India. However, on 30 April, "a group of Pakistani Parliamentarians belonging to the PML-Q and PML-N moved a resolution in the National Assembly stating that the settlement of the Kashmir issue should be 'a pre-condition' for giving MFN status to India" (Kumar 2013: 77).

India and Pakistan concluded two-day water secretary level talk on 13 May 2011 where in both countries decided to explore amicable and early resolution of the Tulbul Nevigation Project within the ambit of the 1960 Indus Water Treaty (*The Hindu*, 11 May and 15 May 2011).

There have been several rounds of talks at different levels between India and Pakistan. The most significant development was visit of Pakistan's Foreign Minister Hina Rabbani Khar to Delhi in July 2011.[4] The Ministers expressed satisfaction on holding of meetings on various issues and endorsed the decision taken by various groups and reviewed bilateral relations. They also decided to revive the joint commission and agree on strengthening cross – LOC CBMs.

Though trade and economic relations dominated the dialogue process reopened in March 2011, there were several diplomatic visits that facilitated trade talks and the two sides also agreed to make effort to create an enabling environment for trade on both sides. They also decided to set up a number of working groups/ sub-groups to explore mutual cooperation. In early November 2011, the Pakistan's Federal Cabinet took a decision to grant the status of the MFN to India. India had already granted MFN status to Pakistan in 1996 but Islamabad linked the improvement of the trade ties to resolution of the Kashmir issue. India welcomed Pakistan's decision. However, a day later, the spokesman of Pakistan Foreign Office somewhat back-tracked by suggesting that the Federal cabinet had agreed 'in principle' to designate India as MFN as a part of the process to normalize relation with India. It will be finally given once consultations within different departments of Pakistan government are complete and the matters involved in this status are settled with India.

Track-II and Track-III dialogues are also used for building support for peace process. The Pakistan Institute of Legislative Development and Transparency took the initiative for organizing joint Parliamentarians Dialogue between Pakistan and India. Similarly the '*Aman ki Asha*' programme was sponsored by the *Times of India* and the *Jang* Group of Pakistan, organized many conferences.

Despite these positive developments, no contentious issue between India and Pakistan has moved towards solution. The Siachen Glacier and Sir Creek have not moved beyond the position in 2007-2008.

Two rounds of talks on the Siachen Glacier were held since the revival of the dialogue on May 30-31, 2011 and June 10-12, 2012. Both sessions were inconclusive as neither side was willing to show flexibility.

On the Sir Creek boundary issue, the final survey was complete by 2007 but the Governments of India and Pakistan have been unable to implement the survey result because of lack of agreement on the precise demarcation of the boundary in the waterway. The officials of India and Pakistan met twice on May 20-21, 2011 and June 18-19, 2012 to agree on the demarcation of the boundary but did not succeed.

Water issues between India and Pakistan acquired prominence during 2012, *Jihadi* militant outfit namely, LeT threaten to blow up India's dams. Pakistan accuses India of water hegemony. The Baglihar project continues to be a bone of contention. The latest controversy was over the Kishanganga river, Called Neelum in Pakistan. India's dam will divert some of the river water down to 22 kilometer mountain tunnel to turbines generating power. Pakistan sought an immediate order from the Court of Arbitration against India's discontinuation of Kisanganga Hydroelectric Power Project. The court accepted Pakistan's argument and stopped from constructing any permanent works on or above the river belt at the Gurez site (Kumar 2013: 264-65).

Terrorism remains India's core concern in the relationship with Pakistan and has been repeatedly raised with Pakistan, including highest level, whereby India has consistently urged Pakistan to fulfill its repeated assurance given to us not to allow the territory under its control to be used for supporting terrorism against India or for any other anti-India activity. There is no evidence that government of Pakistan is taking credible actions to control and penalize the various *Jihadi* outfits avowedly working against India. Pakistan's policy of export of terrorism to India continues. Pakistan's involvement in terrorist's attacks against India was further proved in 2011. It can be exemplified by the fact that Tahawwar Hussain Rana, the Pakistani-Canadian accused in the 12/11 Mumbai terror attack case and David Coleman Headley, co-accused in 26/11 attacks, both confessed before Chicago court that Pakistan's intelligence agency ISI played key role in organizing the LeT's 26/11 attacks. Similar nexus between the LeT was also highlighted the Slain Pakistani Journalist Saleen Shazad in his book *Beyond Bin Laden and 9/11: Insight Taliban and Al Qaida.*

Although peace process was revived in 2011, when it came to the issue of cooperation in the fight against terrorism, India has found itself cheated. Pakistan refused to allow Indian investigators to question LeT commander, Zaki-ur-Rahman Lakhvi, the master mind behind the 26/11 attacks (Kumar 2013: 78). During the meeting of Manmohan Singh with Prime Minister Gilani in Maldives (November 10, 2011), Singh underlined India's concerns regarding terrorism and stressed that it was imperative to bring the perpetrators of the Mumbai attack to justice. A Pakistan Judicial Commission visited India in March 2012 and recorded, the lone surviving accused Ajmal Kasab's confessional statement, and two doctors who had conducted postmortem on the terrorist involved in the attack. The Anti-Terrorism Court in Pakistan upheld the contention of the defence that the report of the Judicial Commission was not legal and could not form part of the case, since the witnesses were not cross-examined. Moreover, continued with terrorist activities. For example, bomb explosion in Mumbai in July 2011 and a bomb exploded in the vicinity of the New Delhi High Court in September 2011, brutal attack on Indian prisoner Sarabjit and his death in Pakistan and beheading Indian soldiers on LOC in April 2013.

NAWAZ SHARIF AT THE HELM: PROSPECTS OF PEACE PROCESS BETWEEN INDIA AND PAKISTAN

With the swearing in as Prime Minister Nawaz Sharif for the third time on 5 June 2013, Pakistan has completed its first successful democratic transition from one civilian government to another. It is interesting to note in the run up to the 2013 elections, Nawaz Sharif made encouraging gestures signaling willingness to normalize relations with India, even before assuming formal charge. However, Pakistan's army Chief General Ashfaq Parvez Kayani urged the Prime Minister designated to adopt cautious approach towards relations with India (*Times of India*, 21 May 2013 : 22). Democracy may be resurgent in Pakistan but one of the biggest challenges is getting the relationship with the country's powerful military right. Nawaz Sharif has had a history of strained relations with the army. Although the army under Kayani has been supportive of Pakistan's democratic transition, it continue to retain pivotal role in the power structure of Pakistan. Since 1988 in the post-Zia Pakistan, army has developed a new pattern of 'non-takeover' intervention in which emphasis shifted from assuming power directly, to playing more subtle, but still ubiquitous role from the sidelines. The military continues to have had an important influence over foreign and security policies and key domestic issues (Kukreja 2003: 67).

Several challenges remain to be tackled for the country to return to political stability. Nawaz Sharif faces an uphill task to tackle Taliban insurgency in North West Frontier Province besides the ethnic and sectarian strife in Karachi, ailing economy, complicated ties with the US, and chronic energy crisis. The new Prime Minister in his inauguration speech vows to strengthen democracy, condemned drone strikes and talked about relations with China and choose to not to mention India and holding back on boosting India Pakistan ties.

It is still too early to predict what shape the India-Pakistan peace process might take. While there is growing acceptance among Pakistan's political class that the principal threat to Pakistan is not from India but from within especially from Jihadists and militant Islamists. Given the rise of Islamist violence in Pakistan and the imminent looming threat to its internal stability in the wake of a US withdrawal from Afghanistan impending in 2014 may also be the opportunity for cooperation between India and Pakistan in meeting the terror threat that could endanger the South Asian region as a whole (*Times of India*, 29 May 2013: 22).

NOTES

1. The officers of the Pakistan Army while taking the oath of loyalty when passing out from the military academy take two pledges – to uphold the ideology of Pakistan and avenge the military defeat of 1971. (Refer Dixit 2002: 361).
2. Pakistan's confidence in dealing with India has received a shot in the arm following its emergence as a nuclear power in 1998. Another dimension of the nuclear power status is that despite the apparent failure of the Kargil adventure in 1999, Pakistan strategic thinking opens up possibilities of such

adventures in future also.

3. The eight baskets are Jammu and Kashmir, Siachen, Wullar Barrage/Tulbul Navigation Project, Sir Creek, Terrorism and Drug Trafficking, Economic and Commercial Cooperation, Peace and Security and Promotion of Friendly Exchanges in various fields.
4. The talks between the foreign ministers did not begin on a happy note, with the Indian foreign minister expressing strong displeasure over Pakistani foreign ministers meeting with Hurriyat leaders on 26 July ahead of the talks. Refer *The Times of India,* 28 July 2011

REFERENCES

Bahadur, Kalim 2011, "Pakistan, India's Neighbour: So near, but so far", *World Focus,* 378 (June)

Dixit, J.N. 1995, *Anatomy of a Flawed Inheritance: Indo-Pakistan Relations 1970-1994,* New Delhi: Konark.

Kukreja, Veena (2000), "Pakistan's Game Plan", *The Pioneer,* New Delhi, 7 May.

Kukreja, Veena 2002, "Agra Summit: The Indian Perspective", *Punjab Journal of Politics,* 26(1).

Kukreja, Veena 2003, *Contemporary Pakistan: Political Processes, Conflicts and Crises,* New Delhi: Sage Publications.

Kukreja, Veena and Singh, M.P. (eds.) 2005, *Pakistan: Democracy, Development and Security Issues,* New Delhi: Sage Publications.

Kumar, Satish (ed.) 2013, *India's National Security: Annual Review 2012,* London, New York and Delhi: Routledge

Kumar, Sumita 2003, 'External Factors Impinging on Pakistan's Decision to Talk with India', *Strategic Analysis,* XXVII (3).

Leven, Anatol 2002, "The Pressures on Pakistan", *Foreign Affairs* LXXXI (1).

Nayar, Kuldip 2002, "Not Enough in it for India", *The Hindu,* New Delhi, 18 February, p.11.

Singh, Jasjit (ed.) 1999, *Kargil 1999: Pakistna's Fourth War for Kashmir,* New Delhi: Knowledge World.

Subrahmanyam, K. 2002, "Washington's Waiting: Islamabad's Tokenism will not Work", *The Times of India,* New Delhi, 11 February, p.14.

The Times of India (New Delhi) 21 May 2011, "Walk the Talk", Editorial.

16

Gyroscope of Indian Foreign Policy: A Case of Pakistan – China

Prof. Dilip Mohite

Asia has become a billiard table of the world with the five nuclear capable states converging with each other. The five powers, India, China, Russia, Pakistan and U.S.A. have been involved in preserving their vital national interest. The three nuclear weapon capable states, India, China and Pakistan have historical enmity with each other, starting from political ambition to unresolved territorial disputes. The confrontation between these powers and their relations with each other cannot be examined in isolation since some key extra-regional powers like U.S.A. and Russia are deeply involved in Asia with their geo-strategic and geo-political interest. This makes the length of Asian billiard ball table gives an appearance of a snooker game, each ball hitting each other with a view to achieve their objective, aiming at serving their vital national interest. Their goal and objectives are demonstrated through their 'foreign policies'. This article evaluates mainly the role of Indian Foreign Policy in it interactions with involved actors mentioned earlier. The major focus would be India's relations with Pakistan, China, U.S.A. and Russia. Occasional reference to some actors like Iran, Afghanistan and some South Asian states in limited way. The essay begins with Pakistan, as India's first adversary.

PAKISTAN

Shashi Tharoor writes, Pakistan ever since its creation remains a biggest challenge to India's foreign policy[1]. It has challenged India's ambition and goal of predominant power in South Asia. Not considering India's size and resources, Pakistan suffered from variety of dilemmas. This includes inherent insecurity infused by its founder Muhammad Ali Jinnah. His statement at the time of creation of Pakistan still dominates the psyche of Pakistan's policy makers. Jinnah in his historical speech stated, *"A weak Pakistan and a strong Hindustan will be a temptation for the strong Hindustan to dictate. I have always said, Pakistan must be viable state and sufficiently strong as a balance vis-à-vis Hindustan. I am therefore against the partition of Punjab, Bengal and we will fight every inch of it"*[2]. Three points emerge out of Jinnah's speech. One, the tremendous sense of insecurity, two, balance of power to overcome its insecurity and three, urge for more territories to be carved out of India. These three factors dominate the foreign policy behavior towards India, creating serious concern for India's political and geo-strategic ambition and its pronounced role in South Asia.

India's foreign policy towards Pakistan has been intriguing. Right from the day one, India committed grievous mistake of taking the Kashmir problem to the UNO Nehru was ill advised by his aides. The UN showed partisan attitude under the U.S.A. sponsored resolutions on Kashmir. It was Soviet veto that saved India. Later in 1965 war, India surrendered strategically important territories like Haji Pir Pass and some key positions in Rajasthan and Punjab. The ceasefire was enforced again under pressure from the U.S.A., denying any advantage that would accrue to India. In 1971 Bangladesh war, India once again failed to take advantage of having 90,000 Pakistani prisoners of war. India fell prey to false assurances from Pakistan at Simla meet. Indian foreign policy also exposed its vulnerability to external pressures.

Towards the fag end of 20th century, Pakistan committed aggression in Kargil. Indian security apparatus was caught napping[3]. India retaliated and drove away Pakistani intruders but surprisingly giving them a safe passage. An aggressive and punitive action would have borne different results.

NUCLEAR CAPABILITY

By the end of 20th century and the beginning of 21st century, both India and Pakistan became de-facto nuclear powers. India's nuclear capability was in response to the Chinese nuclear capability. It was described as 'credible deterrence' and its nuclear doctrine elaborately stated 'no first use'. The nuclearization of South Asia is attributed to 'chain theory'. Given Chinese threat to India's security, it also took into account China-Pakistan bonhomie as collective threat to India's security. Combined nuclear and conventional threat to India raised couple of fundamental issues. The Indian foreign policy was found wanting in addressing this issue vis-à-vis U.S.A. and China. First, U.S.A. connived at Pakistan's nuclear programme, despite the fact that the state of Pakistan had earned the reputation of being a weak, failed and rogue state. The policy makers in U.S.A. largely compromised with its non-proliferation norms. This was simply to use Pakistan as a 'frontline state' against Soviets in Afghanistan. In a way, the American money, arms and expertise was clearly diverted to Kashmiri insurgency. Indirectly, the U.S.A. became the source and threat to India's security. New Delhi was either circumspect or was unable to address this issue with the Americans vigorously. A strong reaction and a punitive action during Kargil or after the attack on India Parliament showed lack of will and determination on the part of India.

Pakistan having insulated itself by achieving nuclear capability neutralized India's conventional superiority. It also embarked on new strategy of 'low intensity conflict' which was the result of nuclear capability[4]. India and Pakistan are interlocked so far as any direct confrontation is concerned but Pakistan has full advantage of interlocking by intensifying cross-border terrorism. Attack on Parliament, 26/11 Mumbai attacks and several other sabotage acts are a result of Pakistan's state sponsored terrorism. This is described as 'bleed India with thousand ants'.

Indian reaction to the attack on Parliament and subsequent declaration of *'Aar Par Ki Ladai'* and Mumbai attack frittered down to mere rhetoric. India's failure to act tough and shying away from any effective action is attributed to China-Pakistan nexus and also U.S.A.'s favorable disposition to Pakistan. It is a NATO ally, strategically significant Islamic state. Indian options to resolve such acts diplomatically is attributed to its weak government and also the economic cost of the war. This has sent wrong signals to both Pakistan and China, where in both keep pricking India by encouraging insurgency in Kashmir or in the North East.

Indian options are limited to diplomatic solution of the problem. The MEA has entered into limited collaboration with U.S.A. to tackle the terrorist problem. India refused to participate actively along with the Americans in their war on terror in Afghanistan. India categorically stated that it is competent enough to deal with the terrorist problem of following rational model of diplomatic recourse. However, overall observation reveals that India has not rigorously pursued UNSC resolution 1373 of the chapter which elaborates that all member states to take whole range of action against suspected terrorist organizations. India should have pursued this matter not only in the UN but also enlighten other members highlighting 'continued inaction by Islamabad', possibility of moving the UNSC to hold Pakistan in breach of resolution 1373 and threatening sanctions against Pakistan if compliance does not follow. The present efforts by the MEA to educate and enlighten world leaders and public opinion lacks will and aggression. Along with the option of diplomatic efforts, India also needs to cultivate strong public opinion against state sponsored terrorism.

India has utilized almost all options to expose Pakistan's duplicity in the areas of LIC (Low Intensity Conflict) by promoting terrorist activities and promoting hate India tirade. But India's efforts lack diplomatic punch. One can recall Mrs. Indira Gandhi's appeal to Americans by-passing official government stand on East Pakistan. There was a marked contrast between Nixon-Kissinger attitude while Mrs. Gandhi was able to influence most of Congressmen and Senate members on the abuse of Human Rights, misuse of American arms and massacre of Bangla people. The Nixon-Kissinger duo was rendered helpless till India liberated East Pakistan and created the new nation of Bangladesh[5]. Two major points emerge out of this episode. First, aggressive diplomacy by which American public opinion was cultivated in favour of India's role in liberating Bangladesh. Second, was the realistic approach to India's foreign policy by signing the 'Treaty of Cooperation and Friendship' with the Soviet Union, neutralizing American-Pakistan-Chinese nexus. Such pragmatic and aggressive diplomacy has not been experienced since 1971 Bangladesh war. All through dealings with Pakistan shows complacency and it is a fact that 'complacency is never sensible in international relations'. What is needed is strong doses of realism while dealing with Pakistan.

Ultimately, discussion on India-Pakistan relations boils down to Kashmir. The by-product of Kashmir problem is the induction of strong Islamist mobilization of the masses in Pakistan and some other Islamic countries. However, there are few geo-political and geo-economic factors which have attracted attention of some scholars. The contest between India-Pakistan has geo-economic dimension. The big question is 'why do people keep invading Afghanistan?' Pakistan's interest in Afghanistan which led Pakistan to take a complete u-turn which resulted into supporting U.S.A. keeping geo-strategic and geo-political factors as futuristic goal of Pakistan's foreign policy. Apart from Russo-American interest in controlling the Afghan landmass, India and Pakistan are vying to have their influence in Afghanistan. The country provides land pathway from Middle East to Asia. Besides Golan Heights and Kashmir are flashpoints because they are high-ground between countries that have been traditionally been enemies. Who so controls high-grounds controls war and peace between two nations. Highlands may also be important for their water resources. The Indus River which is vital to the survival of Pakistan flows through Kashmir[6]. Looking from this perspective, the three Afghan wars fought between the British and the Russian influence pre-invasion of 1979 and then the American interest in ousting the Soviets by 1989-90. The US war on terror also has the side interest of keeping Afghanistan under its control. Further, Pakistan's u-turn and joining the Americans in Afghanistan explains its geo-political and geo-strategic interest in that country. India too has entered Afghanistan quietly by extending development activities, directly trying to erode the Pakistan's role in Afghanistan. Post American withdrawal in 2014, it is going to be a stiff challenge to India's foreign policy makers. It is not only Pakistan but must likely India will have to face joint China-Pakistan in Afghanistan. The US-Russian game plan will have to be taken into account, especially in the views of geo-strategic and geo-political significance of Afghanistan. India, with limited resources and half-backed will, will be found wanting in dealing with quadruple pressure of three great powers (U.S.A., Russia and China) and traditional adversary Pakistan. India will have to be vigilant at the likely global power shifts and strategic transition in the Asia region. The pessimism expressed is in the light of the weak Indian government, domestic political turmoil and decline of Indian economy. The challenge faced by India would need strong government, a fast decision making process, economic and military capability and a government without scams. It is needless to say that it is not Pakistan alone, but host of other powers which will have to be tackled with a strong punch in the MEA establishment.

INDIA-CHINA

India-China relations are like jigsaw puzzle. It is extremely difficult and challenging to assess which way this relationship would go. The options are not many except the two, cooperation or conflict. The contemporary scenario indicates cooperation level on a higher scale while conflict level has been fluctuating from high to low levels. China, a future potential super power, has clashed with India over the territorial issue since 1962. Soon after the 1962 Indo-China war, Pakistan lost no opportunity in embracing China as a bully against India, causing security concern for India. By mid 1980s, India forced two adversaries, which would act in tandem in case of a conflict with India. It is here where the new balance of power game was revived against India. Earlier, the U.S.A. having bracketed India with the Soviet block, boosted Pakistan's military and political capability by providing massive military and financial assistance to Pakistan. After the 1962 Indo-China war, P.R.C. joined U.S.A. in boosting Pakistan's strategic capabilities. In mid 1980s, Raju G.C. Thomas wrote that India should be ready for one full war and another half war[7]. What he meant was that either full war with either China or Pakistan and half war with the other. Now, the Asia's new power game has begun where extra-regional powers like U.S.A., Russia are deeply involved. The global power shift began with the end of Cold War. Asia has become a new arena of power struggle in the world. The focus has shifted from Atlantic (Europe) to Pacific where an intense struggle is in offing. It is a matter of conjecture whether the struggle will involve armed conflict with three major powers, China, India and Pakistan with nuclear capability. Concerned over the phenomenal rise of China, this has prompted the U.S.A. to explore the possibility of using India as a balance to China, while China is using more or less the same strategy of controlling and containing India through Pakistan.

Here, therefore the issues which emerge in India-China relations are that of military and economic balance or one could even describe as competition. How does India's foreign policy strategy deal with China-Pakistan military challenge and also economics as a tool to cool down the conflict level with a dual objective of de-signifying the importance of Pakistan in Chinese as well as U.S.A.'s calculations.

Ashley Tellis eloquently describes U.S.A. objectives in regard to China is to protect U.S.A. primary, interests, extended deterrence obligation in Asia and beyond against Chinese challenges that might materialize overtime[8]. India's perception of China differs from the American perspectives. India is surely weary of Chinese growing power but would be contended if Chinese do not threaten Indian security and other economic interest. The Indian approach is directed towards regional hegemony and rise as 'great power' within the confines of its capability. The Indian policy has been largely directed towards cooperation and not conflict, use trade and commerce as pacifying factors to any aggressive Chinese overtures. It also aims at weakening of China-Pakistan linkage which is evident from Chinese cooling up on Kargil, Kashmir issue and concern over terrorists activities supported and sponsored by Pakistan. Observations by Leo Rose suggest that lately China pursued a rather subtle partnership with Pakistan: it will do minimum necessary to preserve Pakistani security from a distance, but it has sought to avoid overt entanglement[9].

The Chinese have also realized Indian concerns about its security. More pressure from China may force India to move closer to U.S.A. which would be damaging to Chinese goals in Africa and the world. Though, Chinese hold military and nuclear advantage over India, India with its advantageous geo-political location can disturb Chinese oil procurement from the Persian Gulf. At the Strait of Hormuz, Indian Navy, if necessary with the American Navy may enforce blockade of oil supply to China. These are no doubt half-hearted option before India. India's established foreign policy norms would be to keep away from any such military entanglements, either with U.S.A. or even for that matter with Russia, unless pushed to wall by the Chinese. The Chinese knows this fact and would not venture which may encourage India-U.S.A. ties against the Chinese. As such, India had security dialogues with Japan, U.S.A. in 2011. India also has loose security tie up with Vietnam, South Korea, Singapore, Indonesia, etc. signaling collective approach to Chinese designs. A point to be noted is that so far India has avoided any formal defense treaty with any of the East African states or for that matter with U.S.A. Two points need to be noted with caution. First, India's approach to its security is to maintain strategic autonomy and show to the world of its confidence in its military and economic capability. Second,

India feels confident that the border issue which is at present bone of contention between China and India will not blare into any major conflict. The reason being a nuclear deterrence and more than that, economic incentives are far more dominant in Indo-Chinese relations. Both stand to gain by peaceful approach rather than armed conflict in a bigger scale.

While interpreting China-U.S.A. relations, Aron Friedberg highlights five factors which would dominate[10] and can be applied to India-China relation with some minor modifications. First, closer economic benefits and inter-dependence where both states to gain enormously in their pursuit of national goal of emerging as the next super power and as a great power by 2025. Indo-Chinese trade is likely to reach $100 billion in next 3-4 years. Moreover, both sides have shown willingness to cooperate in their respective energy need from Africa, Central Asia and few other regions. Hence, the scale of cooperation weighs much higher than conflict. The second point is that China may become more open and democratic. Third, China is continuing its integration into the international system. This would make China to behave more responsibly to work towards stable and peaceful world order. Its behavior towards India and other nations would stem from this angle. The best example is that of condemning terrorist activities by the Islamic forces, indirectly implicate Pakistan. The fourth factor where India-China cooperation is foreseen is climatic change. India-China have addressed the issue of environment and climatic change though the whole issue is at its primary stage. But efforts are on. Both have shown serious concern over this issue[11]. Fifth is the possession of nuclear weapons which acts deterrence. It is true that there is asymmetry between the number and capability of China and India. Yet, nuclear weapons can act as deterrence. It prevents both from escalating their conflict. Quoting Avery Goldstein, Aron

Friedberg argues that U.S.A. and China have already into a relationship of mutual deterrence that provides not only robust buffer against general war, but also a strong constraint on both limited war and crisis[12]. I would argue that more or less same logic would apply to India-China relations, if not now but in near future. What India needs is to fill up the gap between with China and keep building its military and economic capabilities. If America takes Chinese nuclear deterrence seriously, the Chinese would take India's nuclear deterrence seriously and would not venture into any direct military confrontation. It is more of a win-win situation. Pay offs from cooperation are far greater for both, India and China.

CONCLUSIONS

India-Pakistan rivalry which is not political, confined to political factor that of Kashmir, but has many other dimensions. Claim on Kashmir on ethno-religious ground, helps Pakistan to keep its society united. Pakistan's social mosaic is full of sharp socio-ethnic-religious diversities. Shia-Sunni conflict, ethnic divide between tribals of Balochistan, North West Frontier and Sindhi-Punjabi Muslim divide is indissoluble. The only option that Pakistan has is that of religion. Instead of good governance and welfare measures Pakistan has fallen victim to South Asian destructive element of socio-religious-ethnic divisiveness[13]. By its popular characteristic, Islam has been more proved to be divisive force rather than integrative phenomenon. Further, Pakistan claims to possess geo-strategic advantage but finds itself sandwiched between two hostile neighbors, India and Afghanistan. With India, it is self-created hostility which Pakistan policy makers feel that it is necessary to nurture such hostility for its survival as a state. Indian foreign policy has pragmatically dealt with this phenomenon but fails to convince its counterpart. There is small number of rationale minded people in the Pakistan foreign policy establishment but they are in minority and helpless against religion and war mongering Army personnel. There are different groups which call tune in Pakistan's foreign policy behavior. It is here where MEA finds itself in a state of dilemma. The problem is how to deal and with whom to deal? An example is that of 'bus diplomacy' followed by Kargil. Both Pakistan and India fearing more of conventional conflict, spending enormous amount of resources on propaganda, espionage and insurgencies, low intensity conflict to bleed either on their behalf or on behalf of their client state or groups. If India is also involved in above strategy, then it is counter-productive to its origin from Pakistan. The possession of nuclear weapons by both India and Pakistan may make war less possible but military competition between them would be destructive to that country which has socio-economic and unresolvable internal problems. The Indian foreign policy will have to deal with all these issues with pragmatism since Pakistan is not one state but states within the state.

India's relations with China are showing gradual normalization, except occasional outburst of boundary dispute or claim on Indian state of Arunachal. India is viewing its relationship from three broad angles. The most worrisome is security dilemma that India faces against China. The second one refers to China-Pakistan nexus where China is using Pakistan as bully against India or putting it the parlance of international politics as 'balancer'. The third factor is that of trade and commerce. The issue here is whether the Indian and Chinese foreign policy options favor cooperation or conflict which may arise out of trade rivalry. But at this stage, the situation indicates more of cooperation rather than conflict.

Demonstration of Chinese nuclear capability in 1964 created serious security concerns in India. Having suffered a defeat in 1962, India till today harps on Chinese threat.

China weighs heavily on the Indian strategic think tank. Indian concerns were not restricted to China since Pakistan was quick enough to force security arrangement with China. This nexus came very handy for the Chinese military strategy. Pakistan began to receive double dose of military, economic and political boost from China as well as U.S.A. Emboldened by double support, Pakistan was successful in balancing India including acquiring nuclear capability with the know-how from the Chinese. The Americans, for their own strategic reasons connived at Pakistan's nuclear programme[14]. It is a misnomer that it was only China that helped Pakistan to develop nuclear bomb. J.N. Dixit, states that "Pakistan was helped in terms of material, technology, maps and designs and sophisticated equipments by France, the U.K., U.S.A., Holland, Germany, Italy and Scandinavian countries indirectly apart from larger Chinese help in missile capacities." He also further states, "Aircrafts of US and French origins were given suitable weapons configuration structures to carry and deliver nuclear warheads." With Chinese blessings, Pakistan was able to trigger insurgency and low intensity conflict with India. This was a major strain on India's security, as the Chinese could keep India to pin down to Pakistan and also achieve its objective of containing India to South Asian region. John W. Graver writes to substantiate this point, "India's 1971 nuclear arms capability, coupled with India's substantial conventional superiority would enable India to dominate the subcontinent and relegate Pakistan to the status of a Vassal state[15]. Such an outcome was intolerable to Beijing, which sought to keep India tied down in the subcontinent in its continuing conflict with Pakistan." However, it should be noted that India's efforts of re-approachment process, the Chinese have "distanced itself from Pakistan." This development is interpreted as the Chinese fear of Pakistan as 'failed state' and its support on missiles and nuclear capability may become an issue of criticism from the international community. The Chinese stand on Kashmir has also evolved over a period of time. It does not commit itself to any military assistance. The conflict broke out between India and Pakistan over Kashmir. This fact is highlighted by Susan Shirk. She observes, 'most Chinese diplomats were as eager as their American counterpart to rekindle relations with India'[16]. It is therefore evident that from year 2000 onwards both India and China have shown willingness to dissolve outstanding border issue and concentrate positively to improve trade and commerce which is likely to touch $100 billion by 2014-15. Viewing from this perspective, India's MEA has done a steady progress in improving relations and more importantly distancing China from Pakistan.

The overall conclusion on India's foreign policy addressed to hostile attitude as reflected in the behavior of the state of Pakistan clearly indicates two major traits. First, there is no centralized decision making apparatus in Pakistan. It is torn between the civilian elected government, the Army and religious bigots. This makes MEA's task extremely complicated and falls into treachery from time to time. The best example is that of Delhi-Lahore bus service, which was considered as symbol of new era in Indo-Pak relation. While Nawaz Sharif and Vajpayee were busy signing the pact, the Pakistan military under Pervez Musharraf were planning Kargil. This is once again demonstrated by 26/11, the Mumbai Attack again under the civilian government in Pakistan. This amply proves the fact that there is no central and effective decision making apparatus in Pakistan.

The second factor is hypothetical but it connotes to American military withdrawal from Afghanistan. Pakistan, for strategic depth and for reasons would be roped into Afghanistan with military presence. The Americans would cleverly exploit Pakistan's pronounced goal in Afghanistan and also force Pakistan to fill the vacuum after the American withdrawal. In this case Pakistan would need larger force in Afghanistan there by Kashmir plank would be weakened. Most Pakistani units will be shifted to Afghanistan. Under the circumstances, the support to Kashmiri separatists would also dwindle. The Pakistan strategy would be to accelerate Kashmir separatist movement by attracting international attention. This explains nearly 80 ceasefire line violations by the Pakistani Army on LAC.

So far the Indo-China relations are concerned, the MEA policy has shown consistency of giving due importance to its relations with China. The border issue is too insignificant for both, the Chinese as well as for Indians to invite major conflict. The two ambitions, the Chinese to emerge as super power and India to emerge as great power shows more acceptance and accommodation. For both, economic incentives are far more attractive then entering into a serious border conflicts. The Chinese also know that too much pressure on India would result into U.S.A. taking advantage of the situation which neither China nor India would like. Indian perceptions are clear that it cannot prevent Chinese rise, unless its collapse comes on the same line as the former Soviet Union. Moreover, India knows it very well that if China, while aiming at becoming super power becomes more aggressive, it is bound to have clash of interest with U.S.A. and some East Asian states. The fact remains that this would make China to behave responsibly as an important member of international community. This fact would also worsen China-Pakistan ties which augurs well for India. The MEA should work on consolidating its relations with China, which would alienate Pakistan, and also keep its strategic autonomy intact from any external pressure from U.S.A. or any other power. Ultimately, in finality, the Pakistanis reflect incohesiveness in their approach, while the Chinese have strong centralized decision making process, and while India's foreign policy is a victim of indecision due to coalition government at the centre.

REFERENCES

1 Shashi Tharoor, 'Pax Indica and the World of 21st Century', London: Penguine Books, 2012, p. 55

2 A.G. Noorani, 'Economic and Political Weekly' September 11, 1976, pp. 1500-4

3 K. Subramaniam, 'From Surprise to Reckoning – The Kargil Review Committee Report'

4 See Saira Khan, Nuclear Weapons and Conflict Transformation – The Case of India-Pakistan, London: Routledge, 2009, Chapter 3.

5 Staneley Wolpert, 'Roots of Confrontation in South Asia'

6 Valerie M. Hudson, Foreign Policy Analysis – Classic and Contemporary Theory, Rowman and Littlefield Publishers, Maryland, 2007, p. 146

7 Raju G.C. Thomas, 'The Growth of Indian Military Power – From Sufficient to Defense to Nuclear Defense' in Ross Babbage and Sandy Gordon eds., New York: St. Martin's Press, 1992, p. 41-42

8 Ashley Tellis, 'US and Indian Interest Extended Neighbourhood', in Alyssa Ayres and C. Rajmohan, 'Power Realignment in Asia', New Delhi: Sage Publishers, 2009, Ch. 10

9 Leo Rose, India and China: Forging New Relationship in Asia Pacific in the New Millennium: Geo-politics, Security and Foreign Policy, ed. Shailendra Sharma, Berkeley, California Institute of Asian Studies, 2000, 234-38

10 Aron Friedberg, A Contest for Supremacy: China, America and Struggle for Mastery in Asia, Princeton, W.W. Morton & Co. Press, 2011

11 P.S. Ramkrishnan, 'Growing India-China Economies, Linked Environmental Concerns and Emerging Scenarios', in Alyssa Ayres and C. Rajamohan eds.

12 Avery Goldstein, Quoted in Arona L. Steinberg. op. cited

13 Anatol Livitov, 'Pakistan a Hard Country', London: Penguin Books, 2012, Ch. 1

14 J. N. Dixit, 'India-Pakistan in War and Peace', New Delhi: India Today Group, 2002, p. 337-8

15 John Graver, 'Protracted Contest: Sino-Indian Rivalry in 20th Century', Seattle: University of Washington Press, 2001, p. 50-51

16 Susan Shirk, in Francine Frankel and Harry Harding, eds. 'The India China Relationship', Washington: Woodrow Wilson Center Press, 2004, p. 89

17

India's Policy towards the Himalayan Kingdoms: A Study of India-Bhutan bilateral relations

Sarish Sebastian

INTRODUCTION

India's policy towards the Himalayan Kingdoms had a thrust of retaining the core British strategic framework of keeping these kingdoms as an integral part of India's defence structure. The geo-strategic position of Bhutan and Nepal has transformed the relations with these countries into a vital importance to India since independence. For both the Himalayan Kingdoms, there is no doubt that security imperatives are at the core of the close relationship with India in terms of its security interests and territorial integrity. The long-standing political disputes and border confrontations between India and China, Bhutan have been a part of India's strategic defence plan for a long time. The events that took place in the Tibet region had a major effect on India- Bhutan relations in the past. In the year 1951, when Tibet was taken over by the Chinese Communists, Bhutan moved towards her southern neighbour India for enhanced external help and strong bilateral relations.

HISTORICAL BACKGROUND OF INDIA BHUTAN RELATIONS

In Indian geo-politics, Bhutan occupies a strategic position in the Himalayas on northern border. With respect to the border issues with China, it is natural for India to maintain friendly relations with Bhutan. The relations between India and Bhutan can be traced back to the entry of Guru Rinpoche to Bhutan from India in 747 A.D. Under the Shabdrungs and first two Druk Gyalpos, who followed a policy of isolation from the rest of the world, Bhutan had relations only with India. Formal treaty based relations commenced in 1910, when the King signed a treaty with British India. Even during the periods of isolation, Bhutan had maintained good relationship with India, especially with the bordering states such as Ladakh, Lahaul, Spiti and Kinnaur in the West and Sikkim, Cooch Behar and Northern Assam in South-East. Under the treaty of 1910, the British Government agreed not to interfere in the internal affairs of Bhutan and the Bhutanese government agreed to be guided by the advice of the British government in regard to its external relations. After the independence in 1947, Indian government signed a new treaty with Bhutanese government on 8 August, 1949. Under this treaty, India played a major role in Bhutan's relations with the rest of the world. Though the treaty gives some sort of restrictions in the nation's foreign relations, India respected Bhutan's sovereignty and aspiration and in fact supported the nation for establishing diplomatic relations with other nations.[1]

POLITICAL RELATIONS

The political scene in the entire Himalayan region and Indian sub-continent underwent great changes by the middle of 20th century. The takeover of Tibet by the People's Liberation Army in 1950 and the presence of Chinese troops near the border of Bhutan led Bhutan to re-evaluate its traditional policy of isolation and looked for support from the Indian government, which became an immediate necessity. Such a relationship boosted the strategic interest of both the nations. Bhutan began its socio-economic development and Modernisation process mostly with the assistance of India. With the border conflict between India and Bhutan in 1962, Indo-Bhutan relations began to take on concrete form following state visits made by the Third King, His Majesty Jigme Dorji Wangchuk to India and by Prime Minister Jawaharlal Nehru between 1954 and 1961. A formal bilateral relation between Bhutan and India began in 1968, when a special officer of the Government of India is appointed to Bhutan. The Embassy of India in Bhutan known as the India House was established on May 14, 1968 and formal Resident Representatives were exchanged in 1971.[2]

THE TREATY OF 1949

Aiming for peace and cooperation and non-interference in each other's internal affairs, India and Bhutan signed the Treaty of Friendship on August 8, 1949. However, updating the 1910's treaty with the British India, Bhutan agreed to let India "guide" its foreign policy and both the nations would consult each other closely on foreign and defence affairs. This treaty also established a free trade and extradition protocols between both the nations. The second half of the 20th century saw a major increase in India's economic, military and development aid to Bhutan that helped the Modernisation of its security. By the end of the 20th century, Bhutan began to express its dissatisfaction in being assisted by Indian Government in its foreign affairs. Though the relations between both the nations remained closer, the Royal Government of Bhutan expressed a need to amend some parts of the treaty to enhance the nation's sovereignty. Bhutan slowly gained its momentum of an independent actor in the international relations by joining the UN in 1971 and signing a new treaty with Bangladesh in 1972. The move towards being an independent actor in the international relations does not create any issues with the treaties signed with India in 1949. Both the nation's relations have not been affected by concerns over the treaty provisions.[3]

THE TREATY OF 2007

The Friendship Treaty of 1949 was renegotiated and amended and India and Bhutan signed a new Treaty of Friendship in 2007, which gives Bhutan complete sovereign power in its foreign affairs. The new treaty replacing the provision of requiring guidance from the Indian Government was removed and granted complete freedom over arms import. In the year 2008, the Indian Prime Minister Dr. Manmohan Singh visited Bhutan and expressed strong support for Bhutan's move towards democracy and encouraged deeper bilateral foreign relations.[4]

INDO-BHUTAN RELATIONS AT PRESENT

Since the establishment of a parliamentary democracy in 2008, the relationships between India and Bhutan reached to a new level of cooperation. The relationship between both countries further increased with the tradition of regular visits of the high-level officers. The State Visit of His Majesty the King Jigme Khesar Namgyel Wangchuck to India from 21st to 26th of December 2009 was first such visit to a foreign country since his coronation as the King of Bhutan in 2008. Later from 5th to 7th October 2010, the King visited India during which University of Calcutta conferred upon him the Honorary Doctorate Degree of Law. His Majesty the King again visited India from 20-29 October 2010 for the National Defence College's (NDC) golden jubilee celebrations as Special Guest of Honour. His Majesty the King Jigme Khesar Namgyel Wangchuck and Her majesty the Queen Jetsun Pema Wangchuck paid a State Visit to India from October 23-31, 2011, the first foreign visit after the Royal Wedding on 13th October 2011. The King His Majesty the King Jigme Khesar Namgyel Wangchuck was the chief guest for the 64th Republic Day on 26th January 2013.

On January 14, 2013, the Indian External Affairs Minister, Salman Khurshid, was on an official visit to Thimpu strengthening the ties between both the nations. At present India is more concerned about the political issue of Bhutan's recent talks with China and the internal security concerns of both India and Bhutan. Another important matter of concern between India and Bhutan was the internal security issues that gained impotence at recent time as Bhutan witnessed occasional incidents of IED blasts in 2012 and increased activity of insurgent groups across the India-Bhutan border. A healthy relationship between both the nations is important at the present conditions and given its strategic importance, India cannot ignore the tiny kingdom and should always be sensitive to its relations to create a long-term relation.[5]

ECONOMIC RELATIONS

A planned development in Bhutan began in 1961 with the introduction of the Five Year Plans in the country. First two Five Year Plans were fully funded by the Government of India. Over the years, the assistance from the government of India has increased steadily from Rs. 107 million in the First Five year plan to Rs. 9000 million in the Eight five year plan. A detailed description of India's contribution to

Bhutan's Five Year Plans is given in Table 4.3. Though Bhutan began to get foreign aid from other nations after joining the UN, India continued to be the major donor of external aid to Bhutan. Over the last few decades, India has provided assistance to Bhutan mainly in the social sectors such as education and human resource development, health, hydropower development, agriculture and roads. Gradually, the economic relations between Bhutan and India collaborated on mutually beneficial projects like hydropower development and industrial projects. These projects are taken outside the Five Year Plan programs and considered beneficial to both the nations especially to the Indian companies. Such a mutual beneficiary projects will assure business opportunities in the manufacturing and other industries in both India and Bhutan.[6]

Today, India stands as the biggest development partner of Bhutan. In the year 2011, bilateral trade between India and Bhutan reached Rs. 61.6 billion which constituted 72 percent of Bhutan's total imports and 85 percent of its exports. Almost 70 percent of the kingdom's trade is with India and as of the statistics of 2011, a large amount of development budget of India's Ministry of External Affairs goes to Bhutan. For the year, 2010-2011 Bhutan received almost Rs. 1723 cores as loan from India in which most of the amount goes to development programmes. The recent visit of Salman Khurshid in 2013 was also a beginning process of Bhutan's "Eleventh Plan".[7]

MAJOR PROJECTS IN BHUTAN FUNDED BY GOVERNMENT OF INDIA (GOI)

Besides the assistance for various Five Year Plans, India funds some major projects in Bhutan like the hydroelectric power projects, Penden and Dungsam cement projects, Hashimara-Phuentsholing Railway Line (the "Golden Jubilee Rail Line"), 'Total Solutions Project' (for capacity

Table : India's Contribution to Bhutan's Five Year Plans

[In Rs. crores]

Five Year Plans	Total Allocations	India's Contribution	% of India's Contribution
1961-66 (1st Plan)	10.72	10.72	100%
1966-71 (2nd Plan)	20.22	20.22	100%
1971-76 (3rd Plan)	47.52	42.66	90%
1976-81 (4th Plan)	1,10.62	85.30	77%
1981-87 (5th Plan)	4,44.05	134.0	30.2%
1987-92 (6th Plan)	9,50.00	4,00.00	42.1%
1992-97 (7th Plan)	23,50.00	7,50.00	31.9%
1997-02 (8th Plan)	4000.00	1050.00	26%
2002-08 (9th Plan)	8900.00	2610.14	29.33%
2008-13 (10th Plan)	14800.00	3400.00	23%

Source: http://www.indianembassythimphu.bt/goi_assistance.html

building in ICT sector and establishment of Bhutan Institute of Medical Sciences). In various agreements, Government of India has agreed to provide assistance to Bhutan in developing the hydropower sector and to purchase at least 10000 MW of power by 2020. In order to produce such huge amount of electricity, 10 hydropower projects have been agreed during the first Empowered Joint Group (EJG) Meeting held in Delhi on March 2009. Among these ten projects, the Punatsangchhu-I Hydro Electric Project was signed on 28th July 2007. The GOI had funded a number of projects under the cooperation between the two nations such as the Chhukha (336MW), Kurichhu (60MW), and Tala (1020MW) Hydro Power Projects; the Penden and Dungsam Cement Projects; and the Paro Airport Project.[8] Some of the completed or ongoing GOI funded Mega Projects are:

CHUKHA HYDRO ELECTRIC PROJECT (CHEP)

The Chukha Hydro Electric Project (CHEP) is a 336 MW project located on Wangchu River in Chukha district.

This was built by GOI at a low cost of Rs. 2460 million. This project has a significant share in the revenue generation of the Royal Government of Bhutan (RGOB) through export of electricity to India. This project now is run by the Chukha Hydropower Corporation.

KURICHHU HYDRO ELECTRIC PROJECT (KHEP)

The Kurichhu Hydro Electric Project (KHEP) is a 60 MW project located on Kurichhu River in Mongar district. The project was established in April 2006, with the objective of providing enough and reliable power to eight eastern Dzongkhags to bring socio-economic development in the region. Under the KHE project, surplus power is exported to India which earned revenue to the RGOB.

TALA HYDRO ELECTRIC PROJECT (THEP)

This is a run-of-the-river 1020 MW project on the Wangchu River which was funded by the GOI with 60 percent of total expenditure as grant and 40 percent at low interest rate. This project comprises a 92 meter high concrete dam with a 22.2 km long water conductor system and an underground power house with 6 generating units and three single circuit transmission lines to the India-Bhutan border. All these six units were commissioned during the period of 2006-07.

PUNATSANGCHHU-I HYDRO ELECTRIC PROJECT (PHEP)

This was a 1200 MW project on the Punatsangchhu River which was signed on 28th July 2007 in Thimphu and it is expected to complete by the end of 2015. This project was funded by the GOI with 40 percent grant and 60 percent loan.

DUNGSAM CEMENT PLANT

Dungsam Cement Plant is a dry-process plant with an annual capacity of approximately 1 million ton per year. This plant is located at Nganglam in south-eastern region of Bhutan. the GOI provided funds and agreed to build required road and rail infrastructure for the plant which would commence its production from September, 2011.

PENDEN CEMENT PLANT

Penden Cement Plant is located in Samtse District on Indo-Bhutan border. This plant was built with Indian assistance at a cost of Rs. 142 million with an initial capacity of 300 ton per day. The project went commercial in 1982. The cement factory has contributed to the total GDP of Bhutan.[9]

TRADE RELATIONS

Over the period 1981-2001, the export to India accounted for an average of 86.5 percent of Bhutan's total export and the imports from India was around 79 percent of the total import of the country. Majority of the total trade relationship was with India and in the last decades, Bhutan began to receive import and export from and to the Western and Eastern nations. The major products for export to India are electricity, mineral products, product of chemical industries, base metals and products and wood and wood products. Imports from India to Bhutan include machinery, mechanical appliances, base metals, electronic items, foodstuff and other basic necessities and consumer items. Besides trade, Indian trade involvement was extended to other areas like private and public sector activities in Bhutan. Beyond such big companies operating in Bhutan, a number of small-scale trading and service activities are being operated by Indians. Existence of Indian investors in Bhutan is visible in the manufacturing and processing industries, construction, service, engineering, steel and electronic industries and consultancy in a large scale.[10]

Throughout the history of the country, India is the largest trading partner of Bhutan since the establishment of formal relations between both the nations. The trade agreement between India and Bhutan, which expired on March 2005, has been renewed for a period of 10 years. This agreement also provides for a duty free transit of Bhutanese merchandise for trade with other countries. During the year 2005, imports from India were Rs. 12.80 billion that constituted around 75.1 percent of Bhutan's total imports and exports to India were Rs. 9.97 billion and constituted 87.5 percent of its total exports. In the year 2009, total imports from India were Rs. 23.3 billion and it constituted around 80 percent of the Bhutan's total imports and exports to India amounted to Rs. 20.5 billion which constituted 94 percent of the nation's total export.[11] A detailed data of the trade with India from 2000 to 2011 is given in Table 4.4.

Though Bhutan's economy is inextricably linked with India, an effort towards diversifying the import and export market and products are actively pursued by the Royal government of Bhutan during last decade. Besides the trade with India, imports of consumer goods from Bangladesh, Germany, Hong Kong, Singapore, Thailand, Japan and South Korea have increased in the last few years.[12]

EDUCATIONAL AND CULTURAL COOPERATION

Beyond trade relations, close bilateral cooperation between India and Bhutan is visible in the education and cultural field. The Government of India is providing scholarships to the Bhutanese students both at undergraduate and postgraduate level. In the 10th Five Year Plan the scholarships have been increased from 50 to 85 in undergraduates and 77 for postgraduates. In order to strengthen the cultural ties between Bhutan and India, the

Table : Trade Relations between India and Bhutan from 2000 to 2011

[Rupees in Billion]

Year	2000	2001	2002	2003	2004	2005	2006	2007	2008	2009	2010	2011
Exports to Bhutan (Imports from India)	6.23	6.98	7.58	10.26	10.19	12.80	13.05	15.09	17.33	23.3	29.30	35.2
Imports from Bhutan (Exports to India)	4.37	4.70	5.13	5.92	7.76	9.97	14.48	22.72	21.48	20.5	26.00	21.04

Source: Royal Monetary Authority, RGoB

India-Bhutan Foundation (IBF) was established in August 2003. This foundation focuses more on areas like education, cultural exchanges and environment preservation in the country. On 21st September 2010, Dr. Karan Singh, President of Indian Council for Cultural Relations (ICCR) and Lyonpo Minjur Dorji, Minister for Home and Cultural Affairs of Bhutan, jointly inaugurated the Nehru-Wangchuk Cultural Centre at Thimphu.[13]

CONCLUSION

India always remained committed to its support to Bhutan in its efforts towards economic, social and political development. The bilateral relations between the two countries gained momentum in the areas of hydropower development, information and communication technology, health, industry, education and culture. During the past decades, these relations were further consolidated with regular exchange of high-level visits and strengthening of bilateral cooperation between both the nations. On April, 2010, both the nations signed the Agreements for Punatsangchhu-II and Mangdechhu Hydro Electric Projects (HEPs) alone with the launch of Information Communication Technology Project "Chipen Rigphel" or "Total Solutions project". In the year 2009, Bhutan's total imports from India constituted 80% of the nation's total imports and exports to India constituted 94% of its total exports. Under the Small Development Projects Scheme, India initiated a total of 1259 projects in Bhutan which are at various stages of its implementation.[14]

In the coming years, with the contentious state of Indo-China relations, Bhutan with its strategic location will find a major role in India's security interests. Any change or development in the Indo-China relations will also have a greater impact on India-Bhutan relations as well. The recent border talks between Bhutan and China on January 2010 over the disputed claims line in North Western Bhutan and the meeting of Chinese Premier and Bhutan's Prime Minister on June 2012 at the Rio +20 summits related to border issues and maintaining peace between both the countries generated a fear on Indian leaders over the security matters. The bilateral relations between Bhutan and China will surely be a concern for the nation's closest friend India in the near future.

Ever since both the nations embarked upon the road of friendship and cooperation, India and Bhutan have showed the world that peace and mutual benefits is possible between two neighbours even with the high level of economic disparity and terrorism.

REFERENCES

1. Council on Foreign Relations, *Bhutan's Road to Democracy*, Interview with Prime Minsiter Jigme Y. Thinley by Jayashree Bajoria, September 25, 2008. Available at: http://www.cfr.org/publication/17331/bhutans_road_to_democracy.html
2. Choden, Tashi (2004), *Indo-Bhutan Relations Recent Trends*, Journal of Bhutan Studies, Volume 11, p. 115.
3. Embassy of India, Thimphu, *Treaty Between India and Bhutan 1949*. Available at: http://www.indianembassythimphu.bt/treaty.htm
4. Treaty between Indian and Bhutan, 2007. Available at: http://www.bhutandnc.com/Treaty.htm
5. Bisht, Medha (2013) Jigme Khesar Namgyel Wangchuk's Visit to India: Towards an Assuring Alliance, Institute for Defence Studies and Analysis, February 1, 2013. Available at: http://www.idsa.in/idsacomments/Jigme Khesar Namgyel Wangchuks Visitto India_MedhaBisht_010213
6. Choden, Tashi, (2004), n.9, p.115.
7. Bisht, Medha (2013). n.12.
8. Choden, Tashi (2004), n.9, p.115.
9. Embassy of India, Thimphu, *Mega Projects*. Available at: http://www.indianembassythimphu.bt/mega.html
10. Choden, Tashi, (2004), n.9, p. 115.
11. Ministry of External Affairs, India, *India-Bhutan Relations*. Available

at: http://meaindia.nic.in/meaxpsite/foreignrelation/bhutan.pdf

12. Embassy of India, Thimphu, *India-Bhutan Relatons*. Available at: http://www.indianembassythimphu.bt/indo.html#trade
13. Ministry of External Affairs, India, n.141.
14. Ministry of External Affairs, India, *Annual Report 2010-2011*. Available at: http://meaindia.nic.in/mystart.php?id=500417371